# D.A. Diaries

Kenneth F. Eichner
© 2015

Cover illustration by Matthew Curry
Cover design by Neal Ashby
Book design by Michael Delcour

ISBN 978-0-615-57228-4

For Janjuree and Kinaree Eichner


And for my editors, Michael Delcour and Thomas Blomstrom


And special thanks to editor Tom Jenks for taking time away from the likes of Cormac McCarthy, Phillip Roth, and Tom Wolfe to help an unknown like me.

# Table of Contents

## Chapter 1

# Please Don't Sell Crack from My Office

## DECEMBER 2, 1999

On this particular dawn the painful density of the D.C. courthouse population was reduced to a single car and a single question: "Hey, yo, mister, my friend was locked up last night—are you a lawyer?"

I stopped and a young man got out of a white Lexus. Eminem played at an appropriate volume. He was about six feet four inches tall, wearing a large North Face black winter jacket.

I confessed, "My name's Clay. I'm a D.A., a prosecutor." I thought I'd begin the day with a little in-your-face friendliness.

"Aw, you the man, I don't want to talk to you." His smile indicated otherwise.

I looked down at his shoes. "When I played basketball we had laces on our shoes instead of zippers. The world's gone high-tech." I paused, then asked, "What did your friend get arrested for?"

"Drug bust, search warrant."

"He'll be arraigned at 9:30 this morning in courtroom 160. If he doesn't have a bondsman, walk down Fifth Street 'til you find one. Any drug case involving a search warrant is usually more serious than the average street sale, so he will need a lawyer. If he can't afford a lawyer, go to the front desk at the public defenders. Don't believe the word on the street that public defenders suck. Some of them are better than any private lawyer you could afford. But go early, the line gets real long, real fast."

"Why you helping me?" he asked. "Thought you suppose to put everybody in jail."

"I'm pretty sure I saw you playing basketball in Rock Creek Park a couple of years ago. I feel sorry for you because you can't go left," I told him and began walking away.

"I knew I seen you somewhere before," he said. "That's bullshit man, I can go left," his voice rose. Then he added, "Hey, thanks."

I slipped through the back door of the office. It was just after seven. This was my favorite hour, juicing up on caffeine as I looked at the file, knowing I was about to pick a jury. Pure, undiluted thought without interruptions. With over a hundred and fifty prosecutors and a city filled with gun-lovers that don't hunt, office pandemonium usually broke out by eight o'clock. Silence segued into ringing phones, slamming doors, rising voices, then Scott Cook's voice, and, finally, Alexandra Baker's voice. Once my office brother and sister had arrived, I felt more secure. Our triumvirate was unassailable. We had a pact: anything could be said. No secrets. In an office of friends, enemies, and frienemies, we stuck beside each other. But we weren't just friends, we trusted each other professionally. I could ask either one to cover me at work and know that whatever needed to be done would be done my way, or probably better. Alexandra and Scott probably had thirty I.Q. points on me, but what I lacked in smarts I made up for in unjustified swagger.

Scott was my height and bald by choice; a medium-skinned black man who knew that the world was anything but black and white. Like me, he was thirty-three and one of the few real Washingtonians in the office. We were both retired from the D.A.'s basketball team; we got too busy and too slow. Professionally, Scott was freak-show smart. He could pick up a murder file and tell me in five minutes whether the jury would do murder one, murder two, or manslaughter. His mother taught music, his father was a postal worker by day and a jazz musician by night. Scott was a tremendous trial lawyer, husband, and father. He taunted me relentlessly about my search for the perfect girl, which he thought was an excuse to out-gangsta the gangstas we prosecuted.

Like his parents, Scott was educated at Spelman in Atlanta, Georgia, and then went on to Howard University School of Law. He was raised to do the right thing and championed education over ignorance, fidelity over being a player, and faith over drugs. Sometimes I don't understand why he rolls with me. He says he hopes I will evolve into a father so that I can come to his home more often. (His wife generally disapproves of me. She's never seen me bring the same girl twice to Sunday potluck dinners.) Although a family man, Scott has a sick sense of humor and energy to burn. Oftentimes when I would read aloud some horrific set of front-page facts (Stray Bullet Puts Honor Student in Wheelchair), Scott would just say, "It's the stuff of country music, I can hear it playing softly in the trailer."

Alexandra was just—*vital*. With her long, dirty-blonde tresses and her towering five-foot-nine frame, she would punctuate cutting remarks with a laugh that quickly dispelled any feelings of ill will.

When she smiled men died; when they found out she preferred her own sex, they died again. She came up the ranks with Scott and me; minor traffic, drunk driving, misdemeanors, juvenile, minor felonies, appeals, major felonies, grand jury, and finally, the world of high-profile trials. She declined her first assignment to the drug unit; we all knew that the war on drugs was just a war on poor people. Alexandra, smarter than anyone in the office, chose the sex crimes unit over homicide. While I was the product of bad parenting and an education I ignored, Alexandra was the product of a great family and phenomenal schooling. She did not forget where she came from and even had a few pieces of antique New England furniture in her office. Born and raised in Connecticut (her father was into investment banking and her faultless mother was always throwing herself at one philanthropic cause or another), she had prepped at Concorde Academy in Massachusetts with the Kennedy clan, and did her undergrad at Wellesley and law work at Columbia.

She discovered her love of criminal law after a stint in private practice (the Waspy firm of Sullivan & Cromwell, of course) doing international and communications law. But it was not about her golden resume, it was about her attitude and patience with all the yahoos, psycho witnesses, dysfunctional staff, half-cocked, dingy lawyers, out-to-lunch judges, and their fussy courtroom staff. She effortlessly made them feel great and all she gave them were the crumbs of her affections. If you were a close friend, you were blessed to have her in your life. If you were a girlfriend and she withdrew her affection: ouch. (Last year she had an affair with a pretty Jewess, one Rachael Cohen, aspiring lawyer and office law clerk. When her clerkship ended, so did the affair. When Alexandra dumped her, young Rachael melted down. I had to tell the bat mitzvah girl that one more uninvited trip to the office and we were going to indict her for stalking. Although that was the reality check young Rachael needed, she was shattered. There were ghosts in her eyes as she dragged herself toward the elevator.)

Alexandra has what I love in a woman: zoom. She throws herself into work and play. She was always ready to go to the jail, talk to witnesses, eat, drink, dance, work out, sneak out and go to the movies, smile, and crack a ridiculously funny joke without smiling. The joke this morning, however, was me not knowing whether my star witness would show up. I thought I'd go bother Scott because I knew Alexandra was slammed with work.

"Top of the morning, Scott. What's your idea of the perfect girl? What do you look for in a woman? Or, pretend you are a Catholic priest and tell me what you look for in a young boy." Scott was usually in my office or I was in his.

"It's too early to answer your stupid questions, Chronic," Scott said as he sat down with a file in one hand and java in the other. This morning I was "Chronic." God only knows what he would call me tomorrow. "What do I look for in a woman? I'm married, I look not to get hit by my wife."

"Stop sounding like you don't love Pam," I persisted.

"The only reason you're asking this shit is you probably had another bad date with some woman who suffers from No Personality Disorder. I'm just hoping you got it on video and she was a bad girl."

"If some woman was in the room with us, she would say, 'Typical guys—,'" I commented.

"No, if some woman was in the room, she would say, 'Filming video without consent is a violation of the United States Code and the D.C. statutory code, and will often result in a period of incarceration.' Now, do you have some footage for me or not?" Scott asked.

"Of course I've got footage, and *implied* consent is still consent, right? I even sent a memo last week on Department of Justice letterhead requesting that a screening room be built so we can watch these films in a special setting. It's my way of giving back to my coworkers. They can study my trial skills and cinematography."

He smirked. "Eventually you will get your special setting: a room with iron bars. You'll get a special orange jumpsuit for a uniform, too. Let's go use the back interview room, no one's in there," he urged.

"Okay, let me grab my trial notebook for my murder *du jour*," I said as we headed toward the back of the office. The back interview room held the only remaining VCR in the office after the other video player in an interview room near the front door was stolen by a crime "victim" waiting for a jury verdict. The person worked as a convenience store cashier, testified about being robbed at gunpoint, and went back to the witness room to wait for the verdict; he was told by a victim advocate to come back the next day because the jury had not reached a verdict. The robbery victim then left with the video player—and never returned. Our crack office investigators found no forwarding address. It was so embarrassing that the chief D.A., Tommy Monroe, quickly put it to bed. (Although Scott said he still considers one of our office victim advocates a suspect in the theft.) The verdict? Not guilty on the robbery. The jurors ignored the fingerprint the defendant left at 7-Eleven and felt the identification of the robber was "unreliable." The D.C. courthouse was the land of O.J. verdicts. It was not a place that generously handed out guilties.

We shut the door and locked it. I put the tape in and adjusted the volume. Initially Luscious Jackson was playing "Under Your Skin," which faded into "Fluffy White Clouds."

"Nails!" Scott said in a strong whisper, "Look at that rack." He moved his head from side to side and admired the naked body on the small screen. "Good God, look at that body. What the fuck is that weird music in the background?"

"It's The Orb—not much time for culture when you're married, I guess. Watch this scene coming up when I gently pull her hair," I told him.

"Sounds like ecstasy music. Please don't tell me you're doing E too. We'll have to add that count to your indictment. Oh, man, look at that, she's throwing her hair around and..." Scott was interrupted by a knock at the door.

I moved to the video machine as fast as Bruce Lee. Video ejected, TV off, video concealed. It was Alexandra.

"How dare you leave me out of a porno break?" Alexandra said as I let her in. "Is it you-know-who?" she asked, always up on my dating situation. "She's really cute and I'd like to watch, but you have to go see Tommy Monroe. *Now.* A student just shot a teacher at Carver High School. About seventy square blocks of D.C. are closed."

"I'm busy showing Scott an instructional video," I said.

"The teacher was Bradford Slater, some super-teacher. He received every teaching award ever given. The *Washington Post* did a long piece on him last year. He motivated kids out of the housing projects into some of the best schools in the country. It's your case. Tommy's waiting." Alexandra left, bolting to whatever emergency she was dealing with.

"Put the tape back in. I'll get it back to you later," Scott said.

I grabbed the videotape and left. The last (and only) time Scott said he'd get my tape back to me he "lost" it for two days. Two very long days of ransacking his car, office, and house. Two days of my career on the line. It turned up in my briefcase. He knew where it was the entire time. I still can't figure out if he wanted to torture me or just take the extra time to lecture me on the virtues of marriage, commitment, and fatherhood.

My cell phone went off as I headed down the hall to Tommy Monroe's office. My witnesses had arrived.

Tommy was on the phone but motioned me in. He was a short African American, but worked the phone like a giant. As he covered his phone's mouthpiece with his left hand, he began talking to me.

"You gotta work your magic and win this one. This murder is huge and we gonna get it from both ends. The president and the secretary of education have already called a press conference condemning school violence. Problem is, the kid that killed the teacher is the son of one of our police officers. So you know that motherfucker Steve Duncan of the Fraternal Order of Police is going to go after me. Right or wrong, if I prosecute a police officer or his family, he's in our face. Get ready for that—no matter what the defense is, Duncan is going to do anything to help the cop and his son." Tommy began talking into the phone again and held up his index finger, American business sign language for "I'll be off the phone in a minute." -

Tommy and Steve Duncan hated each other. Duncan was formerly a narcotics detective who was born pissed. He was never really happy with the D.A.'s office, especially when he was always about a freckle away from a perjury indictment. "What time do you need me to testi-lie?" he would joke with the younger D.A.'s. I could never figure out who was worse, the D.A.'s that laughed with him (and allowed themselves to be turned into coconspirators), or Duncan for saying whatever needed to be said at trial instead of what really happened. Since Duncan felt destined for bigger and better things, he reinvented himself as a political activist, becoming president of the D.C. police union. Whenever Tommy indicted a police officer for domestic violence or a police brutality assault, Duncan would be here, there, and everywhere heckling, heckling, heckling. The press loved the feud. It was tabloid gold; a marital split between the police and prosecutors.

I said, "I have to begin a murder trial in thirty minutes. Besides, I don't even want the case. I'm sick of these high-profile cases. I'm burned out, plus these cases ruin my social life. I will cover the bond hearing, but give the case to someone else. Tell me what happened in thirty seconds or less." I owned Tommy and could talk like that to him. Tommy was a clueless trial lawyer, but the ultimate politician. Without me getting him good press and winning cases, the office looked inept. "This case meant a lot to Mr. Monroe, personally," I would routinely tell reporters to get his name in the paper. I was the son of a hard-drinking reporter so I knew what to say and what not to say. It was a lawyer's job to keep secrets and a reporter's job to publish them. My father had taught me about the strange dance between reporters and sources.

Tommy's voluptuous secretary sauntered in and handed him a note and whispered the word "urgent." With pictures of his wife and children silently looking on, Tommy sized her up and down like a soldier on furlough. Their little affair was an open secret. Naturally, Tommy never gave me a hard time about my debauchery. He knew I cruised the courthouse like it was a Vegas hotel. While I never touched employees, Tommy had no problem shitting in his own nest. Nonetheless, his legal heart was in the right place. He once told me that he gave me the high-profile cases because he knew I would win without hiding evidence. He feared that type of scandal, and with good reason. Some of the more desperate and insecure prosecutors routinely hid the goods from the defense.

"I know you better than you know yourself—you'll end up taking the case. Meanwhile, let me tell you what I know: there is a performance at the school, a teacher goes downstairs to get some computer equipment, this little fucker has his father's gun, the teacher is killed in the basement, and the kid starts running. The teacher comes in alive and leaves dead. But it wasn't any teacher; it was Bradford Slater. He's a legend. If you had gone to a black high school

9

instead of that fancy St. Albans private school you'd know who he was," Tommy said.

"Don't play the if-card on me. If you were taller you'd get more women. We are what we are," I puffed, but knew that Tommy was more adept at dating than me. And he was married.

Tommy smiled for a second, and then a hint of sadness suffused his face—unusual for a guy who dealt with death on a daily basis (sometimes two or three homicides in a single day). "This guy Bradford Slater was a maverick. To many families he was like Martin Luther King. He got kids to ignore the poverty and drugs. Bradford helped kids find the musician, dancer, painter, whatever, within themselves. I know. I had relatives that were taught by him. Even if they didn't like art class, they respected him. Lot of those kids in that school come from broken homes and he was like a second parent. I bet if we put that little punk shooter back in the school tomorrow he wouldn't make it through the day."

Tommy told me to get on the Slater murder as soon as I finished my trial, and added, "People will want the father indicted for letting a minor have access to a gun, but you will find a way to avoid that. One sacrificial lamb is all we need."

I began walking away, refusing to commit. If I found evidence proving that the father lent the gun to his minor son, then I would have to indict, prosecute, and orange-jumpsuit his ass. I didn't care if he was a cop. And what was really up with the son? Sex and drugs between the teacher and the student, I wondered. My cell phone went off again. My secretary Annette told me Tomar, the witness I had been looking for, was here.

"I can't talk, I'm in trial and I have to meet with a witness," I said six times as six people tried to stop me on the way to the interview room (front room, no video player). Four out of the six people told me the high school shooting was my case and to get right over there.

Typical. How the fuck could I try today's murder case and run over to Carver High School to look at the crime scene at the same time? I earned one-tenth the salary paid to D.C. lawyers in big law firms and the government demanded ten times the effort of private practice. The government could be such an easy place to hide from work, but if done right it was sheer toil.

"'Sup," I said as I looked at Tomar McKee. I brought him to my office. He had been shot three times and was my star witness.

"What up with you, trial dog, how you be?" Tomar smiled. I shook his tattooed hand. Although it was winter, he was wearing a black t-shirt. Everything was tattooed on Tomar. He was an ageless black man with high cheekbones and a choirboy face; his tats showed up quite well against his light brown skin. Some were pictures, some were symbols I did not understand and others, like the one that said "Bad Influence" on the inside of his wrist, fell into the Department of You've Got to Be Kidding. I asked him about the small Chinese calligraphy tattoo on his left cheek and he told me it meant inner strength. We had met once before when the case had been continued. We had hit it off, but he had been pretty cagey. He promised to help me prepare and then disappeared, effortlessly eluding the detective I sent to find and interview him.

"Did you hear about that teacher getting shot? One of my half-brothers used to hang around the Shrimp Boat, sell drugs," Tomar told me, referring to a large fast-food joint shaped like a boat and located in a nasty northeast neighborhood at the corner of Benning Road and East Capitol Street. "He took Bradford Slater's class. That boy changed. Now he up at some acting school in New York City, 'Jew-yard' or something." I assumed Tomar was referring to Juilliard Acting School. "He doing Def Jam Comedy and shit because of that teacher. Everybody like that Slater and now some little nigga put a cap in him. That fool gonna get hurt in jail. I've been shot. It ain't no fun. I tell you that right now, Clay, I'm gonna kill these motherfuckers that shot me," Tomar said.

"Keep your voice down," I said as I shut the door. "There are people here that take threats seriously." Perhaps I had an ethical duty to report my knowledge of a potential murder or at least put a memo in the file, but there was not enough time. I had plans to get laid tonight, I had to do this murder trial, and then there was this new high-profile teacher homicide I had to avoid. There was never enough time.

"I'm serious as a heart attack. Them low-level niggas is dead."

Again, Tomar was not venting. He meant it and he didn't care if he told me. He was the walking definition of "what difference did it make?" Tomar had been shot three times; if he killed the two people on trial for the murder of his friend, Pookie, everyone would know who did the shooting anyway.

There was a knock at the door. It was my secretary, Annette. "Hey, sweetness. You better get going on that teacher case," she said in a deep whisper, and greeted Tomar, whom she had met once before.

"I'm going to kill you if you don't get out of my office. You know I have to pick a jury on this Novak and Joyner murder case in twenty minutes. The detectives will gather the information on the Slater case. Now get out of here, and *please* put a yellow sticky do-not-disturb on my door."

"I also stopped by to tell you Judge's Chambers called and you're next in line to pick a jury. Just because you got up on the wrong side of the bed this morning don't take it out on me, monster," Annette snapped and slammed the door. Then she opened the door, called me a monster again, told me to do my own yellow sticky, and slammed the door again. Once was enough, I thought. A moment later a new D.A. knocked on the door to ask a trial strategy question. I told her I was jammed up. (Everyone came to Alexandra, Scott, and me for trial strategy questions. I loved the way the new female prosecutors would freshen their makeup before they came to ask me a question. Alexandra would whisper, "You may be a lawyer but you're still a woman," right after a female rookie left.)

I explained to Tomar it was impossible to get anything done during business hours. I wrote "Do Not Disturb" on a yellow sticky and placed it on the outside of my door. I continued to prepare him for the witness stand.

"I'm going to ask you to step down out of the witness box and show the jury where you got shot. Take off your shirt and show them. The judge will allow it, and don't rush it. Walk close to the jury box and make sure each juror gets a look at each wound," I instructed. He began rehearsing.

"After Novak killed Pookie, that nigga capped me here and here and here." He lifted up his shirt and twisted his body around to show me his gunshot wounds.

"Tomar, why do you use that word so much?" I asked.

"What word? Nigga? That's just the way I talk. I don't mean nothing by it," he said as his pager went off. "But the answer is still the answer and them low-level niggas is dead. I'm sorry to tell you, but I'm gonna kill them niggas first motherfucking chance I get. They shot me three times."

"Just calm down, you don't want to do that," I attempted to assuage him. "Listen, let me put them in jail, let me do your dirty work for you. Your tax dollars pay my salary. We don't have the death penalty in D.C. but we have life without parole."

"Hey trial dog, I am the death penalty," Tomar shot back.

"Stop talking about killing Novak and Joyner, and start helping me prepare. You seem like a good guy, you don't really want to shoot them and go to jail. Just between you and me, I'd rather be dead than spend my life in jail," I said.

"I hear dat," Tomar said.

"Help me convict them, that's the way to get even. I want total honesty. This isn't the drug unit and I don't care about that shit. If this was a drug deal that went bad or a drug debt or something, then I need to know, my friend, because their lawyers are going to have every little detail about what went on between you guys — and I don't want them to have more information than me. Without your help, they have the upper hand. Now what's this about? We don't have long. We are going to pick a jury in half an hour and you never returned my letter or phone calls to talk about the case."

Tomar's intentions gave the case a new sense of urgency. I knew Tomar would kill them if the jury came back with a Not Guilty. His pager went off again. I knew what he was up to; his rap sheet was an inch thick. Perhaps his tax dollars did not pay my D.A.'s salary after all.

"Here, use my phone. I have to check in with the Jury Commissioner and see if the other witnesses are here. Dial nine to get an outside line, think about what I said, and I'll be back in a few minutes."

I did my patented courthouse lap, walking as fast as I could walk without running. (Several secretary paralegal types were crying in the hallway because Bradford Slater had been their high school teacher; I overheard their laments as I blew by them.) Note to the courtroom clerk, witness room intros, Judge's Chambers. Half the job was being a producer-director. As for the jury, that was an ad campaign: selling guilt to a small but distrustful demographic. Back to Tomar, wondering how much money he made during my brief absence. Easily more than anyone in the office. It was not hard to beat the anemic D.A. salaries, forty percent of which went to VISA and my law school loan. (Dad could afford it, but he thought law school loans would build my character.) My cell phone went off. It was a detective standing near the dead body of Bradford Slater. I told him to process the crime scene carefully. "This is going to trial. Dude, you have been doing this long enough to know that the plea offer will be a million years, so you know this is going to trial, which means you know everyone is going to be heavily cross-examined about everything. Take all the usual precautions, don't walk in the blood, don't move the body until all the photographs are taken, save the clothes for gunshot residue, interview everyone you can, et cetera, et cetera. I am turning my cell phone off. I have to try this case. You good to go?" The detective said the kiddie killer was still on the run, but everything was under control. I doubted that, but turned my cell off.

I opened the door to my office and Tomar was finishing up his conversation on the phone. "I'll hit your pager back when I'm done here. I got court today and you know how that goes. Yeah, I'm not deaf; I heard you the first time. If you want that much you better do what you need to do because I ain't going there but once, and I ain't spotting nobody. Okay, later." He hung up my phone. I had received awards in the past; maybe I'd get a new one: "First D.A. to Have Drug Deals Conducted from the Homicide Unit."

Since he was dealing drugs in front of me I felt confident he was going to finally give me the details I needed. I pulled out an 8½-by-11 inch pad of yellow paper and said, "go."

"It wasn't over drugs, Clay. Novak think I set him up to get jacked, robbed, ya know. I used to sell drugs in D.C. and over at the Heights 'hood," he began, referring to one of D.C.'s notoriously dilapidated ghettos that included the Capitol Heights neighborhood, right across the D.C. border in Maryland's Prince George's County. D.C. and Prince George's County shared six hundred homicides a year—the highest murder rate in the United States of Honey-Have-a-Good-Day-at-School-and-Don't-Forget-Your-Lunch-and-Gun.

"I made good money too, three thousand dollars a week. I would get ten thousand dollars worth of crack up front, sell it, give my supplier seven thousand in cash, and keep the rest. I did it for the money. I don't smoke cigarettes or marijuana. I don't even drink and I wouldn't dream of doing crack—it was for the money. But those days are gone. Now I work for the D.C. government as an electrician's helper. I got a health plan for my baby and my baby's mama; I be working every day." *Eh-Ree-Day*, Tomar said.

"All right, all right, I don't need to hear how much more money you have than me. Get to the shooting, I had to pick a jury five minutes ago," I said.

"You lawyers make big money, Clay."

"Not when you work for the government. After taxes, this cheap-ass D.A.'s office pays about eight hundred dollars a week," I confessed.

"God damn, is that all? Damn, that ain't much at all. Why don't you go into private practice? Them niggas make a whole lot more than that."

With some witnesses and victims I had to search for something to say in an effort to give some show of ease and purpose that I did not feel, but Tomar was a charmer. He bragged that he had been arrested and jailed twenty-five times and had never once been convicted. His arrest record was as thick as the Sunday *New York Times*. Tomar, the avatar of Street Smart, held nothing back and at that moment, I knew that on cross-examination he would run circles around defense attorneys Jack Shane and Mark Lodge. Shane was smart, but not that smart. Lodge was a goof.

"This is what happened, Clay. You see I love to gamble, it's my hobby," he began. I came from a family of alcoholics and doubted it was a hobby. "We were over at this dude's house playing Nintendo for money, and I lost a couple of hundred to Novak. Later that night he gets robbed, see, then Novak, simple nigga that he is, think I set him up. Which is silly. I never sent anyone to rob him. And for a couple of hundred dollars, no way, that ain't shit to me. Anyway, he sees me and Pookie a few weeks later when he with Joyner. They tell us they know of a gambling party near Georgia Avenue. I say, 'Fine, let's go.' So we driving along, I'm in the front seat, and we get lost—at least that is what I'm suppose to think, if you know what I mean. Then Novak says, 'Hey, Tomar, roll down your window so I can read that sign, brother.' I roll down the window and he pulls a gun out and shoots me in the head, but it grazes the back of my head. I hear a second shot, which is when he shot Pookie in the head. I jump on him, screaming, 'Nigga, what the fuck you doing?' Then that other nigga, Joyner, he gets me in a headlock and they get me out of the car and Novak be yelling, 'Hold him so I can shoot him' as Joyner is holding me down. I hear the gun go off twice. They shoot me in the chest and in the back, then push me into the woods in the back of Rock Creek Park. Pookie died right away. Novak capped him in the face and he just slunked over in the back seat."

"That's what happened?" I asked.

"For real, I swear," he replied. *Fur Reeeel.*

"Did Novak have the gun the whole time?" I asked.

"Seemed like it, but I passed out after the third shot on me."

"Tomar, how did you get out of the woods?"

"I was lying there thinking about my baby, thinking that I don't want to die yet. Next thing I was up on the road and flagged down five-o."

"Flagged down the what?"

"The police, Clay." *Da PO-leese.*

"You're probably going to be a little nervous when you testify because you have to look at the killers. Just relax. Do you understand what I'm talking about?" I tried to comfort him.

"Understand, overstand—you wrong about that. They's the ones gonna be nervous. You watch them niggas when I take the stand, you watch them. I already saw Joyner out in the hall, he wouldn't even look at me. He knows he's dead. How did he make bond? Probably had his lawyer set the bond motion in front of a soft judge. His lawyer is probably friends with the judge too. I don't care. He's dead."

Tomar had a preternatural sense for the flow of the courthouse. His little bond scenario played out. Defense attorney Jack Shane was friends with Judge Watson.

"Let's just focus on the trial. I'm going to go through the questions I will ask you on the stand and then ask you what I think the lawyers will ask on cross-examination. And trust me, after a hundred jury trials, I have a pretty good idea of what they are going to ask you on cross-examination."

"Okay, trial dog, I'm with you. What's their defense? Can't be an accident. Can't be self-defense. Gotta be: 'I wasn't there. That's my bet.' Tomar was thinking like a lawyer.

"You get paid on that bet. Their alibi will be that they weren't there. But don't worry, I already had a detective interview the two witnesses they named in their pretrial motions and he tape-recorded the interviews. I had to ask the detective thirty fucking times to go interview them, but he finally did it."

*

We picked a jury despite Jack Shane's complaining to Judge Joy Watson that I would not withdraw the mandatory life sentence and plea the case out. Super-rich Jack Shane was as smooth as it got; he always had something up his Ralph Lauren sleeve. We went back to Her Honor's chambers so she could smoke one of her Marlboro 1OOs before opening statements. Relentless, Jack continued to lobby the judge.

"The prosecution has the wrong guys. This Tomar character gambled and sold drugs to everyone. You could rent a dance hall and fill it up with people that wanted to kill him. But if you drop the life without parole sentence—good things will happen, a quick plea and we'll go eat." Jack was desperate to stop the trial.

Judge Watson told Jack, "One dead and this young man shot three times by people he knows. I think bad things are going to happen to your client." Her patented, raspy cough-laugh punctuated what she thought was an obvious result. She liked Jack—she liked his tallness, his success, his broad shoulders and slender waist, his clothes, his style, his confidence, even his lawyering—but it was not Jack's day. She chain-smoked and let him rant. Jack launched into another series of reasons not to try the case, along with a bucket of possible dispositions. I looked down at his four-hundred-dollar Salvatore Ferragamo shoes; the cuffs on his nineteen-hundred-dollar Armani suit broke just right, barely touching the little gold buckle on the shiny, reticulated black leather. He had a farm in Virginia horse country, and a house at Rehoboth Beach, Delaware (right down the block from big time criminal lawyers Plato Cacheris and Jake Stein, who represented Monica Lewinsky). Although the white stuff from South America had created havoc in many lives, it had been very kind to Jack.

Judge Watson ignored the courthouse no smoking edict. On the verge of retirement, she did what she damned well pleased. Her smoke-filled *sanctum sanctorum* had a country look and reflected D.C.'s deep southern roots. Stuffed foxes gazed at oil paintings of horses and leather stirrups affixed to the wall. The horse jurist smoked and smiled at me as Jack rambled on. She loved tall, thin, dark men with athletic builds. Her last ten law clerks were built just like me. It was an open secret that she hired to please her eyes, and I would take that edge over a good legal citation. (The female courthouse clerks would volunteer to drop files off at her chambers, affectionately calling it the "Chippendale's Chambers.") She was smart, and a good draw for the case.

"You're done, Jack. Time to go try this case," she said, stubbing out her cigarette. "Jack, you can put all your objections on the record right after opening statement. Let's knock this case out in a day. Clay's got bigger fish to fry, like that kid that just shot his teacher. Man, oh, man, the president already commented on the case. I heard it on the radio. Can you handle the pressure, boy?" she said, and winked at me. (In her heart of hearts she was a flirty, southern girl and she loved to call the male prosecutors "boy" until it became an unusable word, with the rare exception, like today.)

"I'm not going to take the case," I protested.

She ignored me and kept talking. "I can't imagine a student would shoot that teacher. He did it with a police officer's service revolver too. Over the years I have seen letters written by Mr. Slater trying to help some kid I was going to sentence. They were beautifully written about life being a journey and how it evokes character. I never met the guy, but Mr. Slater was special." She paused and lit another cigarette. "I don't think that teacher would want us to seek revenge because he loved his students so much, but that killer has to be brought to justice. And the kid's father, don't get me started. Whenever that cop Rodney Ford testified in my courtroom he lied through his teeth. That's just this old lady's opinion. Oh well, let's go inside and try this one."

There was my cue. "You don't look like an old lady to me," I told Her Honor and smiled.

"Boy, I like the way you lie. I'll take that compliment to the bank even though the check might bounce," she fired back.

I might have been lying, but there was no doubt she would have rocked my world had I been alive during the early sixties when her sultry, cat-on-a-hot-tin-courthouse-roof looks were at their zenith. Then again, although liquor, cigarettes, sun and time had taken their toll she was still a good-looking older woman who kept her Jackie O bouffant hair dyed brown. She had a pleasant smile and blue eyeliner hooded her blue eyes.

Jack and I walked down the non-public corridor leading back to the courtroom. Judge Watson stayed behind to reapply fresh makeup and perhaps check up on her law clerk. Jack made a few comments to me as we strolled down the hallway, but I wasn't really listening. It was seduction time. "Every child needs a story, and no adult outgrows the need," I would tell younger D.A.'s when I gave my standard lecture on opening statements. I liked Tomar, and I was going to get the jury to like Tomar. I was glad to ruin his assassins, and I would convince the jury to do the same. "Stand close to the jury, but not too close. Don't overdress, but don't underdress; don't look like the typical government slob with those wrinkled khaki pants, button-down shirt, and blue blazer that you purchased at the outlet mall ten years ago," I thought, "and remember, it all boils down to preparation." But I felt hypocritical. I was ill-prepared, Tomar was semi-prepared. It was all so imperfect.

"Ladies and gentlemen, in about five minutes you are going to meet a miracle. His name is Tomar McKee and he was shot three times by the two defendants seated over there. They left him for dead. They left him for dead, pushed him into the woods—but with what little consciousness was left in Tomar McKee, he thought of his young daughter, Alisha, and dragged himself to the road and was spotted by a policeman. You'll meet Officer Davis and he'll tell you how Tomar waved once"—I raised my hand—"and collapsed, falling to the ground as if the strings of a marionette had been cut." I heard a startled juror inhale loudly and I continued.

"Defendant Novak thought Tomar McKee set him up because Defendant Novak had been robbed several hours after he had gambled with Tomar McKee. It's not a complicated story. The dots are easy to connect. Mr. Novak wrongly thought he had been set up by Tomar McKee. I will state the obvious: motive. Mr. Novak waited a few weeks and recruited Mr. Joyner to help him kill Tomar McKee. Tomar McKee was lucky. He lived. Tomar's friend, Pookie Smith, was not so lucky. The forensic pathologist, Dr. Lynn Nixon, will tell you how the bullets entered and how life left his body.

"And the way they executed Pookie Smith and shot Tomar was straight out of one of those mafia movies. Are you ready for this? Defendant Novak told Tomar to roll down his window so Tomar's brains and blood would not get all over Defendant Novak's car. Can you believe how cold that is? That is ice cold, isn't it? Anyway, Tomar rolled his window down to help Defendant Novak read a street sign; Defendant Novak then shot Tomar in the head, and then quickly turned and shot Pookie Smith in the head. Pookie Smith died instantly, but the first shot only grazed Tomar's head. He has lived to tell this story, and Tomar will take the stand and tell you how both defendants dragged him out of the car and filled him with bullet holes.

"Naturally, both defendants have been charged with the first-degree murder of Pookie and attempted first-degree murder of Tomar. After Tomar shows you his wounds and scars, after the surgeon explains how he saved Tomar's life, after all the witnesses have testified, you will be asked to convict the defendants of all crimes charged. In light of what happened, perhaps that is the very least you can do?"

The prosecutor always went first, and it was an enjoyable advantage. Some jurors made their decision early and then put their minds on screen-saver.

Jack Shane and Mark Lodge talked about the theories of reasonable doubt and the presumption of innocence, which is what most defense attorneys do when they have nothing else to say, and then added, in a by-the-way fashion, "My client was not even there." But what could Jack and Mark say? *Good morning, folks, my client did try and make Swiss cheese out of Tomar but the plea offer was too high. I thought I'd see if the prosecutor might make a mistake, or perhaps one of you jurors is so galactically stupid that you will acquit.* No, they could not do that, so they had to just throw something up and see if it would stick. What else can you do when the plea offer is life without parole?

Tomar recounted his horrific tale to the jury. He stepped out of the jury box and displayed his bullet wounds before their tabloid eyes. We worked as a team to move his blood-stained clothes into evidence. He spoke smoothly and confidently. When I had Tomar identify the shooter and his accomplice, I realized Tomar was right: Novak and Joyner were nervous as he looked at them. Especially Joyner, who looked like he was going to beg the jurors to convict him just to be safely in jail.

Then came cross-examination. Tomar cradle-dunked on the half-bright Mark Lodge.

"When you were at Pookie Smith's house, before going to gamble, you made a phone call before you left, right?" Mark Lodge asked.

"We all make phone calls, counselor," Tomar said.

Several jurors gave a soft chuckle.

"Just answer the question," Mark Lodge demanded in a tone of voice that was too angry. Lodge was just old school. He did not understand that a white man does not begin his cross-examination by raising his voice at an African American. Not in D.C. Lodge's law practice consisted primarily of bench trials involving petty divorces and small car accidents, and as for criminal law, he would plea bargain everything he got his hands on. Lodge, like all lawyers who did "a little criminal law," just did not understand juries. How Lodge ended up in this case was anybody's guess. Perhaps he had handled a fender-bender for Joyner's family, and, God help them, they did not understand the poor choice they made.

"And when you were on the phone you were having a violent argument with some people, some people that had threatened to shoot you, right?" Lodge asked.

"I was talking to my baby's mother, telling her I was going to be late because I was going to be gambling, which is where I thought I was going. At that time I didn't know they were planning on killing me," Tomar cleverly retorted.

"Didn't you have a conversation with some people that you were beefing with?" *Beefing with?* Maybe Lodge was improving. Next, he'd be sprinkling his questions with "yo."

"How can I have a conversation with a bunch of people unless it's on a speakerphone or conference call?" Tomar answered correctly.

"Your Honor, I demand that you get the witness to answer." Lodge was red in the face.

"Why don't you ask the question the right way?" Judge Watson said with a raspy laugh. "The witness is absolutely right. You keep asking him if he had a conversation 'with some people.' Not only are you asking for hearsay, but no one knows who you are talking about. Ask your next question, and try and ask it right." Her Honor loved to punk clueless trial lawyers when she got bored.

And so it went for Mark Lodge, groping his way through cross-examination. He would not be bragging about this exchange at the next bar meeting. Tomar owned Mark Lodge.

Jack Shane had flashes of caginess, but Tomar handled him by simply being honest. Jack got Tomar to admit that he gambled; Jack also created innuendo that someone else would like to kill him because of gambling debt (which was what Mark Lodge was attempting to do but couldn't because he lacked the fundamental trial skills).

"Pookie's your friend?" Jack asked.

"Was my friend. He dead now," Tomar looked at Joyner and Novak like they would be joining Pookie shortly.

"I'm sorry that happened," Jack offered a little too easily, "but Pookie had a big drug debt hanging over his head, didn't he?" Jack raised his voice.

"Objection, Your Honor. Where's the notice to introduce reputational evidence on the deceased? Defense counsel is just trying to throw dirt on the deceased without an evidentiary foundation," I asserted with a bit of a smile.

"Sustained," she smiled back and let out a slight raspy cough.

When Jack went too far, Judge Watson sustained my objections and freely slapped him down. Even though she liked Jack, she did not allow lawyers to take over her courtroom with fictional nonsense. Judge Watson's downside is that she would get nervous and jittery for a cigarette, but I learned how to play that without ever suggesting she go for a smoke. *The next witness is the forensic pathologist; she is going to take a long time explaining the manner and cause of death. Would Your Honor like to give the jury a quick break?*

Novak put on his stepfather as an alibi witness. The poor man could not pin down the exact times. He struggled with the thirty-minute window during which he supposedly saw Novak on the night of the murder. I had seen this so many times. A family member or friend comes to half-help, to say that the accused was, for instance, in a house but not for the entire evening. *I want to help my son/nephew but I don't want no perjury charge.* It never worked. It was a very simple concept: you just can't be partially pregnant. As for the trial lawyers, why would they put on an alibi witness to say they could account for a defendant's movements for thirty minutes out of an entire evening? My guess was to give some psycho-juror an excuse to hang things up.

Joyner took the stand and said he and Novak had been together earlier in the evening, but then he left and went home. While he was talking to the jury, I gazed down at a package of keys I had not seen before, wrapped in plastic with the standard D.C. police evidence tag. Whose keys were they? Tomar's? I quickly shot to the "property report" in my trial notebook. "Item #17, keys found next to victim." The large key chain said "Cliff." Mr. Joyner's first name. I couldn't believe my eyes, or my sloth. I taught the newer lawyers to examine all the evidence before trial. Was I spending too much time searching for the perfect woman? Was I getting old? Was I treating murder trials like drunk driving cases because they were so routine? During the struggle to kill Tomar, Cliff Joyner dropped his keys. I should be fired for not knowing that.

"Mr. Joyner, you know who Tomar McKee is?" I asked.

"Yes."

"You said on direct examination that you were together, you were with him that night?"

"Yes," he said, bumping his mouth on the microphone when he leaned too close to answer.

"But then you left early?"

"Yes."

"You went home?"

"Yes."

"How did you get into your house?" I asked.

"What do you mean?" *WhaddayaMee.*

"Showing you what has been marked as Prosecution Exhibit 8, are these your keys? This plastic thing says 'Cliff,' and that's your first name?"

Silence. A squeak in a juror's chair. More silence.

"Yeah, oh, yeah, these are my keys. See on the way home I was robbed by two dudes wearing ski masks..." Joyner began a preposterous tale that I hoped would only speed up the jury's deliberation process. "...And those two dudes must have dropped my keys when they shot Tomar."

"Nothing further," I said, but wanted to ask if the "two dudes wearing ski masks" had lift tickets attached to their jackets. I used to ask questions like that when I was younger, but the office division chiefs took me to the woodshed and told me that comedy from the prosecutor in the courtroom is unprofessional.

When the defense rested I had to re-call the crime scene technician to move into evidence the key chain that said "Cliff." Shane and Lodge went buck wild with objections. I told Judge Watson that I didn't move the key chain into evidence earlier because I wanted to lay a better evidentiary foundation and catch the witness by surprise. She looked at me slyly and wondered aloud how I could have predicted that Joyner would even take the stand to testify. "At any rate, I am not going to question the prosecution's trial strategy and I will allow the re-calling of the crime scene technician for the sole purpose of admitting the key chain." Good thing she liked me. If I were short, bald, and unfunny, I would not have received her favorable ruling.

Jury instructions and closing arguments were business as usual. I gave my standard closing argument. The defense beat reasonable doubt into the ground. I turned it up a notch for my rebuttal argument (as usual, save the high drama for the very end).

"Gambling, drugs? Tomar tells the truth even when it makes him look bad. And Pookie? Who will be his voice? Just because he lived in the projects and worked part-time as a security guard does not mean he's invisible or unimportant. Pookie's family and Tomar and the community hope you will be Pookie's voice. By doing the right thing in this case you will help Tomar move on and flourish in life—as the saying goes: healing begins when justice is done," I ended. Now I entered into a universe called Waiting for the Verdict. Like a fifth grade child waiting for recess, time took on its own separate dimension.

As Tomar and I walked toward my office, I was ambushed by the rank and file.

"Clay, there's someone in the waiting room who wants to get his gun back from a case you had two years ago," the receptionist told me.

"Perfect timing, I have nothing to do today. Tell him I'll buy him lunch on the way to the police property division where we will most likely learn that his gun has been destroyed or lost," I shot back. The receptionist, Dranisha, was used to my act and waited for take two. I then leaned over and whispered to her, "I'm in a murder trial and everyone is freakin' over the teacher shooting; please tell him to make an appointment and come back."

"I was gonna do that," she whispered through a half smile.

The next ten feet of movement exposed even more chaos. Someone stopped me and told me that Alexandra's secretary had told my secretary that a transcript from an old hearing was ready. Then she asked me if I had heard about the teacher that had been shot. "Thanks, and yes," I told her. "Please put the transcript in my mailbox."

"Clay, a witness in CT991006X called and said he was going on vacation, can you get a continuance in that homicide?" my witness coordinator asked me. She hated to write anything down and delivered what amounted to oral cryptograms. I apologized for not knowing each case by its number and asked for the witness' name as well as the name of the case and the trial date.

The secretaries, witness coordinators, and victim advocates had no idea what it was like to be in trial, or to feel totally spent after closing arguments. They didn't realize certain demands could be taken care of at a later time. They would not have lasted five minutes at Hogan & Fox, the law firm I quit to come to the D.A.'s office. I hated my old firm but I must admit that it ran with Nazi efficiency. I developed a mental barricade to cope with the government's comical inefficiency, which was a small price to pay for the friendship, challenge, and exhilaration.

Tomar and I walked to 7-Eleven after he caught up on his phone calls. He encountered a woman in the parking lot. (I did not know if it was his sister or girlfriend or a hook up or cousin or what.) I gave him a few feet of whisper space and waited. He handed her an inch of fifty and twenty dollar bills. Although he was clearly selling crack (partially out of my office), I could understand how defense attorneys hated to see their clients go to jail. I genuinely liked the guy and hoped the jury would do the right thing. There was little doubt that had Tomar been placed in a different geographic-economic location, he would have gone to Wharton. Unfortunately, there was no doubt that if the jury acquitted Novak and Joyner, our office would be indicting Tomar for a double homicide. He would kill them both without a freckle of remorse.

"How did I do?" Tomar asked.

"The jury liked you, you did great, you owned the defense attorneys on cross," I replied. "Especially Lodge, you owned Lodge."

"I don't know." He worried like a trial lawyer. "These juries don't convict in Washington, D.C. Niggas know that. Niggas know to stay out of Virginia—they'll convict your ass over there. But niggas know they can do all the crime they want in D.C. because you will be acquitted or you can get the deal of the century." Once again, Tomar's editorial rang true.

"Look, normally you should worry. Juries will not convict if there is any problem with the case, but the guy dropped his key chain next to your body. No matter how dumb this jury is, they cannot overlook that," I lied. D.C. juries create cartoon fantasies to acquit.

"I know a nigga that travel between New York City, L.A. and here because he know that he can do all the crime he want in those places. He will not set foot anywhere else to do his business."

"Tomar, why don't you write an article for *Washingtonian* magazine and call it 'Best Places to Kill People, Sell Drugs, and Gamble'?"

"You a funny man, Clay," he replied. "You wrapped that case up tight."

I exchanged awkward hellos with a court reporter buying iced tea. Tomar could tell we were guilty of something. He whispered, "You a man of the courthouse, dog."

We walked across the street and talked some more outside of 7-Eleven, and then he spotted some friends. I put my hand out to shake before he left and told him I would page him when I got a verdict. He grabbed my hand with both his hands and asked if he could give me a call sometime to just say "what up." I gave him all my numbers. It was always hard for me to understand how some victims of gunshot wounds experienced an unrecoverable free-fall and became a shell of their former selves. Others, like Tomar, "moved on," treated the wound like gladiators that occasionally caught a sword swipe.

I returned to my office and waited for the verdict, unable to eat or work. Half of my thirty voicemails focused on the Slater homicide. Even though I'd told Tommy I didn't want the case, he had already told the press I was handling it.

Locking up Mr. Slater's killer was important, but so was getting laid. Same old conflict. I wanted to find the perfect girl, but until then the perfect body would have to do. The phone was cradled in my left hand, the fingers of my right hand tattooed a beat on my desk; the sound each finger made said Kim, Kim, Kim. The kissable mouth, the rockin' bod. I returned Kim's voicemail with the standard tag-you're-it voicemail. First voicemail, then voice, then hands, then tease, then please, and finally the steamy congress of two work-addled souls. I went to Scott's office to see if he needed any help and discuss how I was going to seduce Kim.

Scott's door was shut. There were people inside, but I did not knock. I never knocked. It was Scott and, except for the judges, no one really had rank on me anywhere in the entire building. Well, maybe Tommy—but he needed me more than I needed him.

"At ease, everyone," I said as I entered, pretending to be the ranking officer. Alexandra smiled. Harrison Collins and Bruce Lebby gave me the finger.

Harrison and Bruce went from office to office entertaining everyone. I did not trust them like Scott and Alexandra, but I loved their twisted sense of humor and the way they mined the office files for comedy. Alexandra was running the task force on priest sex abuse and had assigned Harrison several Catholic priests to prosecute. It wasn't complicated. Once upon a time when the priests had more testosterone in their bodies they played dirty little games with altar boys. Now the boys were grown up. The victims could form their own choir. Cut a CD, call it *Boyz to Victims*. Although Harrison and Bruce acted the part of quintessential conservative Irish Catholics, behind closed doors they were completely irreverent. Three weeks earlier at a party in Georgetown they were having a contest as to who could yell "Stella" more like Marlon Brando in *A Streetcar Named Desire*. It had been three A.M. When the police came, they hid their bottles and showed their D.A. badges and got out of it. It was almost impossible to get arrested when you had a badge. I knew that all too well.

"Come into my office, laddie," Harrison said with a heavy Irish accent. He had made a priest's white collar out of Xerox paper and scotch-taped it around his neck. So had Bruce. "We were just talking about ya, come in Clay-my-Boy, our star trial dog, come in, shut the door, take your shirt off and relax. Let me bear the burden of your sweet load. You've been working too hard on your homicides. Trial after trial, we were worried about ya son. Confess to me, lad. Now you have that big teacher murder to worry about. Imagine if you lose that one Clay-my-Boy. You get a not guilty and then the kid goes back to the same school where he left a dead teacher. That would suck, wouldn't it laddie?" Father Harrison asked. I solemnly nodded.

"Are you coming to choir practice tonight?" Father Bruce asked, in a similar accent perfected by a Jesuit education.

Now Kumar Malik, an up-and-coming trial attorney with huge game, came into the room. Diversity in hiring was part of the Tommy Monroe political machine.

"Bless you, my son," Harrison greeted Kumar and gave him benediction as he mimed the sign of the cross. "Make some room for the young, healthy Kumar. He shouldn't have to stand, but if ye has to stand, stand by me, right by me." Harrison gazed downward toward Kumar's crotch.

"You guys are so sick," Alexandra chided Harrison and Bruce.

Bruce tore off his priest collar and assumed the role of the young confessor. "I want to do something bad, Father, something very bad, something I just discovered about my body."

"What's going on with those priest cases?" Kumar asked in a more serious tone of voice.

"Please, my son, please," Harrison said, waving the real priest's file, The United States of America versus Father McCarthy, "no priest wants to face the humiliation I will inflict upon him if this goes to trial." Clearly, it was on a plea bargain tract. The infamous priests had molested over one hundred and twenty children, several of whom were now prominent Washingtonians and wanted it kept quiet as much as the priests did. I was on the special task force with Alexandra on how to handle all the priest molestation cases. Although I wasn't quite sure how it would all play out, I knew one thing for sure: these ancient perverts were going to jail if I could put them there.

"So let me get this straight: they are caught sucking young cock, so we are going to send them to jail where they can go nuts and suck all the young cock they want," Scott said, with his typical bottom line analysis.

"I don't think elderly white men are going to be a big hit with the brothers in jail," Kumar said. On cue and without direction, black Scott assumed the role of the white Irish priest and white Harrison tore his fake collar off and assumed the role of the young, black inmate. Blasphemous improvisation was off and running. Bruce Lebby assumed the role of a cellmate who was uninterested in sex with the priest because of his age, but "still wanted to be friends." Kumar was laughing so hard a single tear fell out of the corner of his left eye.

There was a knock at the door. I was told the jury had reached a verdict. Forty minutes. That had to mean guilty. Judge Watson had told the jurors they weren't going home until a verdict was reached. She knew that would get them to focus.

I called Tomar and told him that his assassins were convicted of all charges.

"Man, I'm surprised, I didn't think the jury would do that so quick. Big ups to you, Clay, big ups to you. I guess they believed me," he said. "How 'bout my testimony, do you think that helped?"

"Yes." Obviously the adrenaline from testifying and the pulse of the courtroom was still in his veins.

"You were great, the jury loved you," I told him for the sixth time.

"That Lodge dude was simple, but Mr. Jack Shane was pretty slick," Tomar said.

"Jack Shane is a politician, good at manipulating judges and the system. Once it turns into a trial, though, he's nothing special. There's R. Kenneth Mundy, there's anyone from the law firm of Williams and Connolly, several Fifth Street lawyers, and a couple of public defenders that strike fear in my heart—but not Jack."

"You alright, Clay. I really want to thank you. I really appreciate everything you did. Now I don't have to kill them niggas. You know I was gonna do that. If you ever need anything just page me. If any of these low-level courthouse niggas bother you, you call me, I'll take care of them for you."

"Thanks, just stay out of trouble. That would be the biggest favor you could do for me." I momentarily thought of asking him to kill a judge or two that had punked me one too many times, but came to my senses.

"Oh, I'm clean. No more gambling, no more slinging rocks. I got a job, I got a health care program for my baby, I'm done with the street," Tomar lied sweetly.

The office was emptying out. Alexandra and Scott came by.

"Have a good night, and congrats," Alexandra said, then added, "Oh, and I'm sorry, but I can't make Christmas dinner."

Scott chimed in, "That goes for me, too. Looks like I'll have to wait another year for the show."

Scott and Alexandra were practically part of my family—they had joined my parents and I for many courthouse lunches and Redskins games. They had yet to make it to Christmas dinner, which always proved to be a dysfunctional though highly entertaining portrait of Wasps in their native habitat.

I let out an audible sigh and responded, "Well, there's always next year." As Alexandra left, I gave Scott a ninety-second highlight reel of the trial. I told him Tomar had excellent product for sale. Scott told me they caught the shooter that murdered Bradford Slater. He was being interviewed at Homicide. I was relieved about that, and hoped the police would conduct the interview properly. They knew my number if there was a problem.

I was both wired and exhausted as I searched for a parking space near Dupont Circle—often more difficult than winning a murder trial. It was a cold night and the bright florescent crime lights gave the low hanging clouds an orange tint. I headed over to Kramer Books & Afterwords for a bite to eat and to see if there were any interesting women bumping around the Search-for-the-Far-From-Perfect-Man Aisle. After dinner in the café section I attempted to strike up conversation with an earthy, older woman in the recent non-fiction section. I wasn't getting any cougar dial tone. I should have known better. You never find a non-fiction babe looking for romance.

I called Kim on my cell as I headed home. She actually wanted to get together. "At this point it looks better for tomorrow night," I said. *The camera will love you,* I was tempted to tell her.

## Chapter 2

# Tunnel of Love

## DECEMBER 3, 1999

The message light on my office phone was blinking. My guess was forty-five out of the fifty calls were asking how I was going to avenge the death of Bradford Slater. I didn't even have time to think about how I felt about prosecuting seventeen-year-old Kevin Ford. I had another trial next week; I was trying to convict a crazy crack enforcer named Kelly Lord and I did not want to review the case. The teacher homicide was screaming for attention (just returning the phone calls would eat the day), and, most importantly, I had to buy more videotape. Not only would the Slater case ruin my social life, but a loss could ruin my career. I didn't want to turn my back on the community, but Kim's body was sick. I had so much to do I didn't know where to start—so I didn't. Scott was in my office reading the *Washington Post*. That was my cue to open the *New York Times* I picked up along with my triple shot grind-your-teeth espresso.

"Do you think people perceive us as lazy 'cause we're just sitting here reading the papers?" I asked Scott.

"It's a government job. We are surrounded by people that say, 'Thank God it's Friday,' as if they haven't been slacking off all week. We could set up a hammock and a hibachi, and no one would say anything," Scott said without looking up from his paper. "My WorldCom stock is kicking ass."

A bit irritated that Scott had *extra* money to invest, I shot back, "When your stock crashes it will kick your ass—it's like legalized gambling."

"It's only money," Scott responded. He wasn't about to take my attitude sitting down. "At least I come home each night to an actual family."

"You're calling me a low-fidelity kind of guy? Shit, before you were married you were the courthouse slut. You're the one that says, 'Hey, let's cruise through the jury lounge to see if there are any tens bumping around.' Oh, by the way, how's everything at home?"

"Wait until you have children, then you'll understand my state of mind," Scott replied. "I can't wait to see you not get laid."

That thought bounced through my head for a second. "Fuck. I feel work guilt." I put my feet on my desk. "I still should be doing some work on the teacher case for the bond hearing. After that I'll tell Tommy to transfer the case to someone else. I should at least talk to some witnesses before the defense attorneys and reporters get to them."

"It's too late, everybody has already interviewed the kids at the high school," Scott reported. "There was even a group of white kids there giving some ballet performance or something. Once again, your work is done. You don't need to talk to anyone. It's all here in the papers, except the article about you being the laziest trial lawyer in homicide."

"White kids at Carver High? They're lucky they got out alive. Why are you giving me so much shit today?"

"Where's my tape, goddamn it? Where's big Kim, the girl from the Washington Sports Club?" Scott asked.

"Tonight for me, Monday for you," I told him as Annette invaded my office.

"Congratulations on your guilty verdict, pussy man." Annette had obviously forgotten about yesterday's door slamming episode.

"Shut the door and keep your voice down. Please don't call me pussy man or pussy monger, it's unprofessional," I said with faux seriousness. I loved Annette. My ally and surrogate mother—she always had my back. African-American, her age was a mystery— probably thirty-five, give or take a decade. She was five-feet, four-inches tall, weighed ninety-eight pounds, and rumor had it she had a little crack problem the year before I arrived. During that time, she melted down one day in the office and threatened a clique of the support staff at the top of her lungs that she was going to kill them all with an Uzi machine gun. After a few weeks off, she came back and it was basically no harm, no foul. I always found the story hard to believe because she was kindness personified and a great good time. It also made me wonder if there was anything you could do in civil service to actually get fired.

"It's Friday night. Date night number one, Sweetness. Don't lie to your Annette. A monster like you got something lined up." Annette snooped and then greeted Scott. "Good morning soul brother. How are those kids?"

"They never stop eating, but I doubt you'd understand. You look like you could be the Miss Ethiopia contestant in the Miss Universe pageant, let me buy you lunch."

"You used to be nice before you started hanging out with Clay," she responded. "I'm leaving. I got work to do. I don't want to hang around you two monsters."

"Here, take this pile of paper and answer these motions some time over the next month, please," I said, only half-kidding. I love the obscenely slow government work ethic.

"Don't get no AT with me, boyfriend, I'll wash your mouth out with soap," she said. "AT" was her acronym for attitude. Any type of hauteur was forbidden. She took the files. She would answer them in a timely fashion.

"Of course I have something lined up. I'm going to meet her at the gym; we're doing a spin class together. I'm leaving early. If anyone calls, tell them I went to homicide to meet with detectives," I said.

"People been calling all day about that dead teacher. He's a legend. My cousin had him at Carver High, said he was the best teacher he ever had, best teacher in the whole damn school. All of the reporters are calling me because your voicemail is full and won't take no more messages. C'mon now, delete those messages so they stop bothering me." Her deep, raspy voice seemed disproportionate to the size of her body.

"I'll start calling people back, I promise." I could at least work the phone today.

"Okay, Sweetness, and I'll cover for you when you leave early." Annette loved to gather little cover-up chits against me so she could turn them in for little gifts and cover-ups for herself. You scratch my time sheet and I'll scratch yours. "Hey, what kind of date is that? Meeting a girl at a gym? That's a silly white thing. You should take her out to dinner; tell her to put on a nice dress, high heels, and some fish net stockings."

"Scott is wearing fishnet stockings today," I told her.

"You're sick Clay," she told me and ran to catch her phone.

"You going to take the case?" Scott asked.

"No. Will you take it?"

"I have seven homicide trials scheduled over the next ten weeks. I respectfully decline, sir." Scott imitated the overly formal Judge Stone.

As Scott walked out of the office, I voicemailed a good morning to Alexandra and began returning my calls. Thirty calls left. Still not in the mood to work-work, I'd start with Phil, a runaround buddy and *Washington Post* editor (we met when he covered the courthouse). We worked D.C. at night like it was a second job. Actually, he worked it like it was his first job. A man of little patience and big lust, if there was no "talent" at Paulo's in Georgetown he would zoom us down to Chinatown in his black Porsche Carrera. (Speeding? No problem—I put my D.A.'s badge on his dashboard. Phil was disappointed we never got stopped because he was going to tell the cop he was "in pursuit of hot" instead of "in hot pursuit." I told him the cop would not understand either phrase and to slow down.)

"What's up news-boy?" I asked him.

Phil fired away, "Dude, that teacher homicide is going to be huge. The president is milking it for all it's worth. There's a white moustache on his upper lip. Where the fuck have you been? There was a great party last night. You should have returned my phone call; there were some incredibly hot bitches. I got two numbers from women who were about ten feet apart. It was a stressful situation. Where have you been? How's the Slater case going, anyway?"

"You're never going to believe this, but I actually have other cases to try here. So, no, I am not going to do the teacher case. I will do the bond hearing on the kiddie killer, but not the jury trial. I'm burned out. Big cases ruin my social life. Let someone else work fourteen hours a day and eat carryout for six months. I'd rather chase women." Phil was far more decadent than me. Drank every day. Lazy too. I often wondered how Phil advanced to being an editor. The art of failing upward, I guess; it certainly took place at the D.A.'s office.

"That's why I became an editor," Phil said. "I got sick of covering city council meetings deep into the night. I wanted better hours and more fun. Right now I am emailing about four different women I'm working. Surfing the net, watching CNN, flirting online. Lemme tell you about my roster. Hang on, I'm almost done with this email. God, this girl is such a tease. She's asking me what kind of underwear I like. What should I say?"

"Tell her you like underwear that has a picture of you wearing a policeman's uniform, holding up an outstretched hand, and saying, 'Do Not Enter, This Area Is Off-Limits'," I suggested, adding, "And tell her that you want her to wear those panties to keep away all the other guys."

"Okay, that sounds fine—it'll give her the impression of commitment," he said. Phil was divorced and about as anti-marriage as you could get. He once told me that as far as he was concerned, men were genetically encoded for multiple partners and the only thing that got in the way was a woman's demand for monogamy.

"Wouldn't commitment involve you actually being there? I think most women would prefer that over cartoon chastity belt-themed underwear."

"I tried that. I know you want to get married, but wait until you spend Sunday going to Home Depot, coming back to the house, and staining the deck." I could hear the war wounds in Phil's voice.

"I changed my mind; tell her 'no underwear'," I said.

"It's too late, I already sent the email," Phil said. "Are you sure you aren't going to take the teacher murder? It's like shooting Bobby Knight in Indiana. It will be an easy case to win, and you'll end up nailing a couple of court groupies."

"No, I'm not taking the case, and no murder case is an easy win." I tried to change the subject. "What makes the perfect woman? Come on, gimme your list."

"Beautiful, tall, lot of money, thirty to forty, good family, highly-educated, smart, funny—did I say tall?—has her first orgasm while we are kissing, her second orgasm while she is going down on me." He paused for a moment and then continued, "Accepts me for who I am and understands that I'm going to be spending a lot of time watching football on Sundays. And that I will never stain any deck again."

"You're so lucky D.C. does not have the death penalty. If I posted a transcript of this conversation on the Internet you would be arrested and a nine-judge panel of women would unanimously order death by lethal injection. That's your list? You'll never get remarried," I told him.

Then the phone rang. I put Phil on hold and took a call from one of the detectives on the teacher homicide. The evidence clock was ticking. I had to give this case back to Tommy to reassign. Made a few notes, told him I'd call him back, and went back to Phil to hear him defend his stripper.

"She's tall. Plus, she's working her way through school. She doesn't do any drugs and she's just trying to pay for college. She has her shit together and she's not like the other strippers," Phil explained.

"She's not like the other strippers? That's what every guy says when they date a stripper. What about good family and all that stuff? Her family's assets probably depend on how much gas is in their trailer at the time the net worth analysis is done," I said. I was about to give up, but I added, "And what about a family? What's up with that? Are you going to have a child together? I can just hear her saying, 'Put that money down, honey, don't play with mommy's tips.'

I can't keep talking; I have to figure out how to get out of doing the teacher murder." We exchanged Friday night plans in case our dates changed their minds. My other line rang and I picked it up.

"Hi." It was my friend Kara. *Friend?* What do you call a woman you want to marry that is already married? We had met years before at Georgetown University Law School. We studied together during first year, and then she quit and enrolled in the Corcoran School of Art in D.C. The law never trumped her love of art. To no one's surprise, she went on to become a rock star graphic designer. From the beginning, she ignored my overt lust and kept the friendship going; she would waive her ring finger and say, "You must be confusing me with someone who is single," smiling as the diamond glittered. Her smile bested the beauty of the diamond. It wasn't like she hated the law, she just liked art more; in fact, she found criminal law fascinating and came to many of my jury trials. Over the years we would go to lunch, and I gave her dating details, lots of details. Sometimes she shook her head, said I overindulged, then called me a "sick puppy," but she dug it.

"Kara my girl, how are ya?" I asked, but something was obviously wrong. The sound of her voice always bumped me up but now she sounded sad.

"You know about that teacher, Bradford Slater?" her voice started to crack.

"Sure—sounded like more of a saint than a teacher. Just terrible what happened." I struggled to figure out where she was going.

"I just can't believe it. I took a summer course from him at the Corcoran—he was just so amazing. I probably would have gone back to law school without the support he gave me." She paused to compose herself. "Why would anyone want to hurt that guy?" I started to see where this was going. "Are you taking the case?" she asked.

"Well, I'm handling the bond hearing, but the office hasn't decided who would try the case." My lie was practically involuntary.

"I figured you'd grab a case like this and wouldn't let anyone near it." She sounded surprised. "What happened to you?" I could not tell if she was joking. The last thing I wanted to do was disappoint Kara. She told me how Bradford Slater had a tremendous impact on hundreds of students; she had met several artists and designers that chose their professions because of him. Instinctually, I began taking some notes to add to the file. I hoped that a lunch date was on the horizon when Kara suddenly suggested a Sunday afternoon movie and coffee. Her invitation threw me off for a second.

"Sure, that sounds great. Where's Mr. Investment Banker? Gathering equity on the links?" She tolerated my slightly disparaging remarks about her hubby.

"We'll talk. See you Sunday," she said.

I hung up feeling Kara-buzzed (it was her voice—it did me in every time), and began thinking about my next move. No matter how she meant it, her "What happened to you?" remark had stung. I began thinking of taking the case. Maybe I was rationalizing, but it was more than just wanting to win her over. If this teacher meant so much to her, then maybe this thing was worth my time.

At the top of the callback list were the detectives working on the teacher homicide. Messages were left. While I decided whether I would take the case, I would be professional and gather some information for the bond hearing. If I was going to go forward, I had to get the witnesses in the grand jury to lock in their statements as soon as possible, but I still had a few days to nail that down. Next, I had to feed the monster and call the *Post* reporters back. In my no-nonsense tone of voice, I apologized for not calling back quicker and explained that I had been in trial. I gave them the macro-stroke editorial that Tommy Monroe is as outraged as the community, and that the death stunned us all. I knew the minute my voice ceased I would be probed for information, so I preempted that onslaught by informing the reporter that I couldn't comment on the investigative details of a pending case, but I could tell him that I would request no bond for the young shooter. Usually, the reporters ignored the stock answer and kept asking questions, but today they backed off. Probably because they knew more than me, or they knew that I didn't know anything worth reporting. Besides, they had to leave to go hunt down and interview the witnesses that I had yet to interview.

After hours of pushing paper and returning about three-dozen forgettable phone calls, Alexandra walked in, thank God.

"I read the papers at lunch. This kid has got to get life without parole. Slater meant so much to the city." She went on, "This case has your name all over it."

I rolled my eyes and changed subjects. "Let's forget about that case right now and go cruise the corridors of justice for hotties," I suggested. She was also in dating mode. "C'mon, let's go see if the perfect girl is bumping around the courthouse. Maybe one of us will get lucky."

"That sounds like fun, but I can't, I'm slammed." She wore stringy, gold earrings from a country in North Africa, Upper Whatever, a gift from some victim's family for winning a case.

"What is the perfect girl for you? What's your list?" I continued to play, not wanting her to leave.

"There is no list," she said.

"Oh, come on, you don't have a list of certain qualities you are looking for? Good looking, intelligent? Just answer the question," I said, but I knew what she was talking about.

"Sure there are some basic things: the person is emotionally stable, good, real, sexy, and honest. But those feelings I mentioned are like an X-factor—it's either there or it isn't. You just want to be with that person. There are women in this office that married cops or carpenters and are way happy, and women who married lawyers or doctors and are hating life. I'm not sure I buy into the list. It's just the way you feel when you are with them," she said without restraint.

"But no one ever married a real estate broker and has been happy, have they?" I knew Alexandra disliked realtors. As she glanced at the Slater file on my desk, she quickly switched back to a work gear. "So what, you're ducking that case? You are purposely not taking the teacher homicide? I don't get it. This is so not you. You're burned out? You're the one that whines that you hate losing, laziness, and whining. And here you are acting all whiny. So what if you're slammed? I know these cases exhaust us for months on end and then you get some hung jury or some slow-witted juror gives you a bizarre verdict, but what has that got to do with what we are about?"

"Kara wants me to do it."

"True Love Fantasy Kara?"

I nodded.

Again I tried to switch subjects. "And by the way, I am assigning you the worst of the sex priests, Father Dugan. He *accidentally* molested twenty-two boys. You don't back off, and I don't want anything to jeopardize the case of this not-so-holy man. Good-bye, darling." As she walked out, I added, "I have to buy some videotape." Alexandra threw me a faux look of disapproval, then whispered that she was jealous. Enough talking, I was off to the Washington Sports Club to marvel at Kim's body.

I noodled my way through traffic from the courthouse, past the White House, and up Connecticut Avenue toward Dupont Circle. My nerves were a bit jangled. I felt upset because Kara was upset, and a tad guilty for not working on the Slater case. I momentarily wondered whether my brand of fun was the right medicine.

\*

I entered the class a couple of minutes late, of course. It worked. Kim whispered, "You made it" as I adjusted the bike that goes nowhere.

"Newborn Friend" by Seal was blaring out of the speakers at the Washington Sports Club. (They threw in oldies for people in their thirties and forties.) The Lycra-clad spin class teacher encouraged everyone to peddle their hearts out as Seal encouraged the listener to sing harder, my friend. The music segued into a slow song. "Okay, add resistance," the teacher said as The Sneaker Pimps sang "6 Underground."

"Let's go. Push it. If you don't give me a hundred and ten percent, leave now. Stand up, hands on the end of those handle bars. You're going up a mountain. Imagine the sky is blue—I know it's hard because you never see blue sky in Washington D.C., but pretend you're out West, peddling up that mountain. Your hopes and dreams and aspirations will not be denied. Keep peddling, one more quarter of a turn, add resistance..." I tried to peddle through my responsibilities into the suggested upbeat mindscape, but failed. The Kelly Lord attempted murder trial next week was one side of the vice and whether to take the teacher homicide was the other. The Kelly Lord trial had not been thoroughly prepared. When was the last time I thoroughly prepared a case? Was I becoming a soft government worker? Even Kara was losing respect for me. I thought of the six Ps my father taught me: proper preparation prevents piss poor performance. *Less prep, more slop,* I thought. But first I would enjoy tonight. I would deal with my narrow margin of error later.

Kim and I were soaked with sweat. She looked at me and smiled. I wanted to smile back but merely rolled my eyes as comically as I could. She was wearing tight, black, shorts and a small white t-shirt, short above the belly button. I assumed she was wearing a sports bra underneath but when she lifted up her top to wipe some sweat from her face I realized she was wearing what looked like a webbed bathing suit top. The webbing had five or six slits in the fabric about three inches wide between the breasts. Oh, right, Kim, like you just happened to lift up your top to wipe some sweat away when I'm standing in front of you. Puh-leaze. Okay, it worked. An outline of marmoreal luster. Good move. Coming attractions to a theater near me, I hoped.

"That's nice workout gear," I said, and felt like grabbing my cell phone and calling Annette to tell her my date was wearing something very similar to fishnet stockings—over her breasts.

"Thanks, it's from a California company called Carushka Bodywear."

Kim never joked, she always supplied the facts. Does it come with a manufacturer's guarantee to drive men crazy?

"Do you want to meet by the front desk?" she asked as we headed to the showers.

My mind's eye recalled her lifting her top. I saw her sculpted form and the defined line leading down the center of her stomach. And those jutting hips. Not something one should dwell on while parading through a locker room.

I put our gym bags in the back of my car. I could barely wait to get my hands on Tall Kim. "Are you hungry?" I asked.

"Starving," she replied.

I met her at a party a few weeks before and we had made and broken plans twice. Traffic was light and soon we were at the restaurant a few blocks from the White House. The Red Sage put six million dollars into its interior. The ceiling above the bar area had an expansive, three-dimensional western skyscape with thick, plaster clouds; hidden within the artificial cumulus was high tech lighting to simulate flashes of lightning.

She came from the Midwest and was so impressed with Capitol Hill it was ridiculous. Since I had grown up in D.C., it was almost hard to keep a straight face when people from the fly-over states started name-dropping. Senator-this, Congressman-that—who cared? (I was on a mission though, so I counter-dropped the names of the smart and the famous from the world of journalism that my family entertained.) I sipped my margarita, then gulped, and focused on making her feel like the center of the universe. I herded the conversation away from politics toward flirtation. "I want to tell you before I get drunk that you looked totally h-o-t at the gym. Every guy and most of the women in there were checking you out."

She smiled, allowing the compliment to marinate. The sky above the bar brooded, waiting for an impending storm. Kim told me she was never going to get too involved with a man until her "house was in order," which she defined as satisfying all her professional, emotional, and financial goals. She also felt it was important for the man to have his house in order as well. Of course, I wondered if anyone's house ever gets in order. The lightning flashed in the big white clouds.

I wanted to invite her back to my apartment to "listen to music" but was not getting that vibe. Then she swung the conversation toward the Slater homicide. "Do you think you might get that case where that teacher was murdered? I knew this girl on the Oklahoma Bombing trial; right after the case she went straight into a big national firm as a partner. She went from welfare to two hundred fifty a year."

Cha-ching. Typical transient Washington chick. Came to town looking to look up to somebody. East Coast Hollywood. Power, money. Fine, I'd use this as the leverage I needed to get us to my apartment.

"Yeah, that's the dream. I'm actually already working the Slater case pretty hard," I exaggerated; we were both playing the same game. She asked me what the kid was like and I told her that I couldn't interview the kid because he has a lawyer, and explained that pretrial services provides an extensive report about the kiddie killer's life for the court. And in a few weeks, there would come a time when we would argue whether the kid should be tried as an adult or a juvenile. At that time I'd know more about the kid. The hook was in, and the tequila had hammered us.

"Wanna listen to some music at my apartment?" I asked. She paused for a moment, but I knew she wouldn't be too tired. At dinner, I said I was not hungry, and no self-respecting woman—no matter which planet she's from—is going to order heavy while the guy orders light. We split one order of wild mushroom enchiladas. I knew that would not dilute her energy level. I looked into her blue-gray eyes. Her large shoulders cut a nice V down to her waist. I waited for her reply, knowing she had drunk two full margaritas.

On the way home, I was stopped by the police two blocks from my P. Street apartment in Georgetown (speeding, running stop signs, take your choice). After I showed the cop my license, which I kept next to my badge, he asked me to step to the back of my white BMW (leased, of course). I told him I was a little drunk, but my apartment was two blocks away and I needed to go home immediately to perform nude field sobriety tests on my date. He laughed and told me to have fun. Life was a Monopoly game, and my D.A.'s badge was a get out of jail free card.

"Can I hang your coat up?" I said as I dropped it to the ground and began kissing her.

I put on music—Luscious Jackson, the theme song for my videos —as she went to the bathroom. The kissing and stripping of clothes continued. Almost to the bedroom, Kim gently pushed me back, grabbing the chin up bar in the doorjamb.

"I always wanted to be one of those Cirque du Soleil girls," Kim said as she lifted herself in the air. I approached and she wrapped her legs around my waist.

"You've got to let me film this," I pleaded.

"If you turn on that camera, the show's over," she whispered in my ear.

Oh well, a memory was better than nothing. After several acts, an intermission, and a grand finale, Kim quietly dressed and left.

Given a moment to myself, I was right back where I started. Kara. The Bradford Slater case. The upcoming Kelly Lord trial. I was overindulging to escape from something. I was still drunk.

I faded in and out of consciousness as a police helicopter buzzed the roof. Its circular whirling sound was the soundtrack for my spinning head. Police helicopters buzzed D.C. apartment buildings looking for crack-addled burglars, who were looking for anything they could carry and sell for twenty dollars. One more rock to amuse themselves. At the end of the day, we just can't get enough of what we don't need.

# December 4, 1999

I was awakened by the phone. It was Tommy Monroe, our fear-filled leader.

"How's my boy doing?" Tommy inquired.

"I'm fine, just taking a Saturday siesta. How is the Monroe Machine, D.A. for life?" I stroked him.

"An afternoon siesta? You're supposed to be in the office or at the gym."

"Last night got out of control," I said.

"Now that's the Clay I know. Nice tits?" Tommy was not known for his subtlety.

I was creeping back into consciousness. "You're so busy chasing skirts and votes... are you calling about Slater? I mean, seriously, what else could you possibly be calling about on a weekend?

"Have you seen that new show, 'Town Meeting'? The president and the secretary of education were on there, yakking about how we have to curb violence in our schools in light of Slater's murder. My God boy! You'd have to be a pussy to walk away from this case."

"Yeah, of course I'll take it," I quietly declared. I was hungover but the situation had been brewing within me.

"What changed your mind?" Tommy skeptically asked.

"I can't have Scott taking all the glory," I said. "I'd never live it down." That was easier than telling the truth. I'm not even sure I knew what the truth was. All I knew was that I had a chance to impress Kara, which is all I wanted to do after another wasted night.

That's my boy. You gonna win it for me, get me some good ink? There are kids at the school who saw things, heard things. You of all people know that testimony needs to be locked in. I know the homicide detectives are all over it, but I want you supervising and making sure they don't fuck up people's rights like they always do. People are asking about whether the father is going to be charged because it was his gun." When Tommy was under pressure, he would just talk out of sheer nervousness. We both knew the case was going to turn into a great western wildfire with a weather pattern all its own.

"I'll do my best," I said, hungover and at my worst. "Meanwhile you can relax. The little fucker hasn't even hired a defense attorney, the public defender he has right now isn't going to do anything, and the *Post* reporter is not going to go into the ghetto to find the other witnesses. I'll find the witnesses before they do. And as for Daddy, forget about it. Where do you think that is going? Until I find out more, the kid stole his father's gun. You think the father said, 'Here's my gun, son, go out and bust a cap into the most loved teacher in D.C.'?"

"Keep talking," Tommy said.

My mind moved from prosecutorial to political. "At first, I was thinking of indicting the father too, but I don't think the evidence is there. You want to show everyone how tough you are politically, and you can continue to do that by indicting the cops that are stealing cash and drugs or beating people up—not by going after this kid's father. The situation between you and the police is so flammable it's actually a good idea to leave him alone—unless hard evidence turns up. You want me to indict and slam a father? Wait 'til one of those Catholic priests doesn't take a deal in a molestation case. They deserve to be crucified."

"Okay, you got it under control. Just checking. Make sure you bring a detective with you when you go into a tough neighborhood. I don't like it when my boys investigate cases alone. That's too dangerous," Tommy warned.

Tommy was hung like a gerbil when it came to big decisions, but I liked him. He always seemed to err on the side of the humane. He liked the fact that D.C. did not have the death penalty, and he refused to fire an employee no matter how inept they were. (Tommy stood by Annette when she threatened to kill everyone in the office with an Uzi—and he hadn't even slept with her.)

Once I got off the phone with Tommy, I stopped to collect my thoughts. I had ignored this case long enough. It was time to get involved. Kara would be proud of me. Then again, I told myself, *Forget Kara, she's married and I'm sick of wanting something I can't have.* First thing I did was leave a message at homicide for Detective Johnny LeGray (he couldn't handle the case because of the pending corruption case against him, but he'd have inside information concerning the killer's father). I made some coffee, called homicide to find out who the lead detective was, left a message, began reading the paper, and did a little channel surfing. Like a box of cereal that fell on the floor, news bites were everywhere. CLICK, a young black man with elephant-leg baggy jeans told the CNN camera, "There wasn't no reason for 'dis." CLICK, a cluster of young black women cried and hugged. CLICK, yellow police tape surrounded a small area for no reason except to allow police officers to huddle around and ask each other why anyone would shoot this poor guy who devoted his life to kids. CLICK, a chalk outline of Bradford's body at the time of death. A reporter looked into the camera and said, "Teacher Bradford Slater is dead, but why?" *Stupid question.* Motive, as Annette would say, was a silly white thing. Triggers were often pulled for no reason at all. Or for juice, respect. Sometimes curiosity, like trying marijuana for the first time. Slater was extremely popular among the students. He didn't just teach art, but rebirth through art. "Ineffable sadness gripped the school," said the *Post* writer whose name I could not pronounce. I barely recognized any of the new bylines. Shit, I was beginning to sound like my father.

According to the *Post*, Bradford Slater had transformed crack addicts into violinists and painters. And then some punk blew him away in the basement below the stage in the performing arts section of the school. Although there would be community sympathy in the jury pool, unless I had witnesses locked into statements they gave to the police or grand jury, I would have nothing for trial. I had to enter the hard luck world that swirled around the defendant and I needed a gun and a driver, also known as a detective. I was first going to cancel my date with Michelle the Coco Loco Hostess, but decided that she was too sought-after to deserve the courtesy. Why should I call? *Man, did you see that hostess?* she would hear the men whisper as she seated them. I decided to play the mystery card and stand her up. (Sunday I would hang out with Kara. We never cancelled on each other.)

It was the weekend but traffic was heavy. I crept through Georgetown. Third lanes turned into parking lanes, and then there were the tourists. Things lightened up as I headed up Indiana Avenue. Not much shopping around the homicide unit. "Hey Sarge...." I nodded. No need to flash the badge—old-fashioned face recognition. A door buzzed and in I went. Another Saturday evening at homicide (Scott and I called it "Saturday Night Dead"). There were some pictures on a bulletin board of missing children. I avoided their horror movie stares. Couldn't get distracted. First I need witnesses and then I need someone to distract me.

Homicide: fluorescent lights (some blinked, some didn't work at all), battleship gray metal desks, an occasional Washington Redskins football calendar nailed into the cement wall, a mismatched assortment of chairs and mini-refrigerators. Detective Hud Sutcliffe was one of the cops assigned to the case. Hud had been involved in a number of questionable shootings, but somehow he was still assigned to homicide. I guess if I had my choice of being with a cop that was asleep at the wheel or trigger happy, I'd choose the latter. He was one of the few homicide detectives I had not dealt with directly before, so I went through my standard motivational speech. I told him how important the case was, how it would be scrutinized. He was surprisingly enthusiastic to my blah blah blah. We began reviewing the police reports and his notes. He dished out large helpings of fact and rumor.

According to Hud, the kiddie killer, Kevin Ford, brought his father's nine-millimeter semi-automatic handgun to school. Bradford Slater's last moments went something like this: there was a performance in the school's auditorium; Bradford went downstairs to get a piece of equipment; and Kevin Ford—who was a lighting assistant or something—followed him downstairs and shot him in a basement room below the stage area.

"That is quite a show," I said.

After Kevin Ford shot Bradford Slater he bolted up the steps from the basement. Then the events get confusing. On that day the Kirov Ballet of Washington was giving a guest performance. Kevin Ford bumped into a dancer, Galina, with a difficult-to-pronounce Russian name. *Russian Ballerina? I'll talk to her personally. Interviewing a hot dancer is better than reading cold case law.* Then he bumped into another student very hard as he was exiting the school. The male student was about to punch him, but Kevin lifted up his shirt and revealed the handgun in his waistband. Bullets trump punches, so the pissed-off student backed off. Kevin continued his nightmarish getaway run. Then a small group of students (male, of course) broke into a jog and followed Kevin as he ran through a small wooded area and came to a stop behind some failed housing projects. Hud said that he heard a rumor on the street that as soon as the kids went behind a house and approached Kevin, he shouted, "You hangin' with a murderer." I stopped taking notes, looked at him, and he continued.

While the kids were standing around looking at Kevin's gun, every cop and ambulance siren in Washington, D.C. was collectively screaming like a banshee. Despite Kevin's bragging, one of the teenagers assumed the alpha-dog role, and said he wanted the gun for future use. According to more street rumor, the older guy, David Triplett, took the gun and they dispersed. Kevin then ran to the house of a sympathetic family. It was the mother of a friend, and he told her he shot Mr. Slater. The woman, who had been like a second mother to young Kevin, drove him to the police station. But she wouldn't cooperate with the police. Kevin gave a statement saying that it was accidental.

As Hud read, I looked up from my notes and glanced at him. "It was an accident, 'boo hoo hoo', hours after 'U hangin' wiff a mur-der-er'." Hud smirked and shook his head.

"What happened next?" I asked, as Hud continued reading from his notes.

"Kevin then took the police on a wild gun chase, leading them to the small wooded spot and telling them he threw the gun in there. After several hours of dogs sniffing the woods and cops walking the area, Kevin then confessed that he gave the gun away. The cops took him back to the police station and showed him a Carver High School yearbook. Kevin circled a black and white photograph of a student and said he gave the gun to him; however, the picture he circled was *not* David Triplett."

"Now *that* is what I call a busy day: you steal your dad's gun, kill a teacher, give the gun away to another thug to maximize the gun's use, give the police a false statement, take them on an imaginary treasure hunt, and top it off by accusing an innocent person of hiding evidence," I said. "Do me a favor, please call your wife; tell her you're not coming home tonight. We are not going to sleep until we have taken statements from this little clique of guys that heard 'You hanging with a murderer.'" I handed Hud the receiver.

\*

First stop was the home of witness Terrance Overton, one of the teenagers that heard Kevin's boast. The newspapers had already laid it all out before I had interviewed my first witness: accidental versus intentional shooting, and I had to get some language of intent. Hud's police radio squawked out bits of information in the bizarre language of police-eze. Hud translated and informed me that one of the young witnesses was locked up on a theft charge. Already? The murder occurred on Thursday; now it was Saturday and one of my so-called witnesses was already locked up. Why should I be surprised—I mean who hangs around someone who shoots a teacher anyway?

We headed toward a tough neighborhood in the northeast quadrant of Washington, D.C., near the borderline with Prince

George's County, Maryland. The smell of Hud's miniature pine tree air freshener hanging from the rear-view mirror was nauseating (Did every cop car come with one of these?). It was Saturday night, and thank God he was armed. People would be going wild, shooting drugs while they shot at each other. The Nation's Capitol was also the homicide capitol.

At a stoplight I noticed a license plate surrounded by a rectangle of twisted steel. We pulled closer. The driver had a Timothy McVeigh rednecky look but he sported closely cropped blonde hair with a long, thick ponytail protruding from the base of his skull. While I observed his unusual hairdo, which gave the appearance of a Davy Crockett coonskin hat, he rolled down the window of his muscular Dodge Daytona. "What the fuck are you looking at?" he said with a thick Baltimore accent. I was in a cop car. A car with the D.C. police insignia on the door and cop lights on the roof. I was stunned as he sped off.

"That's the kind of balls people have in this neighborhood," Hud said, dismissing the insanity as commonplace. We continued on our mission, driving further into shadows and darkness. We slowed down as we approached the Overton home. Most of the cars in front of the row houses looked typical, except for the occasional gangsta car, which looked to be decorated by an angry Liberace, with tinted windows and over-the-top wheel-rim combinations. We parked behind an Escalade. The driver was talking on his cellphone and watched us as we walked up the sidewalk. The Overton's row house looked well maintained but was surrounded by some pretty beat-up northeast D.C. properties.

The inside of their house was eerily clean. The couch and chairs were covered with thick plastic, and the ceramic animals that decorated the living room shone as if drenched in cemetery moonlight. It felt like punishment was in the air. *You left a dirty glass in the sink? You're grounded for a week. You went and talked to the kid who shot the teacher? I'm gonna tan your hide 'til it falls off.* Hud and I introduced ourselves to Mr. and Mrs. Overton. We flashed badges and gave our cards. Mom said she didn't want our cards. Dad put them in his pocket without inspecting them. Mom disappeared into a backroom and Mr. Overton refused to sit as we interviewed his son.

"Well, you know why we are here. I'll cut to the chase. Tell us what you know about the incident," Hud began.

Mr. Overton was an enormous, forty-something, dark-skinned African American, about six-four. He folded his arms and frowned as Terrance denied hearing anything. "It happened so quick and there was more than one dude talking. I think I heard Kevin say something but I'm not sure. I don't really know much," the kid said, looking at the ground. There was more to it, but I knew I wasn't going to hear it today with his father silently dominating the room. A single tear ran down Terrance's cheek and he quickly wiped it away.

"I know this is hard," I said, looking at Terrance's dad. "Why don't we come back next week? We already took his written statement and now we are just trying to follow up and get a few more details."

"That is probably a good idea," Mr. Overton said.

While I was trying to send a respectful message to Mr. Overton, Hud quietly leaned over and reviewed the statement Terrance gave to the police on Thursday. The statement was short—too short—but the police were interviewing dozens of students that day. Terrance reiterated what was in his written statement—he "might" have heard the "you hangin'" part, but he wasn't sure what else he might have heard. He was a valueless witness for a murder trial. I gave Terrance his grand jury subpoena. It was fruitless to stay there. The teenager's trauma from this ordeal was accentuated by his father lording over him. I would have to wait to find out what, if anything, Terrance knew about the relationship between Kevin Ford and Bradford Slater. What was the motive to pull the trigger?

"He's hiding something," Hud said as we got in the car. "I need to talk to him alone."

"Don't worry, we have plenty of time to talk to him," I said. Actually, I was a bit worried that Terrance was an ambivalent witness —a real problem for a trial attorney because the smallest facts were exploited in the courtroom. "You *might* have heard that? That means you *might not* have heard it, right?" a defense attorney would ask in front of a jury. "You never said you were positive you heard those words," Kevin's attorney would drive the point home at trial. Whoever ended up representing Kevin Ford would use Terrance to show that he knew nothing and there was no intent to kill another human being.

The other kids who were potential witnesses could not be found, so we left free tickets to the grand jury at their respective houses. (Grand Jury Subpoenas were worthless unless properly served, but sometimes people showed up anyway.) We bumped around the city's hardest ghetto, east of the United States' capitol. The next witness on the list was David Triplett, another little punk who heard Kevin Ford brag; he also took the gun from Kevin. He was already locked up in Prince George's County, Maryland, for shoplifting during the weekend. It was almost midnight when we headed to the jail.

# December 5, 1999

It was just past midnight. With some badge-flashing, name-dropping, and arm-twisting, we finally got a jail attendant to wake up the young Mr. Triplett. It was around 1 A.M. when they got him to the interview room. Hud ran his arrest record. Triplett had been popped dozens of times but had never been convicted. (He must have attended Tomar's How to Remain Un-Convicted Seminar.) He had multiple aliases, including "Shoeboot."

"Hello, Mr. Triplett," I greeted him, a big-for-his-age, dark-skinned black kid in an orange jump suit. "You have been working your way through the criminal code. How come you've never been convicted?"

"Shit, man, you shouldn't plea out too quick. If you continue cases, eventually the witnesses don't bother coming to court, and they drop the case," he answered.

"Well, Shoeboot, for someone so clever you stole the wrong pants. You shoplifted Diesel jeans, which are so expensive they'll turn a misdemeanor theft into a felony theft," I said.

We all laughed; even Shoeboot let out a nervous chuckle.

"Who are you? What kind of D.A. be working in *da wee* hours on a Saturday night?" he asked.

I told him my name, and answered his question: "The kind of D.A. who wants to know why one of the most respected teachers in D.C. was shot at point blank range, and why a guy named Shoeboot wants the gun as a collector's item. What's up with those baller moves? Do you have a lawyer yet?" I asked.

"No."

"Talk to me and I'll call the prosecutor in this case on Monday, recommend that the felony be dropped to a misdemeanor, no jail, and unsupervised probation. But if you give us a bunch of bullshit, I'll make sure you do every year, month, week, hour, and minute of a felony jail sentence, and indict your Diesel jean-wearing ass for accessory to first-degree murder, aiding and abetting a murderer by hiding evidence. Comprendo, Señor Shoeboot?" I asked.

"Shit yeah, I'm down with that. Just chill, no reason to get all intense and shit, I'll scratch your back—Señor D.A.," he shot back, cool as ice. "I already help out, I'll keep helping."

"I can't conduct the interview because I can't be a witness at trial in case you start lying in court. Hud will ask the questions and take your statement," I said.

"Straight up man, ain't gonna be no lies," he said. Shoeboot signed the Miranda waiver Hud had dropped on the table.

He told us that when he saw Kevin Ford's nine-millimeter gun he wanted it for protection and to "maybe use in a robbery," but he "would never hurt anyone." Then Shoeboot realized the gun was too hot, so he called the police on Friday and showed them where he had hid it. Hud got on his radio to verify that fact. (The investigation was so decentralized we didn't even know that some cop who had no authority had offered Triplett immunity for the "tip.")

Hud pressed Shoeboot to find out why he was at the school.

"I don't even go to that high school. I was kicked out. I was just up there trying to find a friend of my baby's mother. Ford ain't nothing but a little wannabe. Educator Slater was the last person anyone would want to cap," Shoeboot said.

Hud asked him if he ever heard Ford say "You hangin' with a murderer."

"I didn't hear dat," Shoeboot responded.

"How could you not hear that?" Hud pushed back, his irritation dripped from each syllable.

"Man, I didn't listen to this little punk-ass nigga. I saw the gun and said give it up."

"That's it?" Hud didn't sound convinced.

Hud went back and forth for a few minutes until the subject was strip-mined. The kid denied it, and we left without a critical piece of testimonial evidence.

We gave Triplett a grand jury subpoena. His knowledge of the murder weapon gave us chain of custody value: Shoeboot could potentially tell the jury about Kevin's movements and how the gun was transferred. But still, I was missing critical words of intent. So far I had no one to say they heard "You hangin' with a murderer." A case of this magnitude needed more. Frustrated, I told Hud I wanted to burn through the night to search for the other kids who might have heard Kevin Ford brag.

Next on the list was a kid named Pooh who heard "You hangin' with a murderer." We sped to Stanton Road in southeast D.C., a notorious urban killing field. *The Washington Post* had run a story the year before entitled "An Unlucky Name," which detailed how three young men, all named Andre, died on Stanton Road within three weeks. It was now 3 A.M., and the street was packed.

"Stay close to me," Hud said, then pulled out his gun and took the safety off before putting it back in his holster. I asked him how many people he had shot. He smiled and said, "You don't want to know."

People on the street just assumed I was a cop because I was white. Most of them were so stoned on crack and other goodies that they slowly meandered in the other direction. Some just stared and still others made little taunting remarks as we climbed the cement steps of the apartment building (the elevator was out of order, of course). Isaiah Travers, also known as Pooh, was not home and I apologized to his grandmother for waking her up. She was very cordial in spite of the hour. ("He's not back yet," she told us. *What's the curfew for your grandson, 4 A.M.?* I wondered.)

We talked to people on the street, we knocked on doors, we coffeed up at 7-Eleven, and did it all again and again to no avail. I thanked Hud for his efforts. He told me that he was used to long hours, especially because some of the homicide detectives were on loan to the special priest task force to find and interview a long list of molestation victims. Like a vampire, I entered my apartment during the darkest part of dawn. Too wired to sleep, I began making notes of the special effects I wanted at trial—diagrams, photographic enlargements, et cetera. I made a list of the scientific tests I wanted performed on the gun and Mr. Slater's clothes when I fell asleep.

\*

It was 2 P.M. The phone rang. I thought it might be Johnny LeGray. Why hadn't he called back? The corruption charge must have been keeping him busy. Regardless, I needed to know more about the father of the killer. Instead, I was greeted by the sound of Kara's wonderful voice.

"Hey, are we still on for this afternoon? I'm craving a flick and an Austin Grill enchilada."

"I'm down with that. I could use some breakfast," I said. Where was her husband? I barely knew the guy, didn't want to know him. I'd skipped the San Francisco wedding, and he always seemed to be missing. He was an investment banker who worked crazy hours; what little free time he enjoyed was spent on the golf course.

"Just getting up, are we? Some lucky girl must be exhausted." Kara was that rare combination of ultra feminine and one-of-the-guys.

"I was working that teacher homicide last night. But on Friday night, a hot Amazon was faking an orgasm in the P. Street Palace," I said with a smile. (Kara had coined my apartment "the P. Street Palace.")

"Better to fake an orgasm than fake an entire relationship, I guess." She didn't miss a beat.

We made plans to see *Sling Blade* at The Biograph Theatre in Georgetown with the obligatory cinematic post-mortem conducted over lime-infused beer and salsa. Her voice was soft, clear, intelligent, and nasty-sexy. She was *so it*... too bad she was so taken. I jumped out of bed and went to the front door to grab the *Post*. To my delight, it had not been stolen. I was reading the fat Sunday paper when Kim called. She asked what I was up to, and I told her I had plans with a friend. She didn't believe the truth, and asked me if Friday was a one-time thing because she did not want it to be a one-time thing and she did not usually go that far on a first date (much less climb gymnastic equipment) and on and on. I told her the truth: I worked about eighty hours a week and dated a variety of people. Then I changed gears and lied, telling her I wasn't looking for anything serious.

She didn't buy it. She was one of those: a nice, respectable woman who, when they take it off they expect r-e-s-p-e-c-t. It was the way of the dating world, as simple as a legal arraignment: do you plead guilty or not guilty to the charges? Are you going to hire private counsel or do you need a referral to the public defender? Beneath Kim's passive aggressive friendly Sunday afternoon phone call was my romantic arraignment. Why haven't you called me? Are we a couple? Shouldn't we hang together and see if we are a couple? If you have plans today, why aren't you offering to schedule me in before or after? What about incorporating me into the plans? Why aren't you suggesting we pick another day? Too dazed to deal, I promised to call her early in the week to "do something." On the way to the movies Kim called my cell. She invited me to a Capitol Hill reception of some sort because she had felt she had been too intense over the phone. I accepted but felt like I had been sentenced to three hours of community service.

I parked and waited for Kara. It was a miracle the Biograph Theatre was still in existence. It showed oldies and indies—not much of a product offering in the day of satellite, cable, pay-per-view, and

Netflix. But there it was, the last art house standing, supporting itself with an assortment of film festivals (usually for groups that celebrated their victimization) and by showing XXX-rated movies after midnight. Then I saw it: the SOLD sign. Near the entrance there was a sign that said the Biograph had been bought by a drug store chain. Where tears once fell for *Cinema Paradiso* would soon be aisle number nine where six varieties of tissue would be sold. I bought two tickets and went next door to the newsstand where Kara and I used to meet before the movies.

"Oh my God, Bruce and Demi split," Kara whispered as she came up behind me. I was standing at the magazine rack. She picked up the tabloid for inquiring minds and said, "Splitsville. What are we going to do?" Her incomparable face was blushing with happiness. Although I felt like I was flying at the sight of her, I didn't laugh at her joke and deadpanned it. She struck me in the chest and complained that I never laugh at her jokes. We walked next door to the movie.

After the movie, Kara climbed into my car to head to the Austin Grill. It was never discussed. She always jumped into my car with the understanding that I would drive her back to hers. We drove to the top of Georgetown and hit the restaurant. Tex-Mex again, but this time without fake ceiling clouds. Just a straight-up, take-your-order waitress that was not trying to up-sell tonight's specials or push another margarita on you.

Kara gorged on chips alternately dipped in red and green salsas. It felt great, naturally, to be near her. Was it me, or did every guy who sat across the table from her feel like they didn't have a care in the world?

Kara's Japanese mother was an art history guru. Her Irish father, also a professor, met her while working on an archeological dig an epoch ago. Kara had pale brown eyes, long eyelashes, a long slender neck, and brown hair with festive highlights that spilled around her face in a luxurious way. About five-foot-five, her Amerasian features allowed dark beauty to dominate her blonde genes, creating total allurement. I was grabbing and dipping the triangular tortilla chips, pretending they were French fries and talking like the loveable psycho Carl from the movie we just saw as Kara's laugh shook her frame. And that was another thing that killed me about Kara: when she laughed, she laughed with her entire body. It had been way too long since I had seen her—months and months.

I remembered the first time I spotted her at the Edward Bennett Williams Library at Georgetown Law. As I first approached her, I drank up every juicy curve on her bod, then—*ouch*—I saw the too big, sorta tacky diamond ring on her slender finger. I went after her anyway. I dropped to my knees next to the table she was studying at and whispered, "Please tell me you aren't really engaged but only wear that ring to keep away freak-show jerks and since I'm a great guy, the type of guy you'd want to take home to your mom and your step-mom—this ring does not apply to me. I'm ready to give you the ground-beneath-your-feet-treatment. Where do I sign up?" Her body shook with laughter. She touched my shoulder and told me to stop. She truly was engaged, but we became friends within five minutes. Tonight her eyes beamed. And she wasn't wearing the ring. Did Kara and Mr. Perfect crash and burn? Maybe she rented a crane to take her big-ass ring to get steam cleaned.

"How's my favorite player doing?" she asked.

I felt counter-confessional. "It's fantastic. I'm setting up valet parking in front of my apartment for all my ladies," I said. Kara knew I was full of it.

"How's married life?" I asked. Kara disregarded the question.

"I want to know why this kid killed Bradford Slater," she said. As she rested an elbow on her copy of the *Post* she had folded neatly on the table, her voice broke, and I thought she was going to start crying again.

Without thinking, I grabbed her right hand with my left hand. Her beautiful, slender fingers were covered with a slight patina of salt from the chips. "I worked on the case all last night."

She looked less disappointed, which made me feel better. Kara could do that to me. I took my hand away and licked the salt that had transferred from her hand to mine. "Don't you love salt? They say it's bad for you, but who cares?" She smiled again and asked me what I knew about the case.

"I have some witness problems, but there's nothing unusual about that. The theme will be accidental versus intentional shooting. The strength of the case is that Bradford was this amazing person rather than the typical victim. But I can tell it is going to be a tough case to win. I don't know who the family will hire. They won't stick with the public defender."

"If it's a close case, you'll win," she encouraged. "I went to public school in San Francisco, but no one ever killed a teacher. Bradford's death just seems impossible." She took a slow breath, during which music became audible. The restaurant had the jukebox from heaven. Everything from Frank Sinatra to David Gray to Louis Armstrong to Madonna and back down south to Johnny Cash. "Sing it for us Patsy," Kara said, referencing Patsy Cline's "Stand by Your Man," which had just begun playing. "You have to love that brand of country music, and the way the women sing about longing for some impossible screw-up of a man who never lives up to the promises he made when he was drunk or on drugs or in lust or in rehab or insane." She smiled, but I knew we were talking about more than country music. This girl that brought me to my knees was a free agent. Strangely, I was at a loss on how to react. It was as though I were a child who wished he could drive but couldn't see over the steering wheel.

"Finito, finished, the marriage is over? When? Why?" I asked.

The enchiladas arrived, and she clearly explained the succession of events like a series of slides: the mysterious forest, the clearing, the planting of the field, the beautiful crops, the insect plague, the burning of the field, the subdivision, and a Conoco station at the corner. Love, boredom, annoyance, coldness, take a break, couples therapy, separate beds, separate apartments, and "I bet he was cheating although I never caught him."

"The uncontested divorce is final in ninety days. I have spent the last nine months taking plenty of time off. I visited friends in Boston, relatives in San Francisco and Tokyo. I have been working out like a fiend to get the whole thing out of my system. As the cliché goes, I'm just glad I didn't have kids with him. The guy was so lifeless, dead inside. I thought if I spent one more month in the relationship I would catch his disease." I could tell the conversation was dragging her down, so I changed the subject.

"What are you working on these days?" I asked. Kara designed everything from websites to CD covers. She had lectured me on the use of color for my own trial exhibits. It was good to see the enthusiasm rise up in her before the evening ended. She talked about some of her design projects. I drove her to her car, then we changed our minds and went to Tower Records; then I took her back to her car and dropped her off. I tried to kiss her on the mouth. She grabbed my hair and skull (she grew up with older brothers and knew the basic wrestling moves) to stop me. I told her I wanted to be a home-wrecker. She said her home was already wrecked. I played her favorite Café del Mar CD, and asked her if she wanted to drive through Rock Creek Park. She laughingly declined, but invited me to her kickboxing class the following day.

# DECEMBER 6, 1999

The D.A.'s waiting room was packed. My eyes cruised past Vietnamese families (the people gathered there were friends and parents of a rape victim, in a gang rape trial where the gang ran a train on the poor girl) and Pakistani and Iraqi cab drivers (robbery victims), finally falling on Bradford Slater's parents and his older sister. They appeared sick with grief. This part of my job was difficult. I had been down this road so many times. And the families always asked if I was going to win. I always told them the truth, despising the words as I spoke them: juries were unpredictable.

"Thank you for coming in. I have been doing this job for some time, and I have given up on trying to figure out how to console people about their loss, especially when parents have to bury their own children. I have come to believe that there are no words that exist to comfort you or address the level of pain you are feeling, especially coming from someone you have never met. I offer the usual 'I'm so sorry and I'll do everything to put on the best trial I can,' and you can call me seven days a week to talk about the case or talk about anything you want. But I will not cheapen your son's memory by pretending to understand the level of grief you feel right now. I can promise you that I will work on this case harder than I've ever worked any case. They say that healing begins when justice is done, but folks, not in this courthouse. As you know from the newspapers, any D.A. that promises victory is a fool," I told Bradford's parents and his sister. "Grieve, heal, embrace sadness at your own pace, but it's called the courthouse, not the justice-house, as we D.A.'s say. I want to be here for you any way I can, but I will not look you in the eye and promise a guilty verdict in this or any case."

"Yeah, you never know what a jury is going to do in D.C.," the old man smiled. Both his wife and sister were wiping tears from their eyes. They were a strong trio. After Bradford's mom blew her nose, she fanned herself with a small grief pamphlet provided by one of the victim advocates. Giving her a pamphlet was like handing a cookbook to a person that was starving to death.

"We can't imagine why anyone on earth would want to shoot Bradford," said the sister.

"It makes us very happy that Bradford lived such a giving and fulfilling life," his mother said.

"I couldn't agree with you more. He did more living than a hundred people combined," I said.

"What about you? Do you have any children?" Bradford's mother smiled, trying to be sweet and take a break from her grief-stricken world.

I was flattered by her inquiry. "Not yet, but I'm hopeful," I said, fantasizing about a possible future with Kara. Then I began to discuss details of what I had learned from the weekend investigation and what I intended to do.

We talked for a while and I called Annette to ask Tommy Monroe to stop by. "I'll take care of that sweetness," Annette whispered on the phone, always rising up during the sadder moments. I loved the gospel raspiness of her voice almost as much as Kara's deeply sensual voice.

Tommy stopped by and was the perfect politician. He served up the usual dish of revenge and promised that I would convict the kid, which he shouldn't have said, but that was Tommy. The Slaters gave me a large box full of papers, photographs, letters, awards, teaching videos, and news clippings about Bradford. I thanked them and explained that those materials would become an important part of my trial preparation.

The Slater family left. They did not want to stay for Kevin Ford's afternoon bond hearing. Dealing with families obsessed with revenge like some bizarre made-for-TV movie drove me nuts. I was spared that with the Slaters. They were too smart to think that whispering threats and obscenities at the defendant would bring their son back to life.

I went to court to cover a sentencing on one of Scott's cases because he was in trial. Then I grabbed Alexandra and dragged her into my office. "Guess what? Kara's free as a bird."

"Kara and hubby are finished? I feel bad for them," Alexandra said genuinely.

I was undeterred. "Forget about them. It's great for me. How should I play this?"

"Oh, Clay, it's too early. She probably doesn't want to get involved with anyone right now."

"If I wait too long, she'll find someone else. She looks great; I want to film her while she's in her prime. It's for her own good," I said in an attempt to mask my vulnerability. Alexandra knew I was full of shit.

"Just keep doing things together, you know, *really* get to know her all over again," she said. I had introduced Alexandra to Kara a couple of years ago and they got along great—and even emailed each other occasionally. Scott walked in and greeted us.

"We're doing a kickboxing class tonight," I told Alexandra, and she smiled and shook her head with there-you-go encouragement.

"Whoever it is, I hope she kicks you in your nuts," Scott said.

"You don't know who I'm talking about," I said. "What happened in your trial?"

"Second-degree murder," Scott said.

"What was the plea offer?" Alexandra asked.

"Manslaughter. He should have taken it," Scott said.

My phone rang. It was the chief of the D.A.'s homicide unit in Prince George's County, Bill Morricone, a brilliant trial lawyer who was also an accomplished pianist. Our cases had intersected dozens of times over the years, as killers often had bodies in both jurisdictions. I asked him to reduce Triplett's shoplifting felony to a misdemeanor, and he said he would find out which young D.A. was handling the case, take care of it and pop the young Triplett out of jail immediately. I thanked Bill and bolted to the Kevin Ford bond hearing.

*

"All rise," the U.S. Marshal (they are the bailiffs in federal court) shouted as Judge Floyd King ascended the bench. Good draw for the bond hearing. He's the guy I wanted to be in front of when I am having a tough day; especially after seeing the stress on the Slaters' faces when I told them about the realities of the courthouse. He was laid back, old as Moses, picked cotton in Alabama as a child, and was once a school teacher before the military and law school. Medium skinned and heavy set, he had a moustache, browline glasses, and a wife named Magnolia.

"Be seated, be seated," he said in a weary tone. "Mr. Marshal, bring out that young man who killed the teacher," he directed the U.S. Marshal. King broke me up. He was completely unconcerned with "the court record." No other judge would have said that. Ever. King had not made up his mind about the case but that was just his casual country style—even in a packed courtroom. The kid, heavy set and sad, was brought out immediately. Kevin looked like he built his own face as a shop project. Marshals stood on each side of this large car wreck of a teenager.

"With all due respect, I beg the Court's pardon, but we object to the verb 'killed' and submit that the evidence will show that this was an accidental shooting," the emboldened public defender, Mary Beth O'Reilly, sniped. The Ford family was still conducting a beauty contest deciding which private defense lawyer to hire; the private attorney was probably waiting for the Fords to take out a second mortgage as Kevin Ford's defense would not come cheap. Perhaps the father would have to sell his house. Meanwhile, Mary Beth, the reigning queen of the public defender's homicide unit, was hamming it up for the press. Standing room only.

"Oh, you don't have to apologize to me, Ms. O'Reilly." Judge King just smiled at her over-the-top pretentiousness. "I'm just an old man; that is the way I talk. I did not mean to make it sound like I knew exactly what happened. I do not know anything about your case. Accidental or unintentional, but do you agree with me that a gun was brought to school? From what you just said, it sounds like your client was there and a gun was brought to school, is that correct?"

Mary Beth, who wore her emotions on her Irish Catholic sleeve, glared and said nothing. She had solid courtroom presence and was active in all of the bar association bullshit that I avoided like Ebola. Unfortunately, her clients suffered because she had four children, and her cases were never prepared. After all these years, I never understood her. She was bright but made no effort. She would drive to Maryland and Virginia to protest the death penalty, but God forbid she subpoena a witness or investigate a case. I always felt she could crush me at trial if she bothered to read the file. She would huff and puff and stuff young D.A.'s into seeing it her way. She hated to be wrong, but there she was in front of Judge King without an answer —meaning *yes*, Kevin brought a gun to school.

Silence. Madame Public Defender Mary Beth was quietly fuming. She refused to answer. You could hear the ticking of the large government-issue Seth Thomas clock on the wall.

"Okay, then. Well, that's that. Back when I was growing up it was a big deal to smoke a cigarette in the bathroom. Every once in a while a boy would bring a straight razor to school. That was before your time, hell, that was before the switchblade," King began to reminisce. I knew from years of appearing before Judge King that all roads led back to him. *My Life, an Oral History.* It was fine with me. It was like a mesmerizing radio show with an old country gentleman, a black Mark Twain-like host, and I could listen to his 'Bama Hour' all day. I loved his stories. Play some blues in the background, perhaps Buddy Guy singing, *Here I am a million miles from nowhere in this one room country shack/I'm gonna find me a woman even if she is deaf, dumb, and blind.*

"Maybe we can revisit the bond issue at a later time, but I am not going to release any boy..." King was cut off by Mary Beth O'Reilly.

"Your Honor, I wish to argue the traditional factors of the Federal Bail Reform Act, no criminal record, ties to the community, strength of the evidence, danger to the community..." His Honor cut her off.

"Madame Public Defender, you can argue all you want. But like I was saying, I am not going to release any boy who is bringing a gun to school. It's that simple. Madame Clerk, defendant is to be held without bond, please call the next case."

"But Your Honor," Mary Beth attempted to stop Judge King's ruling.

Judge King dismissively responded, "Please, no more argument. One of the great things about our country is the right to an appeal. Madame Clerk, call the next case."

The public defender stormed out. The court reporter was distracted while reloading his machine with new paper. The kiddie killer looked devastated by the judge's no bond decision.

I was just about to leave when the judge motioned me up to the bench. While the spectators were clearing out and the marshals were bringing in the next prisoner, he told me in a very soft voice that Kevin Ford's father, Rodney, was a notoriously bad cop. "He'll try anything to alter a case, and his own son's case. Be careful, Clay. Be careful," His Honor whispered. Just another courthouse lion in a robe that ignored the *ex parte* contact rules.

*

"Don't you have your own office?" I asked Scott as he rummaged through my file cabinet. I had created a file on every trial issue that came up over the past six years. Pure anal retention combined with a fear of losing made for a good little work boy. He was looking through my research files but said he was looking for a video.

"Oh, man, I forgot to bring in the video from last week. Man, wait 'til you see it. Have you ever seen the Discovery Channel episode of the tigers mating? This woman was big and strong," I lied to him.

"You knock some trees down in your apartment? Spray your scents? I saw a Discovery Channel episode of these lions fucking. Goddamn lion fucked this lioness about two hundred times in a twelve-hour period and the lioness did not make a move or a sound. Just lied there like my dog. I don't know how long those lions had been married, but that lioness looked like she was watching the Lifetime movie of the week while he was doing her," Scott said.

"Hey, it can happen to the King of Beasts as well as a whiney little bitch like you," I said.

"I wish lions would eat that *Washington Times* reporter Jonathan Loeb or whatever his name is. I saw him when I walked by the courtroom today. I win a big homicide and it is in the middle of the Metro section of his little paper, but if I dismiss a case because of bad evidence or dirty cops it's on the front page," Scott said. "When I asked him about it, he said he interviewed the victim's family and they were disappointed the case got dismissed. This from the fucking family that did not exist until someone died."

Annette came in and told us that a field trip to the National Zoo turned into a shoot-out between students. There was a young, dead body, and it was assigned to Scott. "Clay and I were just talking about lions and tigers," Scott said. Nothing fazed Scott.

Annette left, Scott pored over my files, and we prepped cases for the remainder of the afternoon. As evening approached and my focus waned, I headed to kickboxing.

\*

We met at the Dupont Circle subway station and walked to an exercise studio called Joy of Motion that had all sorts of classes. Kara was wearing unassuming workout gear, but she could not hide those Matisse curves. The real joy though was seeing Kara at the end of the day and knowing she was no longer married. The studio schedule revealed everything in vogue: body sculpture, yoga, a variety of dance classes, and finally a class called stretch, which sounded like it came with cookies and milk (soy, of course).

Dance-trance-bass-oriented music blasted the small rectangular-shaped room as a ripped black guy named Desmond led the way. I followed along, occasionally looking at Kara, although our eyes never met. She was in another world, kicking, chopping, and hip-hopping her aggressions away. The class had a collective endorphin-charged panache. The volume of the music was loud enough to get the Branch Davidians to surrender. Sonique, Rui Da Silva, Darude, Fragma, and Kay Cee boomed so loud I thought the steamed up mirrors would fall off the front wall.

There was no shower at this Joy of Motion place, so we headed to dinner in the Adams Morgan neighborhood in layers of soon-to-dry clothing. On the way to the restaurant a homeless person pretended to help park my car with the type of hand signals used to bring a jet into its gate. I ignored his extended hand but Kara gave him two dollars.

"Why do you do that? He's just going to buy drugs or alcohol." I said.

"Aren't we going to buy alcohol right now? I'll ask him to join us for a glass of wine," Kara said and began walking toward him. I grabbed her arm, admitted I was being hypocritical, and pulled her in the other direction. She laughed. Her smile was radiant. My left hand grasped her left forearm as my right hand slid up her back and around her slender, still-wet neck. I pushed my face into her mane of hair toward her ear and told her to behave herself in a stern, mock-parental tone. I blew the softest breath I could blow into her ear. For a second she closed her eyes and revealed the tiniest break in her will. And Kara's will? You could strike a match on her resolve.

Over Italian, she told me about her trip to Japan. Rainy, smoky Shibuya, a crime-free neighborhood in Tokyo with gigantic video screens and people partying with what Kara called "smartphones" lighting up their faces. She explained that the Japanese will never catch up to the U.S. in music and film, but we will never catch up to them in manners and kindness toward others. (A city with no jury trials? What would I do?)

Kara joyfully described all the different design ideas she absorbed during her trip: "Tokyo is dark and rainy, but inspiration is everywhere. The architecture is amazing and the skyline is endless. The neon is not cheesy like Vegas, but bold and vibrant. There are so many great visual cues that I try and incorporate into my work to keep it fresh."

"I'm envious—can't say I ever feel inspired serving subpoenas in Southeast D.C." I paused for second. "You know, I really have missed you."

Kara didn't respond immediately. "I've missed you, too." Then she deflected, "I've missed your family. Your mom and dad are great."

Not exactly what I was looking for, but I decided to run with it. "I'm sure they would love to catch up. Lord knows they would have rather had you for a daughter than me as a son. Why don't you come over for Christmas dinner?"

"I'd love to come over," she smiled and offered me a fork full of espresso-laced cake.

The waiter discreetly deposited the check to my right. As I handed him my charge card, Kara's and my eyes met briefly, but in earnest.

# DECEMBER 7, 1999

"And then we ordered Tiramisu for dessert. She was acting really anal by not putting her fork where my fork had been on the dessert plate," I said to Alexandra and Scott. "Do you think she is afraid of my germs or something?"

"Hell yeah, she's afraid of germs. You'd fuck a girl in a dumpster, sober. Kara ain't dumb. It makes me nervous being in the same room with you," Scott said.

"No, she was just being polite. Relax, you're overanalyzing," Alexandra assured me. "Stop worrying about the little things. You still haven't stated clearly what is on your mind, Clay... under all the bullshit, that is."

"I love her, but I'm worried she thinks I'm just a player."

"You're too easy on yourself," Scott said. "I don't think Kara thinks you're a player. I think she thinks you're a selfish asshole that would never commit to anyone, much less make the real sacrifices to keep a family going." Scott beamed with pride at his own rant.

"Don't listen to him," Alexandra smiled, "just show Kara it's all about her."

Rich Salsbury walked in and said he had a trial strategy question for us. Rich was a phony little aristocrat that had provided God-only-knows-how-much campaign money to Tommy to work his way up the trial food chain. Scott, Alexandra, and I fucked with him constantly. Rich's trial strategy question was probably a ruse to try and get involved in the Catholic priest cases that would get Rich the publicity he needed.

He was the top candidate for the most loathed D.A. in the office. Take any full-of-shit, snobby, lying lawyer, multiply it times a hundred and you had Rich. He acted like I was his fraternity brother because he had also gone to Georgetown Law and done a brief stint at Hogan & Fox. The years were slightly off, and I never really knew him at either place. Slender and five-foot-eight, he favored two-button blue suits from Nordstrom paired with cufflinks, loud ties, and a Coach bag. He wore his brown hair like John F. Kennedy/Ted Koppel, voted Republican, and actually called the support staff "the support staff" to their faces.

He once told a black secretary that if she changed her diet she would have more energy. (The next day she refused to work for him and he was assigned a white secretary from the Virginia suburbs, a practically extinct species. Rich's new secretary was named Dawn and she had "the claw," a redneck version of bangs—well not bangs, but one bang that protruded from the front of her skull and never touched her forehead thanks to gravity-defying hair gel.) Needless to say, Rich's brand of conservatism was just a big hit at the office. Annette said he probably bought his Ku Klux Klan outfit at Nordstrom.

Salsbury was part of the resume-polisher tribe. They did not really want to get their hands dirty with jury trials, but wanted to put a year or three in at the prosecutor's office and go back to some big mega-law firm, and tell the world that they had trial experience. Salsbury wanted to do "white-collar" crime to add a little sex to his otherwise boring resume.

Unfortunately for skinny little Rich, he did not get one of those positions in the Department of Justice Fraud Unit (there were only a couple of slots), so he had to join the approximately two hundred prosecutors who were doing street crime. Rich was just biding his time until he could go back to a big firm and work on the one "white-collar" crime case per year that came into Hogan & Fox, which usually involved pharmaceutical diversion, securities fraud, or international product counterfeiting.

Meanwhile ol' Ken Starr-loving Rich was stuck with blunt objects, drugs, pit bulls, stolen hubcaps, and piles of guns. In the department of expectations, Rich had never conceived of the world he was thrust into. It was as if he expected his witnesses and victims to speak with the eloquence of Samuel L. Jackson or Denzel Washington. Rich thought street crime was a tall young man saying, "Give me your wallet." What he got was a world of incandescent violence where there was often no difference between witnesses and victims, where petite teenagers gathered around a seventy-three-year-old frail woman and, as they were beating her to death, took a pipe and shoved it through her anus into her heart. No, Rich never imagined he would have to read police reports like that, much less talk to the people involved. Rich couldn't conceive that within a mile of the Capitol things were taking place on the street that he thought only occurred in the Congo or Bosnia or Cambodia. Each time Rich thought of going to trial, not only did he fear enhancing his success-less record, he feared his office would fill up with young men in baggy jeans who spoke a language that mystified him ("Cap," "jack," "hoop-dee"—what on earth did these words mean?). Many of these young men were irrevocably recalcitrant, like objects made of stone wearing Sony headphones to a Discman rappin', "*Let me in now, let me in now Bill Gates, Donald Trump let me in now*—and Nelly's "Let Me In" meant their slice of the pie that would never come, much less warm and with ice cream.

Jurors did not connect with Rich. They smelled his fear and condescension and they almost always acquitted. Afterward Salsbury, and the others like him, would brush it off with the ultimate apartheid rant: *If Those People want to find the scumbag not guilty, fine, it's their neighborhood—at the end of the day I go to my home in crime-free Potomac or McClean or Cleveland Park*. But Salsbury was competitive and did not enjoy losing, so to avoid the dilemma he was always looking for a reason to dump a case or make a ridiculously soft plea bargain.

As Rich looked for a chair, we all repressed a sigh. "Hey, guys, how's it going?" Salsbury asked.

"I think you're off by one guy," Alexandra said with a smile. She did not like to be grouped into a "hey guys" greeting.

Salsbury ignored her remark. "Clay, I know you're really busy with the teacher homicide, but I wanted to discuss a case."

"He doesn't look busy to me," Scott said.

"Sure, but first I have a question for you: what is the perfect woman in your book?" I asked.

Salsbury, not really accustomed to improv, paused and said, "Well, nice person, nice family. Jenny and I met in law school, but she actually grew up in a town not far from mine in Connecticut." Not exactly a detail man like my news-boy, Phil.

"If you ever get divorced, I think you and Annette would make a good couple," Scott deadpanned. Silence. Salsbury didn't know how to deal with an interracial dating joke from a black man. I suppressed a laugh that morphed into a cough.

"Basically, the perfect girl is a clone of you with a genital switch," Alexandra smiled her Miss America smile that could get her out of any insult.

"That's not a bad thing," Salsbury laughed at his own attempt at a joke.

"Sorry, I couldn't help you yesterday, but I was mad busy," I said, changing the subject, hoping to answer his question and get on with the day. "Look, before you go through your entire case, tell me what the ultimate legal or factual issue is so I know what to focus on."

"The ultimate issue is whether I should dismiss this case even though I have fingerprints. It's the burglary of the Capitol Hill Radio Shack where the defendant drove his car into the glass entrance and just loaded up. The guy left his fingerprints there, but the defense attorney said it doesn't mean anything because the guy was in Radio Shack shopping a few days before. Clearly, there is a problem with tying him to the theft," Salsbury explained.

"Who is the defense attorney?" Scott asked.

"Jack Shane," Salsbury replied. Scott and I smiled. Jack loved to play with the inexperienced and the fearful.

"Look, fingerprints have a life, a shelf life. The prints are left by the oil on your skin. They are destroyed over time and their shelf life depends on the conditions. Is it hot, cool, dry, dusty, et cetera, and most importantly, what has been done to the surface where the print was left? Was it on a window and are the windows cleaned daily? That type of thing," I explained.

"The prints were left behind the counter, where some VCR and DVD players were taken, but the counter area is sort of open." Salsbury played his usual *Please, daddy, please give-me-permission-to-drop-the-case* game. He would have to prove at trial that the defendant had no business being in a non-customer area except after hours in the burglary. I knew he would not do it. Life was too short to train lawyers who did not want to improve their game.

"Here, take my file on fingerprints. Take a look at it. Good luck," I told him and began going through my messages.

Scott, a real trial dog, tried to encourage him. "Tee it up. Try the case. Shit, make the dude look the jury in the eye and tell him he was shopping behind the counter. But don't ask him where he was that night unless you have some kind of statement from him or he might burn you. Does he have any prior record? Does he own a car? Does it have any scratches? I miss those fun little cases. Now all my cases are serious, like somebody died or something. Go have fun with it, pick a jury, you'll do fine. What is the worst that can happen: you lose. So what? Don't let this dude who is insane enough to slam his car through windows and loot a store plea to some petty theft with a stipulation to probation," Scott said. Nice pep talk, I thought. And damn nice of Scott to jump in with such enthusiasm.

"Yeah." Salsbury, whose face tightened at the mere thought of picking a jury, was not getting the answers he wanted. "Hey, thanks. Let's try and have lunch together next week. Maybe talk about the priest cases. I want to jump in on that, if you big guns will allow it."

"Sounds good. Could you shut the door on your way out?" I asked. I returned to the subject of *my* perfect girl.

"I'm a reformed man. I'm in love with Kara. I am going to stop chasing. I am dropping out of the carpe diem brigade. I've been waiting years for this and I'm going to make this work." I was mostly convinced by my sincerity.

"That is great," Alexandra said. "Isn't she still married?"

"That's what lawyers call a 'technicality'." Scott said. I told Alexandra she will be divorced in three months.

"I've heard you sing this fidelity song before, Son. We'll see, but still, don't drink from my soda can," Scott said.

## Chapter 3

# District of Defendants

## December 20, 1999

It just felt like a dirty day. Before I could dive into the Slater homicide, I needed to get a handle on the Kelly Lord file. This psycho would try anything, do anything. He just killed and killed and killed. He would get caught, win at trial, and kill again. No one in the office had been able to tag him for a homicide before the file made its way to Scott and me. We flipped a coin and the case was mine. Lord's hubris rubbed me the wrong way. I started organizing the file. I actually had a live witness. Kentrel Bishop was in jail, but could identify Lord. I was going through the property reports trying to figure out how many bullets had been fired in his latest rampage, and if there were any forensic matches to Lord's guns. Just as I was getting deeper into the file, Johnny LeGray popped in.

"Thanks for stopping by. I have some questions about Kelly Lord, but first let's talk about the Slater case. Tell me how the shooter's cop father is going to tamper with the evidence."

The detective decided to taunt me instead. "Look at the pictures of yourself," he said as he glanced at the courtroom sketches on the wall from a couple of big cases. (Since cameras weren't allowed in D.C. courtrooms, sketch artists had to draw courtroom scenes that were shown on TV while a voiceover explained the trial. They were drawn on paper the color of grocery bags.) "Don't you ever get sick of looking at yourself?" Between preparing the teacher homicide and getting ready for the Kelly Lord case, I wasn't in the mood for one of Johnny's thrashings. Regardless, that was the price you paid for his under-the-courtroom-table detective work.

"Years ago, the old school D.A.'s had three pictures on their walls: Vince Lombardi, Martin Luther King, and JFK," Johnny noted in a not-so-subtle demonstration of his worldliness.

"Lombardi, King, and JFK never won a jury trial. These pictures are to inspire confidence in the victims that come into my office." The daily boxing with Johnny drove me crazy.

"Lombardi won Super Bowls, King changed the course of history, and JFK got more pussy than every D.A. in this office combined. And, by the way, that's why you have pictures of yourself on the wall." Johnny pointed his fat finger in the air toward me.

"Fair enough, I'm busted. Now tell me about Rodney Ford, that fine police officer who is going to sabotage the biggest trial of my career. C'mon, Johnny." Rapidly tapping my left foot, I was having trouble hiding my impatience.

"Clay, this guy will try anything—I mean anything—to destroy you and this case against his son. Little bastard, if my son shot a teacher I'd pull the switch," Johnny said as his eyes wandered from one corner of my office to the other. Always the detective. He continued, "I've seen Ford plant drugs and beat the shit out of people with a vengeance. Even cops are afraid of him. If he thinks another cop is going to rat on him, he walks by and whispers, 'Snitches lie in ditches.' I ain't afraid of him. He fucks with me, I'll put a bullet in his ass. I don't care if he works out all the time with his bodybuilding buddies. I'm more afraid of Internal Affairs."

"What's going on with Internal Affairs?"

"I met with them yesterday about that old shooting case, the one where I shot the kid that was holding the knife. They said I triggered too quickly." His voice became more stern and he began punching the air with his fist. "They took the case under advisement and will let me know next week if I am suspended. Right now, I can't work on your teacher homicide until they clear me—if they clear me. I am allowed to work on old cases, and can help you with the Kelly Lord trial, but no new cases. Anyway, who cares, fuck 'em. I've got my military pension and if they sack me, I've got over twenty years for my cop pension. I'll go to my condo in Ocean City and go fishing." Johnny's red face barked out words of defiance.

He continued to strut his hulking frame around my office, pointing his thick hands at this and that as he spoke. I watched him punch the air and glanced at his beer belly. "Hey, I caught you looking at my gut. Remember a big horse needs a big shed to protect him from the rain." Johnny grabbed his package to emphasize the point.

"Enough. I sense a Johnny-getting-laid story coming on and I'm too busy. Sit down and tell me what you think the father of the shooter will do."

"Anything he can, Rodney will try anything. I'll see what I can find out, but cops are keeping their distance from me. Once you've been interviewed by Internal Affairs, you're poison. The department is a mess right now. Morale is way down. It ain't like the good old days. My guess is that Rodney will try and tamper with the evidence —physical evidence and testimony. Rodney knows where the property lockers are and how to forge the logbook. All the cops know his son's ass is in a sling. He'll probably tell one of the cops to say there was a second shooter. Maybe he'll tell a cop to manufacture a statement that some kid ran out of the basement and told Kevin Ford to hold his gun. Rodney is the type of guy to make up a fictitious statement and put it into property—he would go that far. Lemme just keep my ear to the street. I'll call you if I hear anything, but it ain't gonna be easy, buddy. Rodney and I don't exactly get along."

Nobody wanted to be on the wrong side of Johnny. When he was in your corner, he was the first person to the hospital if someone's kid was sick, he'd pick you up with a six-pack and subs in his washed car, and badge his way into the Redskins game; he would even interview a witness at midnight. If he didn't like you, he'd set your house on fire and show up with the firemen to help put it out so he had an alibi. You just didn't mess with Johnny. And that's what scared me: Rodney Ford just was not afraid of him.

"You, not get along? Say it ain't so," I teased him.

"Where's Rich Salsbury?" Johnny asked. "I want to go fuck with someone." As he was leaving, I told him I needed his help to do some investigation on the Lord trial. He said he would help me.

Johnny closed the door behind him and I began preparing. I had pizza delivered to the office around 9 P.M. About an hour later I went into the disgusting men's room, flossed, brushed my teeth, and rinsed with mouthwash. I took the miniature plastic bottle of Listerine and threw it down hard into the trashcan. The thud echoed. I looked in the mirror. It wasn't just two weeks of lunches, dinners, movies, and coffees with Kara. It had been ten years and I knew that it was her smile I wanted to see. *This is it? This spent institutional bathroom at the end of the day?* The second I lifted my head from case files I thought of her. *What if she felt the same way? She's not going to call. What if I call? What is the worst that can happen?*

Then the phone rang.

＊

Kara's voice greeted me. "Guess what I'm wearing?" She hung up.

I bolted to my car.

She called back a few minutes later. "I'm taking off that black sweater you like."

"The one that clings? I'm three miles away," I tried to say more but she hung up again.

Another call. "I'm taking off my pants. Slowly. Are you almost here, or what?" She hung up.

Minutes passed. I was flying down Connecticut Avenue, but I started getting anxious and called her back. "I'm one mile away. What are you doing now?"

"Wrong number...." Kara teased. Dial tone.

As I approached her apartment in the Adams Morgan section of town, I struggled to find a parking space. *C'mon, c'mon, my time is valuable here!* I caught a car leaving and nabbed the spot. I looked at myself in the rear-view mirror. I was nervous, seconds away from a life I had wanted for years. I got out of the car and quickly walked to the front entrance. Hit the security code. Buzzer. Elevator. Kara opened the door. My worries vanished. From the point where the parquet floor met her cork-like heels, my eyes moved upward to her beautiful legs, black, translucent panties, and a French blue shirt with only one button buttoned. There were candles everywhere. Crazy Buddha Bar music played in the background.

I walked toward her but stopped short—still two feet away. We had talked and laughed for a decade. Now we were at some speechless interval.

The outfit was out of control, but what really floored me was how she looked into my eyes. She had never looked at me like that. All of our passion for each other had been locked away in deep mineral silence, and now it was alive and molten. It never ceased to amaze me how women could throw the switch from *You're invisible* to *I'd push my mother in front of a truck to kiss you one more time.*

I approached her. Slowly, I ran my fingers through her hair, kissed her neck, kissed her cheekbones, brushed my mouth across hers, kissed her almond eyes, and pressed my hand between her legs. We began kissing. And from there it continued into, as Shoeboot would say, "da wee hours."

"That was worth the ten-year wait," I said around dawn.

"Just knowing me and being friends didn't count for anything?" she teased.

"Shut up. You know I want to be with you more than anything, more than anybody. I'm done dating—I only want you. I don't want to wait another ten years while some guy snaps you up. C'mon—let's just get engaged—you *know* that's where we're going." I was actually serious. This is why people are supposed to get married—passion and friendship—pure and simple.

"You shut up and stop talking like that."

"Hey, I'm serious. I was even thinking about picking up a ring between mile five and mile six on my way over, but I didn't want to interrupt our mojo."

She looked at me with skepticism. "That's the first time you thought of marrying me, on the way over?"

"Don't be ridiculous. I wanted you in my life the first time I saw you, years ago. I've always loved you. I wanted to be with you, but you were involved with someone else."

Kara took a moment to internally review my argument. She responded, "That wouldn't have stopped me if I was in your shoes." I couldn't tell if she was being playful or serious. Kara continued, "Why do you really want to get married? Because you're hitting your thirties and 'it's time'? Because all your friends are changing diapers and now you're asking yourself, 'Where's my little legacy?'"

*Uh oh.* "No, no, no," I interjected.

She let out a deep sigh and went to the kitchen. I heard the plop of ice cubes. She came back with water and offered me some.

"Look, I haven't married or divorced. The experience must have been painful, to say the least. I'm sorry," I said. There was nothing I could do to unring that bell.

"Besides, it wouldn't be a 'little' legacy. I'm six-feet-two, and you're five-five. I'm pretty sure our legacy would be tall." I paused and collected my thoughts.

She said nothing. Apparently, height wasn't the issue.

I pushed on. "Of course I've thought about all of the things you mentioned. But now that you're actually here, all I'm left with is this feeling of not wanting to be away from you. We've known each other forever. I just want to make up for lost time."

She put her hand on my cheek and said, "I don't mean to wreck this with the baggage of my divorce. It was just so… well, I never really thought about going down this road again. But, you're right. You've always made me happy and I've wasted too much time with the wrong person." Kara paused and took a deep breath. She exited the room, cleared her throat, and reentered, leaning on the door frame.

"So Clay, is there something you wanted to ask me?"

"Kara, will you…."

"I accept. I'm locking this down before you realize what a nightmare I am."

# DECEMBER 21, 1999

I checked my voicemail as I drove through Capitol Hill to the jail to see a witness in the Kelly Lord trial. The first message was from Kara. "How's my bitch?" I smiled. Kara gets me.

The second message was from the Slater family. They thought of a few more things they wanted to tell me about Bradford. I left a message telling them that I looked forward to speaking to them. I told them I was conducting another trial over the next ten days and invited them to attend so that they could get a feel for the court process. I wanted them to feel they could talk to me and understand what they were in for when it came time for Kevin Ford's trial.

Jail visits were not a fun thing, especially in a D.C. December. Rain. Thirty-three degrees. But it didn't matter. Knowing Kara was part of my life gave me a surge of energy. She was brilliant and confident, and foolish enough to hang with me.

The first thing I had to do was deal with the kid that Lord shot, Kentrel Bishop. Although the facts were terrifying, I worried that the jury would not believe the crack-dealing Mr. Bishop, who was serving time for slinging rocks. To make matters worse, he sent me a letter: "Dear Mr. D.A., I decide to drop charges and do not want to testify in Kelly Lord's upcoming case." It was written in pencil, with a third grader's penmanship. This guy had about one-twentieth of Tomar's horsepower.

I pulled in front of the jail. No phone allowed inside. I called Kara.

"Hello?" Kara answered.

"Hi, can I ask you a question?"

"It better not be, 'What's for dinner?'"

"Have you come to your senses yet?" I asked.

"Too late to bow out now, buddy," she said.

"Music to my ears. I have to go into the jail right now," I told her.

"Wear a condom. I'll see you tonight."

"Love you, too."

"God, I didn't know you were so hopeless," she laughed.

A concertina of barbed wire sat on the tall, steel fence that surrounded the utilitarian structure. As always, I was treated with suspicion until I flashed my badge. After ear-splitting buzzers and clanging doors and hallways reeking of ammonia and pine-scent, I was in an attorney conference room. Unlike Hogan & Fox, there was no William Merritt Chase watercolor hanging on this cinder block wall. (My old firm purchased Chase's 1894 original *Summers at Shinnecock* with dot-com mergers and acquisitions money.)

Kentrel Bishop, a tall, street urchin of a kid was stubborn at first. Hell, what did I expect? The side of his head was still pocked and cratered from Kelly Lord's shotgun blast. I dropped the letter on the desk.

"Did you write this, Kentrel?"

Kentrel looked at the letter as if it was the blueprint for a new Intel chip.

"You look puzzled—what's up?" I asked.

"Kelly Lord wrote it. His cousin and some big dude came over to me when I was eating. At first I said no, but they said they would have my mother killed if I didn't sign it. I was scared, so I signed it. Just call my mother and tell her to look out. I need some money in my prison bank account, and I'd like to get me clothes like that for trial," he said nodding toward my suit.

"Done. You are a little smaller than me, but I will have the office tailor make the alterations when we bring you to court."

"For real, ya'll got a tailor at the office?" *Fur reel*, the downtrodden request for truth.

I smiled, and he knew I was kidding.

"Aw man, you had me."

"Listen, before we go over the questions I will ask you at trial, I need to know everything: What went on at the house you were staying at when you got shot? How much were you slinging? How many rocks did Kelly usually front you?"

Kentrel's memory was like an old, spent battery. "I can't remember exactly how many rocks, but enough to keep my habit going. Things are blurry."

"Where are your parents?" I asked.

"My mom's staying at her sister's house. I don't know where my father is is." The innate sadness of those words seemed lost on Kentrel, who accepted an absent father as the norm. Regardless, he had clearly fallen into his product. Addresses of houses? He had no idea. His zip code was comprised of smoke instead of numbers.

"I ended up staying in this dude's basement. It was like a bunch of guys. The only adult in the house was Keshon's grandfather, and he be drunk most of the time."

"Where?" I asked to make sure it was the same address in the police reports.

"Somewhere southeast. Lord gave me about ten rocks at a time."

"Twenty-dollar rocks?"

"Yeah, at first everything was fine. I paid him what I owed and got a rock or two. Then I began to smoke what I owed him." My family was addicted to alcohol, I was addicted to sex, and Kentrel was addicted to crack.... I continued to take notes.

"He called my mother's house and told her he was going to kill me if I didn't pay him at least fifty dollar." *Fitty dollar.* "My mother told him, 'Don't kill my son for fifty dollars. You can come by the house and I'll give you fifty dollars.' That's what my mother told him. I was standing right by the phone when she say it." *Don't kill my son for fitty dollar.*

"A couple days later he be seeing me in the Capitol Heights 'hood in Prince George's County right across the D.C. line. I ran from him during the day, but that night he got me. I was in the basement playing with my baby pit bull. Wasn't no light on, but the TV be on. Next thing I know Lord yells, 'This is what happens to people that don't pay me, motherfucker,' and boom. I grabbed the phone to throw at him, but boom, boom, and I was out."

It was an identification case. Lord's shotgun was never recovered.

"How many shotgun pellets do you have in your head?"

"I dunno, enough to fuck up the metal detector."

"Okay, at trial I will ask you everything we just went through, with all sorts of little details, like how far you were from him, how many shots you heard, how long you had lived there, and other questions like that. We are also going to tell the jury all about the letter. When I ask you about selling crack, be honest—totally honest. You will not get into any trouble for that. You already pled guilty to that and you cannot be prosecuted for telling us about any other deals you did. I promise you I will not indict you for that. What is your mom's phone number? I'll call her, bring her up to date and make sure we get some more money into your prison bank account. Anything else?"

"Yeah, I hope we win. He be killing lots of people. Everybody know it. I heard he killed a stripper up on Georgia Avenue. He got her into the crack, and then when she was going to talk to the police he killed her. She had them big, fake titties. And Lord, he cut those silicone things out of her body, cut her head off, too, all so she couldn't be identified. Then he dumped the body in Rock Creek Park. That's what I heard."

"Do you know the names of the people? The person who told you that? The name of the stripper?" *Amber? Destiny? Bad Destiny? Jade? Misty? Probably one of Phil's girlfriends.*

"Naw, it just be street talk. I heard it at the laundromat or the liquor store or shooting dice or something. I'm sorry. It's hard for me to remember exact things."

*

The *Washington Post* reported about five hundred homicides a year, but there were another two hundred dead bodies that no one had any idea what to make of. Unresolvable, unsolvable, unidentifiable, mysterious—and sometimes breastless and headless—dead bodies. Tommy Monroe, D.A. For Life, did a good job of concealing those two hundred bodies—as well as his love affairs. ("Love affairs?" That's just Jane Austin spin for settling sexual harassment lawsuits.)

Defense counsel Lee Pyles was going to portray Kelly Lord as the wrong person, and Kentrel Bishop as a liar and crack-addicted dealer who lived in jail. The police reports were weak, and the evidence gathering was suspect (big surprise). Pyles would exploit those errors. I drove back to my office and developed my attack. Lord was evil, and when you're prosecuting the devil, your witnesses are from hell. I'd keep it simple and let Pyles fall on his own sword. Fortunately, I knew he wasn't going to be much of an opponent. (He'll wear a

Christmas tie and say, "A belated Merry Christmas to you all. I hope you had a nice holiday," then sit down and put his arm around his client who kills people and occasionally disfigures the bodies.)

When I got back to the office, I found a list of alibi witnesses that Lee Pyles had faxed over. The rules said I had to have the list of witnesses thirty days in advance. Trial was less than three weeks away. Typical Pyles. What he lacked in skill, he made up in sleaze. With Pyles, it was always a continuance or a sneak attack. He used to beat up Scott and me when we were new to the office and didn't know anything. He was a solo practitioner with a little office in Old Town Alexandria, across the Potomac River in Virginia. His D.C.-Virginia practice consisted of auto accidents, divorce, and criminal law. He was as shady as they came and buttered up everyone with ante-bellum manners. Scott had even developed a Pyles routine. *Sir, how dare you call me a scoundrel? I challenge you to a duel at sunrise. Sir, a duel at the break of day.* Scott would slap me with an imaginary white glove. *You have offended the family name and you must pay, pay with your life.* Then Scott would whip out his white handkerchief that he had concealed up his sleeve and dab his nose, as if he had just used snuff. *The Pyles' name will not be sullied by the likes of you.*

"Lee Pyles called and said he doesn't have any objection if you move for a continuance," Annette told me as I walked by.

"I don't want no stinkin' continuance. His alibi witnesses are lying, and I am ready to talk to them. Please get LeGray on the line for me." Annette stared at me in disbelief and shook her head. "Did you hurt your finger, honey? Until I see a cast on your hand, you make your own damn phone calls."

It was one of our standing jokes. Years ago, when I would tell her that the lawyers at Hogan & Fox would ask their secretaries to get such-'n-such on the phone, she just laughed. That level of service did not exist in the government. The only time Annette was in her do-anything-for-me mode was when I was in trial. Her maternal instinct kicked in; she knew how stressed I was and totally babied me.

Despite the teacher homicide and fifty other commitments, I was ready to hit the streets with Johnny as soon as I answered the Slater homicide phone calls. I called the F.B.I. to make sure Bradford Slater's clothes had been properly received (the F.B.I. handled the forensics for the D.C. police). I told the examiner I wanted the clothes examined for gunshot residue to determine the distance of the shooter. Then I asked him who had access to the clothes. I wanted to know whether a D.C. cop could badge his way into their unit and tamper with any items. I was assured it could not happen. I asked for the names of the F.B.I. personnel assigned the case. Irritated by my inference, he told me I had to defend the chain of custody of my own damn evidence.

I called Johnny. Voicemail. He had disappeared. Fear shot through me. Alibi witnesses could destroy a prosecutor's case in a cocaine heartbeat. Lord's witnesses would say he was busy the night he shotgunned Kentrel. If the jury believed any of them the case was over. Fear, fear, fear, until the case was over. That was the dark side of this game.

My mind jumped to the Slater case. I called Hud to see if he had any luck finding the witnesses that bragged about killing Bradford. He had been suspended for police brutality. The flip side of fear was Who Cares. Who Cares was always a fun place to hide from fear of losing. I decided to go to the jewelry store and scope out a ring for Kara. I blasted down Connecticut Avenue, parked near M. Street, and entered The Tiny Jewel Box after being buzzed through a glass door. (A much quieter buzzer than the jail.)

"Congratulations," an elderly woman with thick, gray hair said. "What's your price range?"

"I just want something sort of simple."

After about twenty minutes of her "color, cut, and clarity," I selected a small but brilliant diamond.

"I have a feeling she is going to like it," Granny Hard Sell said as she banged my Visa card.

I was five minutes late to my parking meter and there was a twenty-dollar ticket. Bigger fish to fry.

I drove a few more blocks to the gym, feeling amazing. I went from machine to machine, occasionally changing the music (Plus, no sign of Kim, which was nice). I felt impatient so I quickly showered and drove to Kara's.

*

I walked in and greeted her with a kiss. I was too nervous to give her the ring immediately. She was busy cooking so I just began blathering away about work.

"So I call homicide, and they tell me Hud has been suspended without pay. Just like that, I lose my investigator on Bradford's case," I told Kara as she rushed around her kitchen cooking dinner.

"One thing at a time. Focus on Kelly Lord's trial, and then go back to prepping Bradford's case," she said. "You've got plenty of time before the juvenile waiver hearing and then months before trial." I was grateful that she had an understanding and genuine interest in criminal trials. I felt intoxicated before she handed me a small glass of wine. She kissed me, squeezed my shoulder, and went back to cooking. Felt euphoric. Trial stress vanished. I had never really hung out in her apartment. "Their" apartment I guess; I didn't really care. If she had lived here with her husband, I did not see any remnants of their marriage. There were no pictures of the two of them. Pictures of friends and family dominated the walls, in addition to Kara's own artwork mixed with a couple of similar styles from other artists. One picture stood out amongst the others, a beautiful portrait of an Asian woman that bore a striking resemblance to Kara.

"Who's the looker over there?" I asked.

"That 'looker' is Mom from when she was in Japan," she said with a bit of a smirk. "She taught me the value of loyalty. She used to say, 'There is a time to cut ties with a sword and never look back.'"

"Just keep that sword away from my dick. I've already been circumcised once." She swung her spatula toward my crotch, mimicking ancient swordplay. When she laughed, her entire body shook with joy. Her singular talent was combining all these things into one continuous song-like event. I was the straight man. I didn't laugh. Inside, however, you couldn't have kicked the smile off my face.

"What the hell is that?" I asked, indicating a large, tan, oval-shaped machine of some type. "Are we having popcorn for dinner? It wouldn't be the first time, I suppose. Many a night my dinner was a green bottle of Heineken, a slice of pizza, and some popcorn."

"It's a rice cooker. Stop looking at it like it's a spaceship. You'll like it."

Dinner was delicious. Cooking was a gesture of affection for Kara. "The rice has a sour sweet aftertaste—I love it."

"It's the rice wine vinegar," she said. Kara pushed her empty plate into my hands. "I love to cook and hate to clean. Get busy." She walked toward the CD player and put on Tosca. I stacked the dishes in the sink and came back into the living room. I took the ring out of my pocket. I walked over to her while she was standing, my heart pounding a bit, and took her left forearm in my right hand and carefully slid the ring on her ring finger.

"I don't want to wear my ring while I'm washing dishes—will you wear it?" I put my hand on her neck and watched her admire the ring, her mouth slightly open.

"You didn't need to do this," she whispered. "Clay it is so beautiful."

I pulled her closer and said, "I feel great about doing this—this is *right*."

"I know it is," Kara said softly.

"But the ring is too big. You'll have to go over and they will fit it to your finger."

Her face was deeply flushed. "Okay. It's so fast, but I agreed to wear it and I wanted to wear it," her voice trailed off and a few tears rolled down her cheeks.

"Do you really like it? Is it you? I really wanted to get something that you'd love."

"You did. I love it," she said and moved the ring into a different position. "It's amazing, you're amazing," her voice trailed off.

I held her hands and didn't say anything.

"Clay, it's beautiful. I mean it."

"I want to dump my apartment in January or February, move into here. It's bigger."

"It's clean too," she smiled.

"Seriously, is that okay?"

"Of course!"

Kara disappeared into the bathroom. I finished the dishes and heard bathwater start and stop.

I went to bed and started reading my book. Kara came out of the bathroom and dove headfirst into bed, screaming in mid-air. When she landed, she smelled beautiful. She pulled a magazine off of the nightstand and began reading. Kara looked at me, smiled, and fell asleep almost instantly, magazine in hand. What was so different about this woman? Presentation. I began to realize that Kara took all the regular events that comprise our life—eating dinner, errands, working out—and turned them into a more sentient event. Or maybe I was still drunk on fresh love. It didn't make any difference; I was just bowled over by the fact that she let me into her world. I looked over at her sleeping. I had been in love before, but never like this. I felt magnified.

# DECEMBER 24, 1999

Christmas Eve at the Franklin household was not a magical world. It was a big shot in the arm of elite Wasp reality, replete with a cornucopia of addictions, anger, and silence.

Their neighborhood, Foxhall Road, is all about old D.C. money; the houses rival the gated mansions of Beverly Hills. On one side of the road is Wesley Heights, with its old stone houses and Swiss Chalet clapboard facades. On the other side lay Spring Valley, featuring hilly streets and multi-million dollar homes with an occasional view of the Potomac River. (In the early days, the residents had used the courts vigorously to keep out anyone that didn't look like they came from the same gene pool.) Although my parents were empty nesters, they kept the home in Spring Valley. The Franklin household was impeccably maintained. You couldn't ask for a more pristine setting to learn about alcoholism and craziness. The kids I played wiffle ball with seemed more sane than most of the parents. Even though I liked to think of Scott and Alexandra as the brother and sister I never had, I was still strangely grateful for the family I was given.

"Merry Christmas," my mom said as she gave Kara a big hug. "I guess we're going to stay here all night because I am never the first one to let go." Mom knew Kara from my Georgetown Law days, and openly expressed how much she liked her from the beginning. The other women that I brought to family dinners? Mom usually smiled at them and gave me the *what-are-you-thinking* look.

"I'm never the first to let go either," Kara replied. After forever they broke apart and Kara handed her bottles of red and white. (Even though bringing booze to the Franklin household was like bringing a bucket of sand to the beach.)

"Clay, this is the best present you could bring," Mom said, still holding Kara's slender forearms.

In my house, we do not confess to priests—we confess to Mom. So, I decided to throw it down right there on the black-and-white-tiled floor of the front hallway. "Mom, look I should have called you, I'm sorry. I don't want to give an inauguration speech, so I'll give you the short version. Kara and I just got engaged. It happened really fast. I swear you are the first person I told." (White lie. I told Alexandra and Scott first.)

"I don't care if I'm number three on the list Clay, I just want you to be happy," Mom said, kissed me, and whisked Kara away. Mom always had a warm energy, but now she was beaming with joy.

Everyone was gathered in the living room. My father was telling a story (big surprise) and family members and better halves were listening. He actually stopped to greet me. I walked around the room and kissed my sister, shook hands with my dad and my brother, and kissed my brother's wife.

"Merry Christmas, Son. Please tell me your New Year's resolution is to go back to Hogan & Fox so you can stop devoting your life to putting black people in jail."

"Dad, you really have the Christmas spirit. C'mon now, don't you want to see the kid who shot the teacher be put in jail no matter what color he is?" I stood tall and raised my right index finger. "Let's not judge a murderer by the color of his skin but by the content of his character."

"You got me there, Son. Come have a drink and don't interrupt me. I was in the middle of a discussion about our dear president," he said. "A lie is a lie is a lie: Clinton's mistake was…"

There he was, the *Washington Post* superstar editor and resident relic, now headed to the eastern shore of Maryland to teach and be the old man by the sea. (Ben Bradlee and his friends were either leaving the *Post* or dying before they could submit their resignations, and he wanted out too.) I wondered if he ever reflected on the way he militarized and terrorized the house. A former U.S. Marine, he successfully fought in Korea and unsuccessfully battled alcoholism and rage ever since. When he wasn't drunk or berating his kids, he managed to knock out a good column. Still, Dad was most famous for doing Katherine Graham's dirty work. (As the owner of the *Washington Post*, she didn't actually want to fire her own reporters.) He located the talent and, when it fucked up, cut off its head. Mom was a sweet southern woman whose father had been a veterinarian. A couple of hours after one of my father's tirades, she would usually sneak into my brother's and my room with a glass of milk and a goodie. As a kid, Mom always told us that Dad was big on discipline.

And in the other corner of the room: my brother. He tried to follow in my father's footsteps and be a reporter, but ended up a cameraman for CNN. He would sooner cut his tongue out than talk about an emotion. Do not talk or write about the news or life, just point the camera. Dad had somehow muted him. My sister, Melanie, was a stone-cold drug addict and alcoholic. I once asked her if belonging to AA and NA was like having two graduate degrees. She asked me if I got frequent flyer miles for being an asshole. Sometimes it felt as if each member of the family spoke a different language. Dinner was like an assembly at the United Nations, only the interpreters called in sick. My oldest sister, Mary, wasn't there. She cut off contact with the family after she married a dot-com gazillionaire. Apparently, financial freedom segued into reevaluating filial duties. My dad would say, "A toast to the absent ones" at dinner and turn to my mom and ask how his first born was; communiqués were sent via mommy.

"Who is in the kitchen with Mom?" Melanie asked.

"You remember Kara, Georgetown Law student turned graphic artist turned my-new-true-love," I said. "We have always been friends but now we're engaged."

"Oh my God, that is great." She paused. "On the other hand I feel sorry for any woman involved with you," Melanie said. She actually had a nice comedic touch in her lucid moments, which came in spurts. "I'm teasing you. I'll be right back." Melanie was drinking her favorite drink: a large glass of vodka, one milliliter of tonic, and a lime. But before we could begin talking, she disappeared to do God-only-knows-what drug.

"Hey, man, I'm happy for you. I've always liked Kara. I'm glad you guys hooked up," my brother mumbled.

Next to bro was his wife, a freelance radio and print journalist who was too insane to have a full-time job. She said she was delighted to see that Kara was divorced. I joined everyone, had a Scotch on the rocks, and made holiday chat. My father told me to win the teacher homicide and again mentioned that I should then go back to Hogan & Fox where I could practice real law and make some real money. My journalist sister-in-law pulled me aside and asked for an exclusive interview about the teacher homicide. I told her the investigation was confidential. She told me she had a small tape recorder, she could have the voice altered, and I would be a confidential source. I kissed her on the cheek and wished her happy holidays to calm her down. That was Washington, D.C. You worked the crowd, even if it was Christmas and the crowd was your family.

Dad put some Frank Sinatra records onto the hi-fi. The set was old, cherry-veneered, and best of all, built into the bar. Everyone told him vinyl had made a comeback, and that he was in vogue. "I was never out of vogue," he fired back.

Presents were exchanged (my sister fell once, probably the result of some type of barbiturate), and we finally sat down to dinner. Despite Dad's militaristic sensibilities, he was incredibly sweet to Kara. My father tapped his knife against the side of his wine glass.

"I would like to propose a toast to Kara and Clay, and hope they will give us more notice about when they will be setting a wedding date, and to just say how damn happy we are to welcome Kara into our home," my dad said, as we all stood to attention. Everyone lifted their wine glasses to reciprocate.

While the rest of us began to clink glasses, my sister struggled to make it to a standing position. With one hand on the table supporting her lean frame and the other holding her wine glass, she attempted to give her blessing. My sister slurred a word that began with a "g" and fell face-first into a large, untouched pile of mashed potatoes. Her wine glass smashed into the bowl of stuffing, causing her right index finger to bleed.

"Shit, she must have taken a bunch of valium," my brother said. He pulled her head up by grabbing hold of her hair, revealing a face covered with mashed potatoes.

"Mashed potato facial? Which one of the twelve steps is that?" I asked. Kara shushed me, and my brother concurred with a disapproving look.

Mom rushed toward Melanie. Kara tried to wipe the potato sludge from Melanie's face. She wasn't breathing. My dad dialed 9-1-1 and ordered the operator to send an ambulance quickly.

Fortunately, Sibley Hospital wasn't far from our house. Everyone was apologetic to Kara in the hospital waiting area. We began to talk about intervention, inpatient, outpatient, medicines, and therapies. We sounded like one of Dad's old records that had a skip in it. These types of episodes were getting as boring as movie sequels. The doctor came out. She was fine. She was alive, but how she was going to live was another story.

Kara was amazing with my family, engaging in heartfelt communication sprinkled with "I'll call you tomorrow to check on her" and "Why don't we do a girls' lunch next week." The way she was connecting with my freak show family made me feel like the world had softened. In my new, relaxed state, the entire episode lost its harsh edge. I watched Kara as she continued her set of good-byes. She hugged my brother and his aspiring Leslie-Stahl-on-*60 Minutes* wife. Kara pushed up on her toes as she was giving her a hug. It seemed like the good-byes would never end. One person would say, "We're so happy to have you as part of the family" and Kara would respond, "I'm honored to be part of your family." Finally, I had to interrupt.

"We have to go, I forgot I have to stop at my friend Phil's apartment to feed his cat," I remembered. "He's out of town for Christmas and I have to put some food out." After a few more hugs we made it to the car.

\*

Leaving the hospital, I shot down Foxhall Road redlining the Beemer. We drove in silence: Dead Can Dance played in the background. We entered Phil's Georgetown apartment.

"Where's Phil? Can I use the bathroom?"

"He's visiting family in Vermont or some other state where Asians aren't allowed. He told me not to let you use the bathroom."

"I will leave the seat up and keep the bathroom messy. He'll never know I was here," Kara said.

I put out food for his cat. His name was Caligula. He sized me up and disappeared into a hall closet.

From the kitchen, I sneaked into Phil's bedroom and there it was —the cage. I walked over and reached into the four-by-four-foot cell and pulled out the keys that were hanging on a hook in the wall. I couldn't believe how seriously Phil took sex. He had actually bought this twelve hundred dollar human-sized monstrosity for his domination sessions.

"Oh, my God. What is that?" Kara laughed. She paused for a moment and a devilish smile emerged. "Get in there," Kara commanded as she grabbed me and shoved me into the cage.

She turned me around and said, "*Grab the bars*. Your Master says grab the bars." She could barely keep in character.

"Ouch, you're hurting me, Master," I said, playing along.

"Stop resisting, or I'll beat you again," she said with feigned seriousness.

"I'll turn around, Master, so you can take me from behind, and you won't have to look at my ugly face," I said.

Kara hugged my back and was trying to talk through her laughter. It sounded like she was trying to say, "You're such a skank, turn around," but I couldn't tell for sure.

"If you are going to role-play, you have to be able to say your lines," I said, shaking my head as Kara let me out of the cage.

"These are your friends? Your friends have cages? I am engaged to a guy that knows people with cages?"

"My friends and I don't play golf," I said.

She turned me around, kissed me, and said, "My friends don't play golf either, but we don't have cages."

I shrugged my shoulders. "The cat is fed, let's go."

"Maybe we need a sex cage for our apartment. Do they sell them at Bed Bath & Beyond? I have a twenty-percent-off coupon," she said as I started the car.

We drove away through the cold fog of Rock Creek Park and headed home.

# JANUARY 9, 2000

"Your engagement survived a Franklin Family Christmas? It must be love!" Alexandra said and gave me a huge hug and a kiss. "I want to have coffee with Kara this week, hang with her and let her know that I am going to be her sister-in-law. I wish Scott and I would have stopped by for dinner. How did your family react?"

"They were fine, but my sister almost died of mashed potato inhalation." No one challenged the comment—my familial chaos was hardly news.

"How does it feel, Mr. Engaged?" Scott asked me.

"I'm sick of it. The old ball and chain feeling is kicking in."

"I told you. That great feeling only lasts for a week, and then it's all downhill. Did you see all that Christmas memorial stuff in the paper about Bradford Slater? If that punk who shot him doesn't get tried as an adult, Tommy's gonna send your ass back to the juvenile unit."

Scott was referring to the upcoming waiver hearing. Kevin Ford was under eighteen, which triggered a hearing to determine if he was going to be tried as a juvenile or an adult. A juvenile guilty verdict (no jury) equaled being locked up until he was twenty-one and then some outpatient psychiatric treatment; an adult jury guilty verdict equaled life without parole. The waiver hearing was critical.

"Johnny said he'd hit the streets with you after work to help you on the Lord case. He's with his lawyer right now. Don't you just love it? All the cops are now defendants or going to be defendants," Scott said with a big grin. He continued, "Half of them have hired the same defense lawyers they swore they were going to kill some day. I think they realized the toughest lawyers, the ones that have embarrassed them on the witness stand, are the ones they want representing them. Tommy is running all kinds of ads to recruit new police officers because so many are quitting or getting indicted. One ad said, 'High school diploma preferred but not required.'"

"Why should someone need a high school diploma to carry a gun and play God?" Alexandra asked.

"Soon we'll have people with a sixth-grade education processing our crime scenes," Scott said.

"It won't make any difference to me. Kara will become a famous graphic artist designing the covers of CDs, DVDs, and websites for Fortune 100 companies and I'll stop working and become an elite body builder."

"Her success wouldn't change anything. You already stopped working and you're a total gym rat anyways," Scott said.

"Speaking of not working, let's go get some coffee," Alexandra suggested.

I was grabbing my suit jacket when my cell phone vibrated. There was a message from Kara. She said, "My coupon expired, but luckily they still honored it. The cage should be delivered by the end of the week."

I held up my phone and replayed the voicemail for Scott and Alexandra.

"Finally, you found someone with your sense of humor, I am so happy for you," Alexandra said.

"Enjoy it now brother. There ain't gonna be any cage-talk once the kids come. Then it's going to be like ultimate fighting in a cage," Scott said but squeezed my neck, indicating that he was happy for me.

We walked down the hall. We slowed down as we overheard Harrison and Bruce getting scolded by LaDonna, an overbearing division chief that focused on repeat offenders, robberies, and assaults.

"We're really sorry; it was a Friday and we were going to take the message off our phones by the end of the day," Bruce tried to explain but LaDonna was not buying it. She never liked Bruce, and wicked-smart Harrison made her feel insecure. (Although they clowned, they both had accumulated great jury trial track records.) African American LaDonna had heard about Bruce's recent comedy routine in which he made fun of African Americans putting "le" or "la" before their names. ("Since when did black people decide they were French? I don't want to be left out, call me LeBruce," he once said.) And now LaDonna unleashed hell on LeBruce. The three of us slowed down to eavesdrop, pretending to look for a file at a nearby secretarial cubicle.

"Friday? This was a cute little Friday-joke, huh? Is that your reason? This is a prosecutor's office. A prominent prosecutor's office. It's Washington, D.C., the mayor—hell, the president—keep an eye on this place. How am I supposed to run this office when my attorneys are leaving outgoing messages like this?"

The greeting boomed from her phone, bouncing off the walls of the hallway, "Press one if you want to plead guilty. Press two if you want to set the case for trial. If this call involves questions about the upcoming winter basketball league, press zero to talk to an operator immediately."

Fuming, LaDonna continued. "You can't do that and expect to stay here. I can tell you right now, this immaturity is going to hurt your review." She even had her hands on her hips as she scorched them. Harrison and Bruce tried to look worried, but they knew Tommy never fired anyone unless they had been arrested for something more serious than drunk driving.

Scott whispered, "Why didn't we think of that?"

"These guys are good; we're going to have to lobby to get them into homicide," I whispered back.

The cafeteria was in the basement of the courthouse. The large coffee machines spewed a light brown color. A worker wearing a hairnet told us the coffee machines were not working. We grabbed sodas and went back to work. At sunset, I finally found Detective LeGray, who, despite his bitching, agreed to go out and interview alibi witnesses with me for the Kelly Lord trial.

*

"I got better things to do Mr. Franklin," Johnny began griping before I could even buckle my seatbelt. "You see, there is a hockey game tonight."

"I really appreciate it. I will write a letter for your personnel file."

"My file—I don't give a fuck about my file. 'I'll write a letter for your file,'" he mocked my voice in a higher octave as we drove into a hellish neighborhood in his unmarked police car that screamed Unmarked Police Car with its spotlight near the driver's side-view mirror. "Clay, you know what your problem is?"

"I'm too good looking, and it's hard for the female jurors to concentrate on the evidence because they are too busy fantasizing about me?"

"That's not what I was thinking, although I imagine the male jurors are bending you over a chair in their dreams. Do you know what your problem is?"

"Apparently not."

"You take these cases too seriously. I've been doing these cases for thirty years and there will always be another drug dealer, another shooter. You convict one, another will pop up. You don't convict one, you'll get him next time."

Johnny's contrived indifference actually irritated me. "You're one to talk. Don't give me this 'another will pop-up' stuff. Kelly Lord was found not guilty at his last trial. He left the courthouse and popped several people with his shotgun. Is that what you mean by pop back up? Fuck, let's just take care of this case so I can get back to work on the teacher homicide."

"I don't need no fucking lecture about life from someone twenty years younger than me. Shit, a guy like Lord will get himself killed before he's ever prosecuted, you're just too young to know it. Now, what's that fucking address again?" Johnny pushed back.

"Here it is," he said and parked illegally. "By the way, you won't be working the teacher homicide as much as it will be working you. I haven't found out anything yet, but Rodney Ford broke a suspect's arm two nights ago—then he planted drugs and a knife on the kid. You're in for the fight of your life. I'd buy a gun if I were you. Let's go." Johnny was wired into the cop gossip. Maybe I had to worry about more than cross-examining Rodney Ford.

As I got out of the car I began to survey the apartment building where one of Lord's alibi witnesses lived. I didn't even notice two heavy-set women ambling along. Then I heard Johnny approach them.

"Ladies, how are you? Warm winter night, ain't it? I hope you had a delightful Christmas. My name is Johnny LeGray. I'm a detective." He flashed his badge and photo identification. "Look at that picture. Not the best looking guy you ever seen, but I do the best with what I got, two hundred forty pounds of lumbering, loving man. Here to play not to stay—if you know what I mean. And by the way, this Christmas money is burning a hole in my pocket. Which one of you ladies might like to go out for lunch?"

"Aw, listen to this man," one of the women said, and they burst out laughing.

"Man is right, darling. It shows you recognize the real thing when you see it. An old-school gentleman who treats ladies the way they should be treated." Johnny moved on to business as soon as he knew he owned them. "Either of you fine ladies seen him around?" Johnny had a picture of one of the alibi witnesses.

"Oh, yeah, he stay up in apartment nineteen with his auntie," one of the women said.

"Thank you, ladies, and here is my card. You never know when you will need a favor, you never know when you might want a friend to have a drink with and just talk. You can always remember my name, Johnny LeGray: like the gray fox, an older distinguished gentleman who can truly appreciate a fine woman."

The two forty-something women were eating it up. They took his cards and carefully placed them in their purses. "I'm keeping this in my handbag," I heard one of the women say as they walked away.

"Dat's right, it's good to have a PO-leese officer's card in your handbag. It's like he say, 'You never know.'" Their voices faded into the darkness.

"How did you get that picture?" I asked.

"I ran the names you gave me. He's the only one that has an arrest photo and a record."

"What was he arrested for?"

"Insider trading," Johnny said cynically. "What the fuck you think he was arrested for? Drugs. Possession of cocaine."

Lee Pyles never gave me an apartment number. Johnny got the fat ladies to sing, pulling the lead out of thin air. We knocked on number nineteen.

A shirtless young man slowly opened the door. He was wearing bright, Tommy Hilfiger boxer shorts and elephant-leg baggy jeans that were resting at the top of his pubic area. The *de rigueur* six inches of underwear were showing. He had clearly been sleeping.

"Yeah?" the young man said in a barely audible voice.

Johnny was in the door in a flash, and I followed him. There was no air in the apartment, and the heat was blasting. Johnny was unfazed by the oxygen deficit. He sat down at the dining room table and whipped out a small pad and a pen. The young man sat down across from us.

"How are you my man, my name is detective Johnny LeGray. I'm looking for Billy, would that be you?"

"No, my name is DeWayne. I'm Billy's cousin."

"DeWayne, does Billy live here?"

"He stay here sometime."

"DeWayne, what is your last name and your date of birth?" Johnny asked. Continuing with great speed, he added, "DeWayne, are you married, single, divorced, gay, lesbian, against marriage, cohabiting with a woman, living in sin, in psychoanalysis deciding what your sexual preference is, widowed, or currently more interested in watching sports than dating?"

"I'm a lesbian," DeWayne said, and the three of us laughed. "What the fuck do you want?" DeWayne had finally drifted out of his sleepy state. He looked at Johnny and said, "You a crazy cop, I can tell."

"DeWayne, your cousin Billy's name was given to me because he has been listed as an alibi witness in an upcoming trial. Billy is in no trouble whatsoever, and I am not lying to you. I repeat: Billy is in absolutely no trouble. I just need to talk to him. Here's my card. No, here's two—one for him and one for you—you never know when you need a favor. Please have him call me. Sorry to have bothered you."

"Hey, man, no problem, no problem," DeWayne said and looked at Johnny's card.

We drove around trying to find another alibi witness named Dorris. Even Johnny was lost and had to get on the radio to talk to a dispatcher. The conversation was mostly in numbers, flavored with "roger this" and "copy that." We finally ended up in a rotten part of southeast D.C. filled with low-rise housing projects and grassless courtyards. Poverty and misfortune had conspired, leaving broken glass everywhere.

"Look at this neighborhood. Crime is completely out of control, and the residents complain that Nordstrom won't put a shop in this part of town. What a joke." He punctuated his editorial with a single laugh. "What do I know? Here's the house, or what's left of it."

Johnny knocked on Dorris' door. No answer. Johnny then took his business card and stuck it in the mailbox. He placed a second card in the crack of the door about a foot above eye level. It took forever because he wrote notes on each card asking the person to call him. Johnny then dropped me off at my car and congratulated me on my engagement to Kara. As I was getting out, he grabbed my arm.

"Listen, I will find out what I can and feed it to you—just keep it to yourself. Don't go running to Tommy or feed it to your dad at the *Post*, you got that?"

"No problem."

I checked my messages. Galina, a witness in the Slater case, had left a message. I had to listen to it a second time to decipher her strong Russian accent. "Hi, my name is Galina, I am a ballerina with the Kirov. I got your number from Hud or some such name, and was told to contact you. I would have called sooner but I was performing in *The Nutcracker*. We should have coffee so I can tell you what I saw on that horrible day. My mobile is…"

It was only 9 P.M. What the fuck, I decided. I wasn't married yet, and Galina had valuable information. I called her, and she said she was hanging out with other dancers at a Starbucks on Connecticut Avenue.

"Which one? There are a hundred Starbucks on Connecticut Avenue. There are Starbucks inside of Starbucks. A new one probably opened up during our conversation."

She didn't laugh, but conferred with other soprano voices and gave me the location near Dupont Circle.

"Thanks, I'm on my way. I need to gather information from you and get you ready to testify. See you soon," I told her.

I completed three laps around the block before I finally found a space. As I walked toward my destination, several homeless people asked me for money. Two were literally decomposing; the third, right in front of Starbucks, had a latte cup in one hand and the *New York*

*Times* at his feet. He demanded the sum certain of one dollar. I ignored him. He yelled, "Don't you fucking ignore me," and blocked the entrance. I reached into my jacket and pulled out my D.A.'s badge. He looked confused, like I was going to arrest him. Instead, I reached into my wallet and gave him a dollar. Kara would have given him a buck. Plus, guys like this, so far off on the margins, why bother?

"Ooooooo, that guy is so gross. He spit on Pam because she said she didn't have any money," said one of the ballerinas. I hadn't even introduced myself to Galina's entourage. Apparently, they had watched me through the window.

"He did not *like* spit on me, he just *like* spit on the ground near me and a little piece of it *like* hit my ballet bag," a young girl with a heavy gothic look said. She added, "You know what I mean."

"Puh-leeze. I'm going to throw up," another one said.

"Get in line. Meredith is already in the bathroom doing that right now," one of the other dancers said. "She's all bent because Vladimir said he couldn't pick her up today. Vladimir needs to lift some goddamn weights. Hit the fucking Nautilus instead of the vodka bottle. I'm sick of these men telling us they can't lift us."

"Hi, I'm Galina," she said in a deep voice with a Russian accent, "and you're cute." The others giggled.

I smiled, looked down to feign embarrassment and gave her my card. Galina was blonde and had the type of tall, athletic body that would make a bishop kick a hole in a stained glass window. Her blonde hair was in a tight bun, her eyes were blue and her arms were long and slender. It required a muscular effort not to stare at her incredible jean-clad thighs. Galina was seated. I could see how outrageous her waist, hips, and ass were; I forced myself to look at the other dancers.

"Hi, my name is Clay Franklin," I said, as I smiled and shook each one of their gracile hands.

One of them said, "How come she got a card, and we don't? Don't make up your mind yet, Clay Franklin. All of us were at the school when that teacher got shot, and we all want to get laid." They all laughed. Unabashed girl power, power-in-numbers, gang mentality—whatever it was, uncensored words flew from their lips. They wore their blonde hair in buns, tightly wound on the top of their skulls. "Angel" by Gavin Friday was playing, and half of them were smoking. Smoking inside a fucking Starbucks.

"I didn't know you could smoke in here," I said, deciding to get into the conversational waters, not wanting to be ignored or talked about as if I were one of those cardboard cut-outs of the president with which tourists have their picture taken.

"We know the manager and he doesn't care as long as no one complains," Galina said and took a drag.

Only Galina had seen the shooter, but they all began talking at bullet speed about the killing of Bradford Slater: "What kind of country is this?" They were wired on caffeine and nicotine. Meredith, the last member of the creative quintet came out of the bathroom. She was as emaciated as ET. I had to do my best to paste a smile on my face when we exchanged introductions because her bulimia was so obvious. Her limbs were concentration camp thin. Poor girl, phone home and tell them to cook up some food.

Unlike cigarettes and lattes, the dancers could only handle sadness in small doses. They quickly changed the subject from a dead teacher to dating. I ordered coffee and came back. I told Galina that Hud or another detective would be showing her some pictures to identify the shooter. In her original statement she said that Kevin Ford had bumped into her when he was running out of the basement. She got a close look and even saw the gun in his waistband. It was foolish to try and prepare Galina for trial tonight, so I just listened.

The ballerinas began exchanging stories about guys hitting on them at the Metro… Safeway… the mall… Georgetown… busses. These five women? Girls? Nymphs? Bunheads? Kate Moss clones? Whatever they were, men gave them enough cards to fill up a Palm Pilot on a weekly basis. And the way they were talking, almost any man who had a car got a date. They bitched endlessly about how broke they were, and I learned that the players in their Renaissance game got paid virtually nothing. After pointe shoes, cigarettes, and lattes, they had to depend on the kindness of strangers. Every shopping trip and cell phone bill threw them deeper into charge cards. The men came after them, thicker than flies, confusing svelteness for sweetness, but could never figure out that any one of those bunheads would commit murder for the lead role in *Giselle* or *Romeo and Juliet*. As far as what I felt: it wasn't love I wanted. I wanted Galina on film for my bachelor party. I chided myself for even thinking it. I began to get up to leave.

"Don't go yet. You just got here," Galina said and touched my arm.

I was thinking the unthinkable again and told Galina that I was going to use the restroom and would be right back.

When I returned, they were still yammering away in dance lingo.

"…I thought she was a little bitch when we were at the Bolshoi." A dancer with black mascara around her eyes was on a tear. "She was *like*, 'Excuse me, that's my section of the barre.' I'm *like* 'Hey bitch, you might have been teacher's pet in Moscow but we're in D.C. now and I'm not moving.' Then we do adagio and she is *like* way off the music. God, did you see her do Clara in *The Nutcracker*? It was *like* with no feeling."

"I couldn't stand her in *Coppelia*," said one of the other bunheads, sticking an invisible knife in a boney back.

"It was nice meeting all of you. Galina, I will call you and set up an appointment to talk about the case. I really appreciate your help," I told them.

"Where are you going? It's early. Do you have a second date? Why can't I have a second date tonight?" one of them teased me.

Galina stood up and took a couple of steps with me toward the door.

"I want you to know I will do everything to help you." Galina said, standing inappropriately close. I said nothing.

"Why don't you come watch rehearsal at the ballet studio, then we will go out for coffee and you can go over my testimony," she asked.

This was one of those dangerous moments. I watched Galina write her phone number down. I glanced over at the other dancers. "You Oughta Know" by Alanis Morisette was coming out of unseen speakers, and Meredith was off on her own little foodless planet, silently mouthing the words to the song. Another ballerina lit a cigarette with the end of the one she was smoking, and said that I had a nice ass for a lawyer. These girls were too fucking much—too sexy, too overt, too physical.

"Sounds like a plan," I told Galina.

# JANUARY 10, 2000

I had to pick a jury for the Kelly Lord trial, but first I went to Scott's office to tell him that he was going to be the best man at my wedding (I would somehow include Alexandra, of course). Being my best man, I couldn't resist describing my entertainment plans to him.

"There's this Russian ballet babe, she's a witness in the Slater case and she wants some action. Hey, lights, camera, action, fine by me; I'll shoot some video of this Galina-chick for my bachelor party. "

Scott sized up the situation: "There are two problems. First, there won't be a wedding once Kara realizes what a sorry excuse for a man you are. Second, and far more important, ballet dancers usually don't have much of a rack. I don't know much about dance, but I do know if their tits are too big they lose their balance."

"Think outside the box for God's sake. You are not seeing the possibilities. I am going to call Phil over at the *Post* and consult with him. You are really not exhibiting the kind of *esprit de corps* that I need right now. This isn't some skank. This is a professional dancer—think of the positions I can get her into." I was annoyed with Scott's lack of imagination.

"Okay, just settle down my little Caucasian. There's no need to bring in all sorts of consultants. You might as well get in one last fling before you get married; then, when your wife gets pregnant, you can look for your 'one last fling' again." Although Scott talked the macho talk, he'd never walk into a hotel room with any other woman. He'd shoot himself before he would cheat.

"Just shut your door. For a second there I thought I was going to have to yank your best man ticket," I said as I punched the small, plastic numbers on the phone.

"City desk, this is Phil."

"Hey buddy, you're on speaker phone with Scott and me."

"Scott, how are you doing, man? Congrats on your last murder trial victory. Why don't you get a hall pass from your wife and come out to dinner with us?"

"How about we skip dinner and go right to a sick party with hot *Washington Post* interns who want to blow a homicide trial lawyer?" Scott replied.

"I'll get to work on that but here's my question for *you*," Phil said. "Say you're handling a homicide case and the father is killed, right?" Phil took a dramatic pause. "So, after the trial, you know, once you start banging the mother, do the kids call you 'Dad'?"

"Shut up. Both of you. Just stop talking shit and fucking listen to me." I interrupted. "There is actually something important to talk about here. As you all know, I am getting hitched."

"Big mistake. One out of two American couples tank according to a poll in my paper," Phil interjected.

"And it is important that we have an evening of special entertainment for a select few. There is a ballerina at the Kirov Ballet here in our Nation's Capitol that wants to share some precious moments with me for the last time as a bachelor. And then I will have ten beautiful children with Kara and suffer happily ever after."

"Get her on video. We'll have a small get-together at my condo. We run the video in the background on my big TV, and I will get a stripper from Camelot to do the foreplay in the foreground," Phil said.

"The stripper is for me," Scott said. "What are you guys going to do?"

"We'll play Trivial Pursuit," Phil said.

There was a knock at Scott's door.

"Where have you been? The Kelly Lord trial is going to begin without you, baby," Annette said. Phil heard her voice and said hello.

"Phil, can you put my daughter's picture on the front page of the paper? She won her fourth grade spelling bee contest," Annette asked.

"Give me your direct line. I can't put her picture in, but I'll get someone to follow up. The Metro section loves spelling bees. Oh, shit, I have to go into a meeting. Bye everyone."

"Clay, get to court," Annette commanded. We began walking toward my office.

"Tell them I am stuck in grand jury or something. I have to make ten minutes of phone calls on the teacher homicide. Tell them anything. Just go to judge's chambers and sweet talk them. Go."

I shut the door to my office and put a do-not-disturb yellow sticky on the door.

"Hey, you know what to do," said Tomar's voice on his voicemail.

"Tomar, this is Clay. I need your help in finding a witness in that teacher case. Our detectives couldn't find a dead body if they fell over it. Call me." I hung up and called the F.B.I. lab.

"Forensics," a soft Indian voice said.

"Hi, this is Clay Franklin—prosecutor, homicide division. I'm running the Bradford Slater case."

"This is Sakar, Mr. Franklin."

"Excellent. But don't call me Mr. Franklin. Call me Clay. Mr. Franklin is a crusty old bastard teaching journalism on the western shore of Maryland."

"Okay, Clay." Sakar loosened a bit.

"I want to turn you into an evidence guarder; a guarder of evidence instead of an evidence technician."

"What do you mean?"

"There are a number of routine things that need to be done to Bradford Slater's clothes, such as gunshot residue tests to determine the distance of the shooter. Fine, no problem. That is very easy for you. What I am worried about is evidence tampering—something unusual like pouring gun powder all over the dead man's clothes so that you can't determine the distance of the shooter. Anything really."

"Who do you think would do this? This is the F.B.I." Sakar sounded a little hurt.

"I hate to say this, but perhaps someone from inside, someone from law enforcement."

"I promise you, Mr. Franklin—I mean Clay—that I will keep an eye out for that."

"Who else is working on the case?"

"My partner is Allison Melville, also an F.B.I. evidence examiner. She's not here today. I think she's at a training seminar in Virginia."

"Sakar, could you kindly tell her everything I told you, and put me through to her voicemail? Thanks for all your help."

I left her a message as long as a college physics lecture. She'd probably file some government overtime form just for listening to it. Next was Hud. I called homicide and left a message on his voicemail. Was Hud hiding a close relationship with Rodney Ford? I couldn't tell at this point.

I left a voicemail for Johnny saying I wanted to do a flow chart of everyone Rodney Ford was close with on the police force. I left a voicemail for Kara: "Hi—just wanted to say, you smell beautiful and you're just the right amount of nasty. Miss you. See you soon." I ran to court to take a crack at nailing Kelly Lord.

*

"Excuse juror number seven," Pyles screamed, as if giving a military command (but not like my father's U.S. Marine scream). He was a strange bird, this Pyles. It was not that he was just a born-again Christian, which was healthier than my drinking and extreme sexual escapades. It was that he was a born-again Christian, an Amway salesman, and a dangerous liar with a *faux* southern accent. His behavior had bizarre conflicts: he attempted to strengthen his clients' relationship with God, then he'd show up at discovery conferences with prosecutors and try to convert them to a new long-distance plan (his new venture into telecom).

We took the better part of the morning picking a jury. Because attempted first-degree murder carried a life sentence, Pyles could strike twenty jurors. He used every one of those strikes too.

Judge Ramsey was a good draw for me. A former prosecutor and partner in a major Washington law firm, he was steady at the helm. He was well respected in the legal community. He could have come to the bench earlier in his career but waited until his children finished college because of the pay cut: as a law partner his salary was six hundred fifty thousand a year and as a judge it was ninety-seven. Why did he accept the black robe? Did he have money stashed? A rich wife? Did he love trial work that much? Did he grow tired of his wind-filled partners and big firm politics? Did Pyles talk him into a new long-distance plan, which now allowed him to take a pay cut? Some days nothing made sense in this courthouse, but one thing I did know—he was a solid judge.

The best thing about Ramsey was each ruling was like a fresh clock. Certain judges who were not great thinkers tried to "balance things out" and divide up the rulings. If Judge Ramsey ruled for the prosecution or the public defender nine times in a row, the tenth ruling would be based on the law. There was none of the *Well, I've been ruling your way all day counselor, I think I'll throw a bone to your opponent, and sustain the objection.*

It was time for opening statements; time to get in the water. A case is only as strong as its victim, and my victim was a biased crack head. I knew it was going to be difficult, especially with a bucket of alibi witnesses. I had been so busy with my love life and trying to keep my finger on the pulse of the Slater case, I had not even written an opening statement in this one. My theme would be Kelly Lord equaled death. It was essential that the jury understood that if Lord walked out of the courthouse there would be more death. I would risk going over the top because I just did not have a better option.

"Madame court reporter, do you need to change the paper in the machine or get water? Are we ready for the jury?" Judge Ramsey asked.

"I'm ready," she said.

"Mr. Bailiff, kindly go get the jury," His Honor ordered.

Off in the distance, airy inconsequential chatter and high-pitched laughter floated from the jury room. Suddenly, it stopped. They filed in.

I stood up, walked over to Kelly Lord, thrust my index finger about six inches from his face, turned to the jury, and said, "This man is The Terminator. It may sound overly dramatic, but, ladies and gentlemen of the jury, that is the best description of him. When you don't pay for your drugs, he is the guy that shows up to collect the bill —and the interest is paid with your life. You will meet Kentrel Bishop in a few minutes, and he will show you how expensive the interest payment can be: his entire head is pocked with pellets from Mr. Lord's shotgun."

Then I walked over to the podium, paused, lowered my voice a bit, and continued.

"Defendant Lord advanced young Kentrel little pieces of crack cocaine, what are referred to on the street as 'rocks,' that are sold for twenty bucks. Young Kentrel fell into his product, began to smoke what he was supposed to sell, and became indebted to Mr. Lord. There's your motive with a capital M, but we don't have to prove motive. Judge Ramsey will tell you we have no burden of proof concerning motive, but there it is anyway. Mr. Lord came after him; Kentrel ducked him for a while until one night Mr. Lord decided to terminate the account along with young Kentrel. An account, ladies and gentlemen, that equaled the sum of less than one thousand dollars. Kentrel is shy, and I ask for your patience in advance. He is young and shy. While he has two-dozen shotgun pellets still in his head, he will identify Mr. Lord as the shooter.

"Good morning ladies and gentlemen, my name is Clay Franklin, I represent the community in this matter, and convicting Mr. Lord in this attempted first-degree murder is our duty as citizens of Washington, D.C." I hoped that I sounded serious, but not too severe. I left the podium and walked over to the courtroom easel. I drew a floor plan of where the young Kentrel Bishop had been sitting when Lord broke into the house to shoot him. I drew an arrow between them to show that he could see him clearly.

"Perhaps convicting the defendant is the very least we can do for the community. That is all I have to say at this time. I invite Mr. Pyles to present his opening statement," I said and sat down.

"Mr. Pyles, would you like to give an opening statement?" Judge Ramsey asked.

"I guess so, your honor. I didn't think the D.A. was going to be done in two minutes," Pyles said as he grabbed his notes and began awkwardly walking toward the jury.

"You can talk for up to half an hour or be as short as you want Mr. Pyles, it makes no difference to me. However, if you had planned to write your opening statement during Mr. Franklin's opening statement, that was probably a mistake."

The jury chuckled at Judge Ramsey's deadpan humor. He was beside himself with a comic's satisfaction. A formal jurist, he cracked about one joke in front of the jury every five years. Inside, however, I wasn't smiling; I felt a strange sense of underachievement. I knew Pyles was not a good sparring partner for the upcoming Slater case. Who would the Ford family hire in a city of five hundred thousand lawyers? Would they sell the house and get Johnny Cochran? Whoever the Ford family hired would be soaked with talent. And if he or she kicked my ass, my ass was out of the D.A.'s office. I just leaned back and enjoyed this Gomer Pyle goofball. Hell, at least my career didn't depend on this case.

"Mr. Franklin here gave such a quick opening statement you good people probably forgot that he has this heavy, heavy burden of proof. The prosecution has two problems. First, the U.S. Constitution protects Kelly Lord. Second, Mr. Lord is the wrong person. He wasn't even around Kentrel Bishop the night he was shot. Mr. Bishop is a crack addict who dealt with multiple drug dealers. Lots of people would like to see him dead," Pyles rambled on. I liked his lead, but it went downhill from there. Why, for instance, would people like to see him dead? After another minute I couldn't even follow what he was talking about. I looked over at the jurors, and I don't think they were following either. His opening finally petered out and the judge asked me to call my first witness.

"The prosecution calls Kentrel Bishop to the stand," I announced.

"Ladies and gentlemen of the jury," the judge said, "Kentrel Bishop is incarcerated. We are going to bring him in. He will be in handcuffs and perhaps leg irons. Due to recent problems in the courthouse we have increased our security. The marshals will stand near the witness stand when he testifies. Please draw no negative inference from this. You are to weigh the credibility of this witness the same way you would weigh the credibility of any witness."

"State your name for the record and tell the jury why you are locked up," I began with Kentrel.

"Kentrel Bishop; I stay at the D.C. jail for selling crack. I pleaded guilty to distribution of cocaine. My public defender said it was a good deal, so I took it." There he was—in my clothes. I had given him an old suit with an out-of-style, too-narrow pin stripe. He still looked better than if it was an orange jumpsuit. He told his harrowing tale of being shot. We went through every conceivable detail and moved in dozens of exhibits from the crime scene, including his bloody clothes.

"Did there come a time, after you were incarcerated, that you were threatened about testifying?"

"Yes, Lord's cousin and some big dude made me sign this letter that said I don't want to testify in this case."

"Do you want to testify?"

"Hell, yeah."

"But this is your handwriting, your signature—why did you sign it?" I asked.

"He said he'd kill my mother if I testified."

"Kentrel, is the person that shot you and threatened to kill your mother in the courtroom today? If so, please point to him."

Kentrel did that, and then the judge gave the standard instruction, "May the record reflect the defendant has been identified."

"Your witness," I said and looked at Pyles.

"So you're in jail for distribution of crack, huh, Kentrel?" Pyles began.

The jurors had a collective look of *So what, we already knew that.* Pyles then began to chip away at Kentrel's perception of the event. This was the area I feared most because, truth be told, I hadn't spent much time with him. A witness' improvisation was a D.A.'s nightmare.

"Isn't it a fact, sir, that it was dark in that basement when the unknown assailant shot you?" Pyles emphasized the phrase "unknown assailant."

"Yes." Kentrel was flatlining. He was too young and nervous to assert himself. Inside, I was screaming, *Please, Kentrel, say it was not an "unknown assailant." It was Kelly Lord.*

"Isn't it true that the television was on, and you were facing that television? The light was in your eyes?"

"Yes," he said softly. I didn't object to Pyles' compound question. Why allow Pyles to have Kentrel repeat damaging answers three different times? It would have just made matters worse.

"You bought crack cocaine after you smoked what you were supposed to sell, right?"

"Yes."

"And you certainly bought crack from a number of different crack dealers?"

"Yes."

"You owed money to some of them too, didn't you?"

"Yes."

"No further questions."

The judge stroked his chin in thought, and then offered, "Any re-direct, Mr. Franklin?"

"Yes, thank you, Your Honor."

Pyles created doubt, reasonable doubt. All I could do on re-direct was patch things up a little bit.

"Kentrel, Mr. Pyles referred to an 'unknown assailant' several times in his questioning. What is the name of the person who shot you?"

"Kelly Lord."

"Nothing further on re-direct, your Honor."

"Mr. Pyles, based on Mr. Franklin's single question, do you have any re-cross?"

Pyles shook his head no.

"Mr. Pyles, the court reporter must put your response in the record. Yes or no?" Judge Ramsey ordered, getting a little impatient.

Pyles coughed up a "No questions," and Judge Ramsey sent the jurors to lunch. I ran back to my office to call the F.B.I. on the Slater case. I left a message with ballistics wondering if they had the gun and the bullet from Bradford's body to do a match. I called Kara.

"Hey, what are you doing?"

"I'm talking to some band guy in California who wants me to design his group's CD cover. I'll get rid of him so we can talk," Kara whispered.

"No, I have to go back to court anyway. I just called to tell you I love you."

"I'm going to vomit if you tell me that one more time," she said. "I'll be super nice and cook you dinner tonight. You don't have to lie or buy me anything. Do you want something special?" Kara teased me.

"I'm always up for something special." I paused. "I guess I should get back to court. Bye."

"Wait."

"What?"

"Nothing." I could tell she did not want to hang up the phone. I said goodbye.

*

"Whom do you want to call to the stand next, Mr. Franklin?" Judge Ramsey asked off-the-record. We were waiting for the court reporter to come back from lunch. "Judge, my witness coordinator just handed me a note saying that the treating physician is in Florida. Nice of her to tell me on the day of trial. I think I am going to have Kelly Lord shoot her too."

The defendant had not been brought up from the jail yet, so everyone gave a soft chuckle: the judge, the judge's law clerk, the marshal, the court clerk and, to my surprise, Pyles. The judge was going to give Lord a fair trial and Pyles was going to vigorously defend, but even Judge Ramsey didn't mind a little humor from time to time.

"What do you want to do?" Judge Ramsey asked.

"Move Kentrel Bishop's medical records in through the custodian of records, but I need to call my secretary to get her in here. I'll call a short witness while we are waiting for hospital personnel. I need five minutes to step out in the hall and make a call."

"You've got three minutes. The defendant and the jury are on their way. I'm sorry about your office's disorganization, but we're not slowing down."

I was too annoyed with the witness coordinator to call her; I felt a loss of control coming on and was worried I might say something truthful about her work effort. I called Annette, knowing she'd lecture me endlessly.

"Do I get two paychecks?" Annette asked. "Answer me, do I get two paychecks?"

"No."

"I am your secretary. I am not your witness coordinator. I do not get two paychecks and two sets of sick leave."

"Are you done? Now I have one minute left to get back into court."

"Alright, baby, I'll get my records girl Simone from D.C. General Hospital up there. But you're buying me a Curtis Mayfield CD and giving me a twenty-dollar cash bonus."

"I love you for this."

"As soon as I get that custodian of records in that courtroom you'll stop loving me, you monster." Annette was going to get every Curtis Mayfield CD I could get my hands on.

The marshals were waving at me to get back into the courtroom. I walked in and the jury was already seated in the box, and I had to call a witness.

By the time I was done with the first officer on the scene of the shooting, Simone, the custodian of records, arrived. When I went to move the records into evidence Pyles screamed, "This is the first time I have ever seen these medical records. The prosecutor never gave me a copy of the hospital records, and this is a low-down, dirty trick." Good old Pyles, right in front of the jury. The judge looked annoyed and told us to approach the bench.

"Okay, Mr. Pyles, I understand your discovery complaint. Mr. District Attorney, your response?" His Honor inquired.

I pulled out my special log. I'd had this odd-shaped spiral notebook for years. I had been schooled in dirty defense bar tactics during the early stages of my career. Tell the D.A. something quick in the hallway, then change it and spin it in the courtroom until it looked like a rape case was pled down to disturbing the peace. I had been horse-fucked by dishonest lawyers so many times that several years ago I began keeping what was now labeled as "Phone, Fax, and Hallway Contact Log." People teased me about the anal-ness of it, but it was great for moments like these.

"Your Honor, either a messenger service or a member of Mr. Pyles' staff picked up the medical records on October 7, 1999; on October 14, I sent a fax thanking him for picking the records up and asking him if we could stipulate to the medical records, thus saving the time of bringing in the custodian of records or the trauma surgeon. On November 10, I saw Mr. Pyles in the hallway and asked him again. He told me since it was an identity case he didn't have a problem with the stipulation. Here is the fax and the proof-of-fax transmission sheet." I handed the documents to Judge Ramsey.

"Mr. Pyles, did that conversation take place?"

"I don't remember Judge," Pyles lied.

"Mr. Pyles, is your fax number 703-627-1565?"

"Yes," Pyles said, his face frozen like a ballerina caught with a dozen donuts.

"I find no discovery violation, Mr. Pyles. And the next time you have an objection of this magnitude, you are to approach the bench and not leap up and indict the prosecutor for sleazy behavior in front of the jury. Do you understand?"

"I can assure this Honorable Court that the fax slipped through the cracks, and the objection was in good faith," Pyles lamely said.

"Let's not bring 'faith' into it. Now get back to your trial table." Even Judge Ramsey grew tired of Pyles' Holy Roller Amway bullshit.

I finished up with the hospital witness and moved the medical records into evidence. The judge sent the jury out.

"Before I break for the day," the judge spoke with a troubled look on his face, "we have a bit of an issue. During the noon hour one of the juror's sent a note to my bailiff. It says, 'Is there any way to avoid releasing our names and addresses?'"

Pyles leaped up like he won the bingo game at his church. "I want a mistrial. That shows the jurors are irrationally afraid of my client, and he won't get a fair trial."

"Slow down Mr. Pyles, and please let me finish. You're not getting a mistrial, but you have the right to make an appellate record in a minute," Ramsey said in his steady-at-the-wheel voice. "I am going to inform the jurors that I am ordering both attorneys to give their jury lists to me. Furthermore, those jury lists will be sealed by the Court so there is no possibility of their names being released. Also, over the noon hour I researched this issue, and it is the Court's position that I will not be reversed on appeal if I deny Mr. Pyles the right to go interview the jurors after the trial to question them on their level of fear. Counsel, give me your juror lists. Mr. Pyles make your record."

"As I stated it is so obvious this jury is too terrified to judge my client fairly. He has been denied his due process rights and…" Pyles droned on.

When he ran out of legal gas and paused, Judge Ramsey asked, "Anything else you want to add?" After a second of silence, the Judge ruled. "Motion denied. Tomorrow morning we'll finish the prosecution's case. Mr. Pyles, have your alibi witnesses ready. I want to finish this case tomorrow. Because of our budget crisis, I will not let the jurors deliberate past 5 P.M. I will see everyone here tomorrow at 8 A.M. Court is adjourned."

The office had pretty much cleared out. Alexandra and Scott were there, of course. I blew by everyone and went to my office to call Johnny about the alibi witnesses. The combination of Kentrel's weak testimony today and good alibi witnesses tomorrow equaled a not guilty. On any given Monday, any of us could lose, as Scott always joked. It didn't feel funny. I was going to call Kara, but she had already voicemailed me that she was working late.

"I'm fucked," I told Alexandra when she poked her head in.

"You always say that," she laughed. "And I always say, 'It always feels like that in the middle of trial.' Let's see what we can find out about the alibi witnesses tonight. I'll come with you," she insisted.

The phone rang. It was Phil. I held my hand up to Alexandra not to go. She mimicked me and added air traffic control hand signals.

"There is a young metro reporter who wants a quote concerning the arrest of NBA player Chris Webber for resisting arrest and drugs."

"Tell your fellow reporter I think Webber has a solid all-around game, and he's an exceptional passer."

"That's not exactly what we had in mind," Phil said.

"It's not my case. I'm in a trial, and I might call you back later to go have a drink on the other side of town. I have to check out an alibi witness. Bye," I hung up and started talking to Alexandra again.

"No, Johnny will go with me. Get out of here. Go have fun." I was not going to ruin her evening for this case.

"I'm going to yoga and then a bunch of us are going out for Indian. Why don't you join us after the witness?"

"Sounds good. I'll hit your cell. Kara is working late."

I called Johnny LeGray to see if he would go out with me and try to find another witness.

"Pyles got to the witnesses. They are hiding from me. That's what happens when you wait until the last minute to interview witnesses. I need more time," Johnny said.

"Like it's my fault? Pyles just dumped the names on me. I couldn't move for a continuance because the case has been continued so many times."

"The only thing I do know is they were all hanging out at a bar named Jimmy's on Georgia Avenue. Lord was probably putting coke up everyone's nose as they partied on the weekend. Pyles probably told him to give him the names of people who didn't have criminal records, so he could stick them on the stand to lie. That's all I could get out of one of the witnesses. He told me they hung at Jimmy's and then he hung up on me."

"Stop by the courtroom tomorrow," I said. "I am going to demand that the judge let me interview them in the hall. You, Scott, and Alexandra will each talk to one of the witnesses. Walk them about fifteen yards apart. Pyles can't stand in three places at once. I'm sure we will find inconsistencies in their story."

"You take your cases too seriously," Johnny responded. "This is what I was talking about in the car the other day."

"Are you going to be there?"

"Hell no, I am not going to be there. The system don't care about me. I put thousands of bad guys behind bars, and now they want me to join them. Fuck 'em," Johnny said with exasperation.

I knew Johnny would be there. Too bad he wasn't allowed to help me on the teacher homicide. I drove home fast and careless, as usual.

*

I changed, ate cold pasta and began looking at my trial notebook. The evidence scene was poorly processed. Shotgun shells had never been fingerprinted. The detective wrote that two thousand dollars was recovered off Kentrel when the evidence bag contained two hundred. Then I saw on a different page it was two hundred dollars. Pyles was going to have a field day. The detective never returned my phone call to prep him.

I awoke to the piercing sound of a siren. Shit, I had fallen asleep. Within seconds my mind was racing and my heart palpitating. *Everyone is going to say they were at a bar named Jimmy's and I don't even know what it looks like inside!* How could I effectively cross-examine Lord's witnesses tomorrow? They could say they served sushi on waterbeds and I wouldn't know if it was true or not.

*Bam!* My old white BMW was rocked by a crater-sized pothole. Street repair, education, snow removal, jails, police, fire departments and other ordinary city functions were ignored in D.C. Nothing in the city worked except parking enforcement. The latter was carried out by platoons of black women with attitude, or, as Annette would say, serious AT.

I trolled the block for a parking space. I stopped at Starbucks for coffee. It was the same Starbucks where I met Galina. Tonight it was smoke-and-ballerina-free. I was climbing back into the car when the caffeine kicked in. I looked at a piece of paper with the address for Jimmy's on it.

I drove along Florida Avenue, a tributary off Connecticut Avenue that meandered between august embassies and outposts of despair, until it finally dumped into Georgia Avenue, placing me in front of Jimmy's Bar. No parking problems here. No upscale restaurants or movie theaters—in fact, no curb period. Someone had torn the heads of the parking meters off. (But who, *Cool Hand DeLuke?*)

As I was walking toward Jimmy's I noticed a person coming up on my right. A black teenager asked me if I was "looking for something?" I politely declined. I was wearing Air Jordans, Diesel jeans, and a leather jacket (Shoeboot would have been proud of me). A second kid ran up and said in a soft voice, "Yo, white boy, I got some rocks for you." I slipped my badge out of my right pocket and quietly said, "No thanks." He froze, thinking that I would radio a car to pick him up if he ran, or grab him myself if he didn't.

"Wacky world, ain't it? Between the police profiling African Americans and now you profiling me, it's getting so a guy can't go out for a drink on a warm winter night." I had learned a couple of things from Johnny LeGray over the years. "Do me a favor, and I won't arrest you. Take a look at this picture, and tell me if you know this guy."

I showed him a picture of Kelly Lord. The low clouds reflected the yellow-orange fluorescent crime lights, which, in turn, threw a patina of orange over the black and white mug shot of Lord.

"I don't know who he is," the young man said.

"C'mon, take another look. He hangs around Jimmy's over there."

"I live northeast. I just started working this area with my cousin to buy some shoes and a PlayStation for me and my little brother."

"Let me guess, you're under eighteen and your cousin is over eighteen, so if you get caught it's a juvenile parking ticket and if he gets caught it's a felony. Take it from me, get another job, dude. Sooner or later, you're gonna get arrested."

He gave me a long look and then said, "I ain't got no drugs on me."

"Of course not, the drugs are on someone else who is watching us or hidden somewhere close. As my father used to say, 'I'm wasting my breath trying to lecture you.' Just keep an eye on my car."

"No one is gonna touch your ride, man," he said as we began moving in opposite directions.

Things may have been jumping on the street, but it was dead calm inside the bar. A Jamaican waitress brought me a beer. I asked her to send over the manager. Off in the kitchen, I heard her shout a name. "Ray!" I took out a pen and began sketching the floor plan of the bar. There was nothing like being on a witness' turf to understand the lies they're going to tell in court.

"Can I help you?" A large black guy in a cook's uniform about forty, maybe forty-five came out and sat down. He lit a cigarette aggressively, snapping his wrist hard when half the effort would have extinguished the match.

"You must be Ray. How are you? My name is Clay, and I am a lawyer working on a case. I can see you are busy so I won't stay long, but first, let me buy you a drink." I tried to be as enthusiastic and friendly as possible. Ray reeked of vodka. *Yellow sticky mental note: bring Ray to next family gathering to meet my sister.*

"Who told you I'm Ray? I'm not Ray. And how do you know I'm the manager?"

"You look like the man in charge." I continued to joke, suck up, and assure him of his alpha-dog status. Ray, who said he was not Ray, was going to give me a hard time. Fine. Same old story. In criminal justice, there were more hostile witnesses than friendly ones. It was a Washington fact, like big potholes that went unfixed and politicians passing family-oriented reforms during the day and chasing interns at night.

"Cherry, bring me a vodka and orange juice," Ray yelled at a waitress. "So you are a lawyer. Well, counselor, how do I know you are who you say you are? You could be anyone."

"I work down at the D.A.'s office. Here is my badge and my card. I am just trying to find out whether Kelly Lord and his friends come around here much. That's all. I'm harmless." There was nothing left. I couldn't beta-dog this anymore.

The vodka and orange juice arrived. I assumed the good-looking black waitress was Cherry.

"So you a prosecutor, huh?" He took a sip from his drink before plucking the badge from my hand. "Let me tell you something, motherfucker—you come into my bar acting tough when you don't know what I'm about, what I been through…"

"I'm sure you've been through a lot." I struggled not to roll my eyes. "I'm just trying to find out if you have ever seen Kelly in here. But if I'm not welcome, I'll leave." I reached for my badge, but Ray would not give it back to me.

"Now Ray, it is not a good idea to keep that badge. I am not a policeman. I am just another suit. But, I do represent the entire D.C. police force. If you don't give that back I can fill this place with cops, and they won't be ordering vodka and orange juice," I said with a stupid half-smile. I could feel anger rising up, filling my body with primal fuel. There was a strong metallic taste in my mouth. The advantage of getting my ass kicked as a smartass kid was that it shortened the list of people I would take shit from. Judges and Annette were on the list. Ray was not.

"Let me tell you something, Spunky," he began, stopping to take a drag off his cigarette. "Maybe I keep this badge and call the police tomorrow to see if it is real. Or maybe I'll keep this fucking thing longer than that, teach you a lesson. What do you think about that? Maybe I seen Kelly Lord, maybe I never heard his name in my life."

I wasn't really thinking. There was so much adrenaline pumping through me, I was on the brink of vomiting. I knew if Ray were sober he could destroy me, but drunk—he would not be able to react in time. There was a heavy-set guy on a stool at the bar. He couldn't get to me either. Unless Cherry had a gun, I could make it to my car quickly. Ray interrupted his drunken diatribe to put his cigarette out with his right hand. His left hand held my badge with only his fingers. He picked up his drink. His neck was completely exposed as he lifted his glass. I simultaneously snatched the badge and punched him in the throat. He dropped the glass and grabbed his neck. His chair tipped back. I kicked it so that he crashed to the ground.

"You're right. You're not Ray," I growled, "you're just a little bitch." I kicked him in the stomach as hard as I could and came flying out of the bar so hard the door struck the brick facade with a thunderclap.

Outside, I began running with the keys to my car in my hand. About ten yards before my car, I fell to my knees and puked up the pasta. I dropped my keys. I heard steps behind me. It was probably Ray with a weapon of small destruction. I stood up, and, as I turned, I saw the kid I had stopped earlier.

"What happened?" he asked and handed me my keys. He stared at the regurgitated chunks of food.

"Jamaican jerk chicken, man, don't eat the jerk chicken in there," I said as I opened the door of my car and fired up the Beemer. I heard the same thunderclap as the metal bar door swung open. In my rear-view mirror, I saw Ray. The light reflected off an aluminum baseball bat.

I hurtled down Georgia Avenue, the copper taste in my mouth mixing with the horrible aftertaste of vomit. *Ray has a bat. I have a car.* I wanted to turn around and run over him but even I wasn't angry enough to be that foolish. I didn't need to add an auto manslaughter charge to the simple assault I had committed. Time for me to head home for my own vodka and orange juice.

## Chapter 4

# Terminating the Terminator

## JANUARY 11, 2000

At dawn, I told Kara all about my night with Ray. Her jaw clenched and brow furrowed. "What were you thinking?" She wanted to hammer me with maternal regard.

"You're right. I reacted instead of responded and did all the wrong things," I replied meekly.

"I'm really surprised," she said.

"Don't worry, everything is going to be fine," I attempted to assuage her.

"How can you possibly be ready to get married? Think. Everything you do is now connected to me, as well as your family," Kara told me as her eyes softened.

She immediately got dressed and came to the office with me, ignoring my protests. When Johnny arrived at the office, he sweetly persuaded Kara to go to work. He assured her, "If Clay's arrested,

I'll have him bonded out in five minutes." As she left, Scott and Alexandra entered, shutting the door behind them. I told them what happened.

"This is the best thing that ever happened to you, Clay. Pure class. A beautiful woman who stands by you like that? Don't screw this up buddy boy," Johnny said in his 1960s Rat Pack jargon.

I said nothing. Instead, I stared at the floor. I was hung over and more than a bit appalled at my behavior. "I have to go tell Tommy. I have to self-report so the office isn't embarrassed. I can't let Tommy get blindsided by reporters."

"You don't have to do that," Johnny shook his head.

"I know what you think Johnny. Let's get other opinions," I said, looking at Alexandra and Scott.

"Here are the crimes I think you have committed," Scott began. "Assault and battery for the first punch, a second count of assault when you kicked him, disturbing the peace, disorderly conduct, destruction of property if the chair broke, and littering when you vomited. Then there are the traffic offenses of reckless driving and careless driving when you sped out of there. Maybe a bunch of little stuff I can't even remember because I haven't done traffic cases for more than six years. That's all I can think of, Spunky."

"That is un-fuckin'-helpful, Scott," I told him.

"Tell Tommy about the fight, but don't mention that you said you represented the entire police force. That is another crime involving a public official's misrepresentation. In case you forgot, we don't represent the cops," Scott shot back.

"Next time I am going to use your name and leave your card," I said.

Letting out a loud sigh, Johnny addressed the room. "You fucking lawyers and your imaginations," he began, strictly bar and grill.

"What's this Ray going to do? Go to Skadden Arps or Williams and Connolly and sue you for battery? He's a cook. Not to mention the guy was probably so fucking drunk he doesn't remember what happened. Maybe Ray is on parole or probation? Maybe Ray knows he is guilty of attempted theft? He don't want to charge you with anything. Besides, he's got his reputation to think of. Pride, think pride. This big black guy is gonna call up the police and tell them some little white guy beat him up in his bar? Not on my mother's grave. Go finish your trial, convict this Lord guy, and start prepping the teacher homicide."

"Look on the bright side. How's Ray going to find you? It's not like you gave him your business card," Scott said. "Oh, that's right. You did give him your card."

After internally weighing the options, Alexandra spoke. "You and I are going to go see Tommy. Johnny's right—emphasize that Ray was stealing your badge and acting belligerent. There is an advantage to self-reporting this. After all, if Tommy were ever called as a witness about this fight, he could honestly say you were acting in self defense."

"Nobody can cook up a conspiracy to lie and obstruct justice like a bunch of Department of Justice lawyers," Scott said. "And we have a great tradition of it. The way J. Edgar Hoover used the Justice Department to hunt down Martin Luther King, Charlie Chaplin and other dangerous people. That's why I like working here."

"Alright. If you fools think Clay should tell Tommy, fine," Johnny barked. "You're doing it the right way. But I'm telling you, this guy will never pop up. I'll call my contacts in that district, see if anyone called in. Then I'll meet you all up near the courtroom to help interview these alibi witnesses. By the way Clay, congrats. You're the first lawyer I know who attended Georgetown and got into a solid donnybrook. I might have to stop calling you a pussy."

"Johnny, thanks for coming here and helping me through this. I owe you one, and you can count on me to be a character witness at your next police corruption trial," I said.

Johnny smiled—another favor in the bank.

"I have to cover Tommy's back in case someone calls him," I added. "If I tell him now, at least we can get prepared if something happens. He won't fire me and maybe he'll admire me in the same sick way you do."

Johnny took off. Scott asked me if I wanted him to come along to Tommy's office.

"No, that's alright. Just having you as a friend here today meant so much to me. After I'm done with Tommy, why don't you meet Ray and me for a drink at Jimmy's Bar?"

"I might take you up on that—if you're not in jail by happy hour," Scott said, leaving the room as Alexandra took me by the arm to walk me to the principal's office.

"We need to see Tommy right away," Alexandra told his personal assistant.

"Come on in. How are my superstars doing?" Tommy was reading the paper. "Alexandra, you are doing a great job on these priest cases."

"Thanks. Some are jailed; some have moved out west; and some have Alzheimer's. But we are nailing them, pervert by pervert," Alexandra said, and then shut the door. I sat in a chair. She remained standing.

"Look, we came without an appointment because Clay was in a fight last night. He went to some dive bar on Georgia Avenue to investigate the alibi witnesses testifying in the Lord case today. A guy at the bar grabbed his badge, Clay punched him, the guy picked up a baseball bat, and Clay ran. No biggie, but if the guy from the bar calls the cops, the whole wide world is going to call you." Alexandra turned it into a light, breezy film review: Good summer fun, lots of car chases, plenty of hard bodies, and a shiny baseball bat.

Tommy turned to me. "I've told you many times, we go out in pairs in this office. I want my lawyers with a police officer for safety. A lawyer can't be a witness in a case, you know that. Are you alright?" Tommy asked.

"Yeah, I'm okay. The guy is okay too, or at least I think he is. Shit, he chased me with a baseball bat. What do you think will happen? If he hasn't dialed 9-1-1 by now…"

"You ain't the first D.A. to get into a fight with a witness. You're about the tenth." Tommy looked at me sternly.

"Alexandra, you go make our churches safe again. Clay, you stay with me. I want to talk to you alone for a minute."

Alexandra squeezed my shoulder and left.

"You alright?" Tommy asked again, and I nodded yes. "Good. So here's the situation: with all the press scrutiny surrounding the Slater homicide, I can't take any chances. If this fool makes a complaint all the reporters will run to him. During a high-profile case all the newspapers and magazines profile the attorneys. A bar fight is a great sidebar piece—a piece I don't want to see."

"Jesus Tommy, if you're going to fuck me, just come out and say it."

"Fuck you? You fucked yourself. Still, you should know: if you're busted, I'm giving Scott the case. You'll take three of his homicides to even it out. There's twice the number of people looking over my shoulder. There's the local community and this congressional oversight bullshit. You'll have to see the team doctor; he treats cops after shootings, things like that. This falls in that category."

"All for one fucking fight?" I asked.

"Go talk to this doctor, Terrance Hanlow. There are lots of shrinks on the list, but he's the best. I want you to see him today in case reporters get wind of this." He glanced at the phone, as if he expected it to ring. "Clay, I wouldn't fire you even if you got arrested. You're my boy, you know that. But I have to cover my ass. You go see this doctor. Now get out of here and go to court," Tommy said.

*

I headed back to court with Kelly Lord on my mind and the name Dr. Terrance Hanlow in the breast pocket of my white shirt. When I arrived, it was almost 8 A.M. No one was in the courtroom yet. I called Johnny on his cell.

"Did Ray call the cops?"

"What? I don't know—forget that shit for a second. I just overheard Rodney Ford asking about you. Some rant about how a cop's son shouldn't be prosecuted, the gun went off accidentally, that kind of thing. I think he's trying to see who will join his gang. And that's not all; I hear he's passing the hat so he can hire a big-time lawyer. He also said he was trying to refinance his house for lawyer money. You ain't going up against a public defender on this one. Someone big is entering the case. I'm on my way to court, see ya in a minute."

I stepped back into the courtroom. It was booted up: Judge Ramsey, Pyles, the court reporter, and the marshal were ready to go.

"Good morning, Mr. Franklin," His Honor said. "Where are we?"

I heard Alexandra, Scott and Johnny enter the courtroom and sit down. "I want to call my evidence technician to the stand before the prosecution rests its case. I know the Court wants to finish today, so I am suggesting that Mr. Pyles make his witnesses supporting his client's alibi available for interview. While we are finishing up in here, my investigator can interview the alibi witnesses in the hall."

"They've had over a year to interview my alibi witnesses," Pyles lied. His case essentially rested on a group of shady characters claiming they saw the even shadier defendant doing something other than trying to murder people.

"Judge, Mr. Pyles dumped the list of alibi witnesses——"

"Be quiet Mr. Franklin," Judge Ramsey ordered. He strummed through the court file.

"Mr. Pyles, according to the file, you noticed these alibi witnesses on Mr. Franklin less than two weeks ago. How can he interview someone he doesn't know about?"

"They were a Christmas present for Mr. Franklin." Pyles tried to humor the judge, but His Honor wasn't in the mood.

"Mr. Pyles, you will have your alibi witnesses in the hall in five minutes. Tell them it is their choice whether or not to talk to representatives of the D.A.'s office. I repeat, tell them it is their choice. If it gets back to me that you told them not to talk, you are going to be in hot water. We will take a five-minute break to get the jury in; then we will begin with the evidence tech. Get rolling gentlemen. Remain seated; court is adjourned."

By the time we got to the hall, Pyles' alibi witnesses were waiting for us. "You can talk to these guys if you want, we have nothing to hide," Pyles told them with faux confidence. I smiled. Mr. Southern Sleaze had his tricks and I had mine.

By setting it up this way, Pyles could not interfere with the interviews. He would be cross-examining the evidence tech while the interviews were being done. Using multiple interviewers allowed us to separate the alibi witnesses, improving our chances of finding inconsistencies in their stories. They agreed to talk as instructed. Alexandra immediately began charming the woman and walking her down the hall. Scott smiled as he introduced himself to the other alibi. And Johnny, shit, he owned his guy in two seconds. Alexandra, Scott, and I had used our little SWAT team interview technique many times over the years. I went back into court to watch Pyles make mincemeat out of the horribly trained evidence technician.

The judge spoke to the jury: "Good morning ladies and gentlemen. I warned you at the beginning of the case that there would be many delays. For that, I am sorry. But we are ready to go. This case should be in your hands by lunchtime. Mr. District Attorney, call your first witness."

"The prosecution calls Officer Garnett, the crime scene evidence technician" I said. As Garnett was taking the stand, I told him to state his name and introduce himself to the jury. Next, I asked him to walk us through the crime scene, from the moment he was 9-1-1-ed to the collection of the shotgun shells.

"Your honor, can we approach?" Pyles asked.

"Come on up."

"Judge, as Officer Garnett is testifying, I don't want him stating that he is part of the Metropolitan Area Homicide Task Force. A jury hears "homicide" and they'll presume guilt. This is an attempted murder, and I don't want that mentioned," Pyles whispered.

"Response," His Honor ordered me to answer before ruling.

I wanted to taunt Pyles about all the murders Lord had already gotten away with, but I didn't want to alienate the judge. "No response, I defer to the Court," I said.

"Mr. Pyles, your motion is denied for two reasons. First, you should have filed a written motion prior to trial or at the very least submitted the motion orally before I got the jury out here. Second, I do not believe that revealing the technician's background and training to the jury will establish a Constitutional violation. Can you direct my attention to any authority stating that it is a violation of your client's due process rights for a witness to state his background?"

Pyles struggled to construct an answer, but before he could answer His Honor interrupted. "Motion denied; let's keep moving."

Garnett rolled through his testimony from securing the crime scene with yellow tape to interviewing Kentrel Bishop.

"Mr. Pyles, you may begin your cross-examination," Judge Ramsey said.

"How much money was found in the room?" Pyles asked.

"Two hundred dollars."

"Well, here, right in your report, Officer Garnett, it says two thousand dollars."

"I don't remember."

"Why don't you look at your report on page two, under the 'Property Recovered' section?"

"Yeah, well, I typed it late at night. I must have made a typo."

"So that's wrong, and if that is wrong, everything could be wrong," Pyles said in a loud voice.

"I disagree with that."

Pyles was so unsubtle it was hilarious. He moved in for the kill in four questions and then fizzled.

"There is a big difference between two hundred dollars and two thousand dollars, right?"

Eighteen hundred to be exact, I thought. But Garnett did not even answer, so Pyles went on to the next question.

"I am showing you a picture of the crime scene. Is that another officer in the photograph?"

"Yes."

"Doesn't that contaminate the crime scene?" Pyles asked.

"No. I had already picked up the shotgun shells and marked where they were found before the other officer entered the scene."

"Why didn't you fingerprint the scene?"

"When the ambulance folks were putting Kentrel Bishop on the stretcher, he told us ten times, 'I was shot by Kelly Lord. In case I die, I was shot by Kelly Lord.' So we didn't fingerprint the scene because we had a strong primary suspect."

Pyles broke every rule of cross-examination. He asked questions he did not know the answer to, which made my day a little easier. The forensic examination of the crime scene was horrible, but Pyles refused to take his time and break it down. Lord must have been low on money when he hired Pyles. This was a twenty-five thousand dollar case and Pyles probably did it for five. While Pyles was finishing up, Alexandra slipped into court and handed me a piece of paper with her notes.

"Officer Garnett, since Mr. Bishop sold crack there are a lot of people that might want to harm him, right?" Pyles asked.

"Objection—calls for speculation," I said.

"Sustained," His Honor ruled. Pyles sat down.

"Any re-direct from the prosecution?" the judge asked.

"Briefly, Your Honor. Officer Garnett, directing your attention to page four of your property report. Defense counsel asked you about two hundred versus two thousand dollars. What number did you use on page four?"

"Two hundred dollars."

"Which number is correct?"

I straightened that out for any slow-witted jurors and rested my case. Pyles made several routine motions, requesting that the judge dismiss the lesser counts. The judge denied his motions. Pyles began calling alibi witnesses.

As the first alibi witness came in, I began reviewing Alexandra's notes that explained the inconsistencies among the witnesses. As I turned around to look at the alibi witness, I also checked to see whether Ray was in the back of the courtroom waiting for payback. I felt like I was back in junior high school.

Pyles introduced alibi witness number one, a sassily-dressed gentleman named Jamal wearing an orange shirt. Pyles helped Jamal provide the jury with a little background information before asking him the most obvious question.

"How do you remember that night in particular?"

"We were relaxing and drinking, like we all do every Saturday night," alibi witness number one said.

Apparently, Pyles had not rehearsed, prepped, or paid this witness. He was frustrated, so he supplied the answer he wanted in his next question.

"Was it someone's birthday that night?" Pyles asked.

"Objection—leading," I said, and stood up and faced the judge. "Your Honor, defense counsel is testifying for an alibi witness."

I smiled and looked over at the jury. I allowed myself one theatrical look-at-the-jury per trial. More than that, and you were invading their domain.

"Sustained," Judge Ramsey ruled quickly. "Mr. Pyles, please try and refrain from asking leading questions and kindly move on."

"Oh, yeah. It was Dorris' birthday," alibi witness one said.

"Sir, when one of the lawyers makes an objection, please wait for me to make a ruling before you answer." His Honor shook his head in frustration from the sloppy display of trial advocacy. "Ask your next question Mr. Pyles."

"Sir, what else do you remember about that night?"

"Nothing much. Kelly Lord was there."

"Was he there the entire time?" Pyles asked, putting the final layer of cement on the story.

"Oh, yeah. The whole time."

"Nothing further."

"I pass the witness," Pyles shouted.

I gathered up my notes and went to the podium.

"Good morning, sir. How are you?" How was he? How was I? Fucked, that's how. My face looked like an ad for an anti-depressant. Can't sleep at night? Filled with despair? Maybe it's time for better living through pharmacology…

"Fine, sir. Fine."

The only thing I could do was appear confident and get the witness to "yes" as much as possible. I had nothing—except a basic idea of what Jimmy's Bar looked, smelled, and felt like.

"Jimmy's Bar is on Georgia Avenue?"

"Yes."

"It has a brick facade, the front is all bricks?"

"Yes."

"It has a big steel door?"

"Yes."

"Let me draw a floor plan. Can you tell the jury where you were sitting?"

"Near that little stage. There was a reggae band that night."

"Can I put an X over here, is that fair?"

"A little to the left."

"Fine, is that okay?"

"Yes."

"What was Mr. Lord wearing that night?"

"Black pants, nice shirt."

"Thanks for coming. Nothing further. Judge can I move in this drawing of the floor plan of the bar?"

"No objection," said Pyles.

"It shall be received into evidence," the Court ordered.

Trials are won with details, and I was lucky to have Scott and Alexandra in the courtroom—they were the fastest minds in the office. At the bottom of the notes was a matrix showing exactly where these people conflicted with each other: dress, music, and floor plan. Pyles called alibi witness number two, Billy, the guy we tried to find when we went to DeWayne's house. Billy was a large man dressed in black. Looked like he used to play football. Glad he wasn't in the bar when Ray and I had our chat.

"Please state your name and introduce yourself to the jury," Pyles said.

"My name is Billy Spencer. I work at the United States Post Office."

"How often do you go to Jimmy's with Mr. Lord?"

"We go a lot, almost every weekend," Billy said.

"What specifically do you remember about the weekend in question?"

"Kelly Lord got arrested, and I helped bail him out," Billy said.

"Anything else special about that night?" Pyles asked, itching to mention the birthday but knowing Judge Ramsey would eat him alive if he did.

"Hell, I put a lot of money up for that bond. How I gonna forget that? He didn't do no shooting either."

"Sir, that decision is for the jury. Kindly answer the question and only the question." His Honor was polite but firm.

"Nothing further. I pass the witness," Pyles said.

I put a fresh sheet of paper up on the easel, intending to run through the same drill.

"You helped post bond?"

"Yes."

"How many years have you been friends?"

"Since high school."

"You have been to Jimmy's Bar?"

"Yes."

"On Georgia Avenue?"

"Yes."

"You go there a lot—with the defendant and your friends?"

"Yes."

"To drink and listen to music?"

"Yes."

"Do you do cocaine together when you go there?"

"Objection—can we approach?" Pyles was quickly on his feet.

"Where are we going Mr. Franklin?" His Honor asked.

"He has a conviction for possession of cocaine. All we have talked about for a day and a half is cocaine. It's relevant."

"Your Honor," Pyles protested. He was getting red in the face.

"Shut up, Mr. Pyles—I'm about to rule your way," Judge Ramsey whispered. Mr. Prosecutor, it is not a crime of moral turpitude to test the veracity of the witness. It is drug possession, not distribution. The prejudice outweighs the probative value. I know it is a felony, but I'm not letting it in. Objection sustained. Ask your next question."

Even when Ramsey ruled against me, I liked him. Besides, at least one juror probably heard every word we whispered, so mission accomplished. I placed the police report back in a folder conspicuously labeled "prior criminal convictions." I only brought the manila envelope into the courtroom when my opponent was sleazy. I hated to sink to Pyles' level, but when you bring in a bucket of lying witnesses, the gloves come off.

"What kind of music played that night?"

"Rhythm and blues."

"What was Kelly Lord wearing?"

"I don't remember, probably shorts."

"I am drawing a floor plan of the bar. You and I are in happy agreement that that is what the bar looks like, right?"

"Yeah, it looks like that on the inside."

"Kindly step down and put an X where you were sitting, if you can remember."

"Sure."

"Thanks, you can return to the witness stand."

"What were you drinking that night?"

"Captain Morgan rum and Diet Coke."

"What was Kelly Lord drinking that night?"

"Same thing."

"Any special celebration that night?"

"Not that I can remember."

"Thank you for coming in. I move to have government exhibit nineteen admitted into evidence."

"It will be received. Mr. Pyles, if you don't have anything on re-direct, please call your last alibi witness," Judge Ramsey said.

Pyles walked Dorris through her special birthday celebration that Billy couldn't seem to remember. I wanted to ask Dorris to show the jury her driver's license to verify the date of her birthday, but I didn't have the balls to take that risk. I could just imagine her answering, "Oh, Lord, I have my driver's license and my birth certificate right here in my handbag Mr. White Cracker Prosecutor Asshole."

"How long had you known Kelly Lord as of that night?"

"Not long. I met him through Billy."

"How long had you been partying together as a group?"

"A couple of months."

"At Jimmy's usually?"

"Yeah."

"On Georgia Avenue."

"Yes."

"The front of Jimmy's Bar is brick?"

"Yes."

"It has a metal door?"

"Yes."

"You have a good eye for detail, don't you?"

"Yes, I work in retail. Lord 'n Taylor clothing store. I pay close attention to style and people and things in general."

"Here is the floor plan in general. Can you put an X where you all were sitting that night?"

"I don't remember where. I had been drinking to be honest."

"What was Kelly Lord drinking?"

"He always drinks gin."

"What was he wearing?"

"Oh, he had on a nice suit for my birthday," she said and smiled.

"What color?"

"Green."

"Ma'am, you said you have a sense of detail, a good eye for things. Could you tell the jury why you didn't call my detective back? He left cards on your front door, back door, and mailbox."

Dorris stopped smiling.

"I thought you said you notice things. Here, let me draw up your house and show the jurors where the front and back door is. Is this your house?"

"I didn't see no card," Doris said.

"The question was, 'Is this your house?'"

"How you know about my house?" Dorris was getting irritated with me. Sorry, not my fault; you came in to vouch for a killer.

"Ma'am, I don't mean to be impolite, but you have to answer the question. The question was, 'Is this your house?'" Judge Ramsey stated calmly. .

"Yes, it's my house."

"Have you been home all week?" I continued.

"Yes."

"Did you see any cards from Detective Johnny LeGray asking you to call him?"

She did not answer.

"Ma'am, I'm afraid you have to answer," His Honor said.

"No."

"Nothing further," I said.

"Ladies and gentlemen of the jury, we'll take our morning break. When you come back, we will finish up and go right into jury instructions. Mr. Marshal, please escort the jurors back to their room.

"Mr. Pyles, if you have not already done so, you will advise your client that he has the right to remain silent. You will further advise him that I will give an instruction to the jury, telling them not to hold it against him if he chooses not to speak. Should your client wish to testify, I will allow admission of relevant felonies only." Judge Ramsey raced through the formalities. Having done so, he turned to Pyles and asked, "What do you want to do?"

"My client does not wish to testify," Pyles said.

That's too bad, I thought. I'd have liked to have seen the jurors' faces when they heard about the prior charges for drug distribution and possession of a sawed-off shotgun.

"Fine. I will advise Mr. Lord on the record," Judge Ramsey said. He paused, waiting for the defendant to stand up. But Lord did not

stand. He remained in his chair, dressed in some damn nice Polo gear
—defiant to the end. Pyles whispered, "Stand up." Lord ambled
upward. "Sir, I need to advise you on your right to testify or not
testify…" Ramsey droned on about Lord's Constitutional rights. Lord
politely told the judge he understood his rights, and that he chose not
to testify. Not as brave without a shotgun and a chainsaw.

"The defense rests," Pyles announced.

"Any rebuttal witnesses?" Judge Ramsey looked at me.

"One brief witness: Detective Johnny LeGray."

"To rebut what?" Pyles shouted.

"Mr. Pyles, please maintain the decorum of this Court. Mr.
Franklin, give me an evidentiary proffer if you will."

"Detective Johnny LeGray will testify that he papered Dorris'
house with his cards and she never called. I am calling him to attack
her credibility."

"No, I object. He is calling LeGray to show Dorris has a guilty
conscience for not calling. There's no law saying you have to call the
police when they leave their card," Pyles asserted.

Judge Ramsey flipped through a stack of papers lying before him.
"I am looking at U.S. v. Garcia as well as the Smith and Mouton
cases and I don't see anything to support your position Mr. Pyles. Do
you have any points or authorities?"

Points or authorities? Pyles was research-phobic. The only time I
ever saw him in the courthouse law library was to use his cell phone
because it was quieter than the hallway. "I can't really talk, I'm in the
library, but let me say this…" Then he would chatter away.

"No, but I've known LeGray for twenty years, and I never trusted
him," Pyles took another run at humor.

"We've all known Detective LeGray for twenty years. You can explore that on cross-examination," Judge Ramsey shot back and kept it moving.

"That's fine, Judge," Pyles said.

"Mr. Marshal, go get the jury. Mr. Franklin, you may call Detective LeGray."

The jury came back looking a little confused. Maybe they were buying the alibi, but they would think twice once they learned that Lord refused to take the stand. Not taking the stand created a guilty vibe in the deliberation room.

"The prosecution calls Detective Johnny LeGray." He climbed in the witness stand and took the oath. "Please introduce yourself to the jury," I requested. No stunts, please, Johnny, I thought. It had been a long two days.

"My name is Detective Johnny LeGray. I have been a police officer for twenty-six years." His voice conveyed a player's confidence. I thought he was going to segue into and by the way ladies, if you're not doing anything after the trial, I'll pick you up after dark. Single moms are okay in my book. I'll even kick in a few bucks for the sitter.

"Did there come a time when you were tasked to interview the alibi witnesses in this case, and if so, what steps did you take?"

Johnny gave an overview of the steps he took to interview each witness and said that he left his card at Dorris' house. "Your witness," I said.

Lee Pyles and Johnny LeGray had battled in the courtroom since the pre-Watergate days when Washington was a sleepy southern town and the D.A.'s office was run by a handful of Irish Catholics whose wives worked part-time as support staff between pregnancies. Nothing had really changed over the years: Johnny was still bigger-faster-stronger.

"Detective LeGray, you and I go back many years," Pyles said, smiling away, trying to show that he was just a fun-loving good ol' boy. Hell, even one of the older male jurors smiled.

"That's right, counselor, over twenty years. But that doesn't change the fact that I am here to tell the truth, the whole truth, and nothing but the truth. Even if I didn't have to, I would tell the truth because that's the kind of guy I am, and that's what I teach my kids."

Pyles moved on immediately, realizing it was not a good idea to play games with Johnny.

"Detective LeGray, can you give me one of your cards?"

Johnny reached into his pocket as Pyles approached the witness stand. He held out a card, and Pyles took it.

"Detective, wouldn't it be fair to say that my witness could have overlooked such a small card? If it was placed in the mail slot it could have slipped in with the other pieces of mail, right?"

I could have objected twice. It was a compound question and, more importantly, it called for speculation. But I didn't say a word— you couldn't have paid me to object.

"Well, counselor, I have been doing police work for over two decades and developed a sure-fire method for leaving my card." DEE-vell-loped. Johnny faced the jury and began to perform. "First, I toss a card through the mail slot or place it in the mail box. Next I place one in the door jam low. Finally, I place a card two feet above the doorknob. That way, when a person opens the door it comes fluttering down right in front of her face." Johnny's hand mimed an object fluttering to the earth in slow motion. "Unless she's entering through the chimney, one of those cards gets noticed. But that don't mean they aren't ignored."

Poor Pyles. No one ever told him the courtroom is a bad place to go fishing.

"Nothing further. Thank you, detective."

"Ladies and gentlemen of the jury, the time has come for jury instructions. Afterwards, we will give you a restroom break, you will listen to closing arguments, and begin deliberations."

While the judge read aloud the usual cookbook on direct and circumstantial evidence, reasonable doubt and elements of the crimes, I nearly fell asleep. Ray, his baseball bat, stunt driving, fear of getting arrested, fear of being fired...there wasn't much left in me. During the break, I threw some water on my face.

My closing argument was flat. I went through the elements of attempted murder. Then I started in on the smaller crimes. There were ten different counts. Finally, I did the best I could to negate the attack on Kentrel that was coming.

"Mr. Pyles will argue that Kentrel Bishop doesn't deserve justice because he is an imprisoned crack user. Many of you know our elected District Attorney Tommy Monroe. You see his name in the paper. Do you think Mr. Monroe has a special form that victims fill out? Do you think it asks how much money a person makes? Do you think it asks whether you vacation in Aspen or use your vacation time to clean and paint your garage? Mr. Pyles will talk about justice for the defendant, but what about justice for Kentrel? Is he some invisible man with no human rights? Justice is not one-sided."

It was the type of lame argument that could never win a case in Washington, D.C. without good evidence and a silent defendant. I could barely focus on Pyles' summation. "These people have no reason to lie. They have nothing to gain. They would never risk perjury to help their friend."

"Rebuttal argument from the prosecution?" Judge Ramsey asked.

"Briefly, Your Honor. Motive? Kentrel fell into debt. Proof? Kelly Lord threatened to kill Kentrel's mom if he testified. Alibi witnesses? Kelly Lord's friends are trying to help him out, which is understandable." Like all D.A.'s, I was saving my best arguments and my voice for rebuttal. I was always louder in rebuttal argument than the initial closing argument—all the better to drive home those high-octane, rousing facts that I hoped would sway the jurors to my side of the debate. That was the power of having the last word.

I continued, "Perhaps they have never seen the other side of Mr. Lord's personality. Maybe they don't want to accept that, without any hesitation, he fired a shotgun into Kentrel's head and that he threatened to kill Kentrel's mother because the young man had the audacity to survive and testify. Maybe they want to ignore the facts the same way Dorris ignored Detective LeGray's card when we were investigating the case. What did we learn from these alibi witnesses? Why is one person saying the defendant drank rum, and the next person saying he drank gin? Why is one alibi witness saying he's in shorts and another in a green suit and yet another in nice black pants? How could reggae turn into rhythm and blues? Why are they out for a birthday celebration, but not everyone can remember?" I pointed to the floor plans the alibi witnesses helped draw. "These drawings show Xs in three different places. Why are they sitting in three different parts of the bar? You can connect the dots and find the defendant guilty of all the charges. On behalf of Kentrel, his family, and our community, that is the very least you can do."

"Ladies and gentlemen of the jury, you will be sent to lunch and then right into the deliberation room to begin your verdict," the judge advised. "Do not discuss the case until you are all together. If you break off into twos and threes during lunch, you are not to discuss this case. Attorneys, give your office and cell phone numbers to my clerk. Be no farther than five minutes away. Court adjourned."

\*

I got back to my desk, called Kara, and told her everything was alright. I rested my head on my forearm and drifted off. I quickly awoke as the sound of the doorknob turning signaled Alexandra and Scott.

"Sleeping on the job when you should be preparing cases? You are pathetic." Scott had no mercy for me.

"I no longer prepare cases, I ship them off to Indonesia. Overseas labor is cheap and they are sent to a factory of child lawyers. They write all the motions and develop cross-examination, then ship them back to me. You obviously haven't been reading the office memoranda highlighting our new procedures."

"Leave him alone, Scott." Alexandra assumed the role of protector. "What did Tommy say? Are you all right? Were our notes helpful? Did you call Kara?"

"Yes to everything. Tommy's fine. He just wants me to make a couple of visits to a shrink." My phone rang. Back to the courthouse.

*

"I understand the jury has reached a verdict?" Judge Ramsey asked. He received a collective "yes" in return.

"Who shall say for you?" His Honor continue-eth his seventeenth century traditions.

"Our foreman," the collective body answered.

"What say you as to count one, attempted first-degree murder?"

In identity cases, it was all or nothing. Either Lord was there or he wasn't.

"Guilty," the foreman said. The clerk picked up the phone and called for additional marshals.

I listened as the word "guilty" was repeated ten times, and I felt a bit of energy return to my body. Last-minute, sloppy preparation had pulled me through.

"Ladies and gentlemen of the jury, I want to thank you for performing your civic duty, without which this system would not exist. You have made a very important contribution to our community and our country. The marshal will take you back to the jury commissioner's lounge. The lawyers may want to chat with you. You can either talk with them or, if you choose, not talk to them about the case. Thank you again and have a nice day."

Judge Ramsey waited until all the jurors shuffled out.

"Okay, back on the record. Mr. Pyles, do you object to proceeding to immediate sentencing? The reasons I ask are two-fold. First, I have Mr. Lord's record here in the file, and I have studied it. Second, and, more importantly, attempted first-degree murder carries a mandatory life imprisonment. I see no need to spend government resources during this budget crunch for a lengthy pre-sentence investigative report."

"That's fine with me judge—if it's fine with my client?" Pyles said. He knew he had lost and he was ready to move on to a new case with a new client and a new retainer.

"Whatever," Lord mumbled.

"Sir, is that a 'yes'?" His Honor asked.

"Yeah," Lord mumbled again, looking at the judge. Pyles told Lord in a whisper to stand up when he spoke to the judge.

"Okay, then, let's proceed to sentencing," Judge Ramsey said and waited patiently for Lord to stand up.

"Stand up, Mr. Lord," His Honor commanded. "I am losing my patience. You may not respect me, but you will damn well respect this Court and what it stands for."

Lord ambled upward in slow motion with his head cocked to the left. Gangsta to the very end.

"Sir, you are an obvious danger to this community. Without hesitation, it is the judgment of this Court that you are sentenced to life plus twenty years. You have thirty days to notice an appeal of this trial and one hundred and twenty days to appeal this sentence, but I can tell you right now—I under-sentenced you. Based on this verdict, you could easily be sentenced to life plus eighty years. I took the liberty of merging several of the sentences and running others concurrently when I could have run them consecutively. Is there anything you want to tell this Court before I have the marshals escort you out?"

"Yeah—you an asshole and your mother's a bitch," Lord told the Court.

"Mr. Lord, you must be referring to my mother-in-law." The judge waved to the marshals and said, "Take him away."

The marshals cuffed him twice and took him away hastily. Pyles packed up and began shooting the breeze, happy that Lord was gone. He joked that he was glad he got paid up front and complained that being in trial was always a money loser. I was ready to leave but the clerk said the judge wanted to talk to me in chambers.

I liked Ramsey. He knew my dad and even lived near us at one point.

"Clay, come on in. Have a seat."

I looked at the vacation pictures and world's greatest dad stuff in kid scrawl.

"You hang with your kids?" I made small talk.

"Being with them is very special. I hope you will get that experience. I hear you are engaged?"

"Word travels fast."

"Well, I'm happy for you, Clay, but I have something to tell you. It is a bit awkward...."

Shit. He must know about my fight with Ray the bartender.

"I am the son of a U.S. Marine. I can take anything, go ahead," I said and smiled.

"I like your dad, which makes this even harder, but here goes. You dodged a bullet today. That trial was pure slop," he said.

I shifted in the dark brown leather chair in an attempt to convey to His Honor that I was taking his words seriously while hiding my joy that I seemed to have dodged a bigger bullet.

"Your level of preparation has dropped. Now, I'd very much like to see you win the teacher homicide, but you can't win it doing what you did here. A one-minute opening statement? You look exhausted, and you were clearly unprepared as it related to the forensics of this case. You just got lucky. The alibis were a joke, and Lord didn't take the stand. What if it had gone the other way?" He paused to gather his thoughts.

He continued, "This Ford kid who killed Bradford Slater—his family is going to hire some of the best lawyers in the world. I don't want to see any O.J. verdict—not in this courthouse, not with this case."

"I hear you loud and clear, Your Honor, and I thank you for it." I may have won the trial, but I still felt like a clown.

"Bring your A-game, Clay. For that matter, get a second D.A. on the case and make sure they bring their A-game too. I am not your boss, but if I were I would encourage you to take the rest of the day off. You earned it. You are hereby dismissed."

*

I was going to take the rest of the day off even without Ramsey's two cents. Outside it was cold and bright. I stopped my car outside a coffee shop on Dupont Circle and called Dr. Terrance Hanlow's office. He answered after the first ring.

"Hello," a voice said.

"This is Clay."

"I am ending a session right now and can't really talk. Tommy already set this up for five o'clock today. I will see you then." Dr. Hanlow hung up.

I read the paper but couldn't concentrate. I checked my voicemail five times in twenty minutes. Ray still hadn't contacted the PO-leese. I decided to call Scott.

Not surprisingly, Scott was mostly unhelpful: "By not reporting you to the police I am concealing a crime. We could both go to jail. Of course, if we do go to jail, I could make some great sex videos. My first one is going to be you getting slammed by some decomposing old priest." Switching gears, Scott added, "Big ups to you on the guilty. I was getting sick of seeing Kelly Lord's name appear in homicide task force reports."

"Thanks, man. Call me later if you hear anything about last night."

I walked toward my new psychiatrist's office. Washington, D.C. was a city of lawyers, journalists, and shrinks. You couldn't say which one came first or how it all fit together.

I pressed the security code and entered the 1920s Art Deco apartment building. Shrink-man was on the first floor. It was a quarter to five, and I was in the front waiting room. At the courthouse, I bribed the marshals with sodas so I could eavesdrop on the jurors during their deliberations. Now, I put my ear to the door and listened to an ongoing session. It was a female lawyer complaining about her firm. "At first they wanted eighteen hundred billable hours, but now these young speed freaks are clocking in twenty-two hundred billable hours a year." Between work pressures and loneliness, she was melting down. I called Phil at the Washington Post on my cell phone. "Hey, I think I found a lawyer for you to date."

"Why are you whispering?"

"I'm at my new shrink's office, and there's a woman in session who says she's lonely."

"Fine, what does she look like?"

"I can't see her. I am listening through the door."

"Call me back when you get a look at her. If she's hot, tell her I'd like to have a glass of vino with her, maybe talk about the porous boundary between love and sex."

"What are you working on anyway?"

"I am editing a piece on the Privacy Act that is being debated in Congress. How does that make you feel right now?"

"We are both going to burn in hell. I better go into the waiting room and look at magazines. Bye."

The anteroom, I quickly realized, protected the anonymity of the guests. I reviewed Washingtonian magazine's top ten lists. Poor Tomar. No category for best drug dealer in Washington (and if Kelly Lord had been best murderer, the recent trial would have knocked him off the list). I picked up People magazine. I was checking out cleavage shots, tragedy, and sudden-success stories when I heard multiple doors shut. Time to go play the patient.

"Nice to meet you."

"Call me Terry. Sorry about this." He lit a cigarette. "It's a nasty habit that I am trying to break."

Maybe therapy was irrelevant to my health. Between Terry's smoking and Ray chasing me with a baseball bat, I probably wouldn't be around to enjoy my new psychiatric enlightenment.

"What do you intend to get out of therapy?"

"I just want to keep my job. It means a lot to me."

"Being in a fight, how did that make you feel—excited? Embarrassed?"

"Embarrassed? Not really, he's the one that lost. I'm the good guy here—I send assholes like him to jail every week."

Terry took one more pull on his cigarette before stubbing it out. "I know you do important work for the community, but that is irrelevant to what goes on in here. I've treated vice presidents, secretaries of state, senators, real estate moguls, you name it. Title does not mean much in here. Tell me more about yourself, outside of work."

"Sir, I have two books by my bed: the King James Bible and the federal rules of evidence. Each night I pray that I can move my exhibits into evidence," I said in a deep southern accent.

"Tommy said you were funny." Terry didn't smile, which meant he wanted me to answer his question. Fair enough. I dropped the accent.

"I'm thirty-three years old. I come from a typical drunken Wasp family. I squeaked through Princeton undergrad and Georgetown Law trying to keep up with the family tradition. Graduated too close to the bottom of my law school class. Through family connections I got a job at the law firm of Hogan & Fox but I hated it. I got my shit together and left for the D.A.'s office six years ago—took a hundred thousand dollar pay cut to do it. The workload is crushing, but it gets my adrenaline going. I prefer to deal with people rather than corporations. My main hobby has been chasing women. But those days are over now. I am engaged to a great woman."

"That's a big change in lifestyle," Terry said. I was distracted by Terry's white Abraham Lincoln beard and his Birkenstock sandals—and socks. I was in treatment with Socks & Sandals Guy.

"So, do you think I am a threat to the community?" I quipped.

Terry jotted something down. "There are worse things than chasing women. There were several patients in here today who haven't had sex in years and they feel dead. Other patients are depressed and they have no commitment, passion, or depth of feeling toward anything. They'd give a finger to wake up and do something they love." Terry took a sip from his cup. "But I think most people are happier in an intimate relationship rather than acting like a sex clown. Of course, making the transition from player to family man can be a little dicey."

This guy was better than I expected. Maybe I should give Phil his card.

Terry looked me square in the eye. "Tell me about your family."

"My dad is insane, my mom is sweet, one sister disappeared into dotcom money, another into drugs, and my brother is a quiet drunk. Family dinners are tricky."

"Okay, tell me about the fight. Why did it happen?"

"This asshole grabbed my badge in a bar when I was interviewing him. He wouldn't give it back, so I took it."

"You're a D.A. Wouldn't it have been easier to simply call the police? They would have sided with you."

"How long do I have to see you?" I asked, ignoring Terry's question.

"This can be your last day if it doesn't seem like a good fit. Normally, there is no timeframe. You can come here a couple of times and terminate the sessions. Or, you can start up again at a later time. Of course, your situation is a little different, especially if you are arrested for the assault."

"This guy Ray has my fucking card. He knows who I am. I have already prepared a statement in case I get busted. The guy was drunk, he obstructed an investigation, grabbed my wallet, and there are witnesses that saw him come after me with a baseball bat."

"Sounds good. It's important that you have a plan to protect the career that you care about."

"I guess we should finish the session," I tried to nudge things along, wishing we were done.

"Fine, go home. I will see you next week," he reached over and grabbed his black, At-A-Glance appointment book and fingered through the pages. "How about next Tuesday. I have an evening appointment at six."

I nodded begrudgingly. "I'll see you then."

Once I was out of the office, I called Johnny.

"Do me a favor—tell the dispatcher that you want any complaint out of Jimmy's Bar assigned to you. Tell them it's part of an ongoing investigation," I suggested.

"That shit is the least of your problems. Rodney Ford's been telling people that he wants you off the case. Says if you weren't around, another D.A. might plea-bargain it down to a manslaughter in juvie hall. Clay, Ford wouldn't think twice about planting drugs in your BMW. And you're worried about an old drunk named Ray?"

"That's funny, I thought the police and prosecutors were on the same team."

"Try telling that to internal affairs. That's just the way the world works these days, buddy."

## Chapter 5

# Kiddie Killers

## FEBRUARY 15, 2000

As another month of living with Kara went by, the reality exceeded the fantasy. I looked out the office window. It was a freezing cold February day; the sun popped out briefly and melted more slush. Water was dripping off the roof. Alexandra and Scott were in my office. We were quietly looking at our files. As usual, my office was like study hall. We kept quiet unless we saw something amusing in our files or hit a puzzling legal issue. I decided to hit the streets in preparation for the Slater trial.

"Alexandra, I'm going to the Kirov Ballet. Want to check out the dancers?" I asked, putting on a long overcoat. Time to meet with Galina the witness-ballerina-cock tease.

"Damn, can't go. Why don't you take Scott?" she said looking his way.

"Can't go. Why would you plan a meeting with a bunch of half-dressed women while I'm stuck in court in the middle of a motions hearing?" Scott complained.

"You should have interviewed twinkle toes last month, slacker," Scott said.

I shook my head in mock irritation. "I wanted to but the dance hall was closed and she left town. She went to some place called Europe. Now she's back. C'mon, we're going. Let's bounce."

"Sorry—I need to bounce back to court."

\*

I made my way out of the courthouse and through the maze of fjords that practically sprung from the potholes in the street. I pulled out of the parking lot slowly. As I accelerated, the swishing sound of tires and water became louder. I drove down North Capitol Street toward the practice studio for the ballet troupe near Catholic University in northeast Washington. The sun had disappeared and it was raining again. I pulled up near the front entrance and rested my badge on the dashboard, hoping to avoid a parking ticket. As I walked toward the auditorium, the occupant of a parked car turned up his hip-hop to an ear-splitting level. I walked through a small crowd and entered the ballet studio. The room had a tall, curved, white ceiling with ample lighting, wooden floors, and ballet bars on the side—basically, a basketball court without the backboards. The sound of the bass from the car out front was now replaced by Aaron Copeland. The inspirational, larger-than-life notes were was the score from Billy the Kid, one of my mom's favorites.

There they were. The chain smoking, non-fat latte chugging clique I had seen at Starbucks, plus a few dozen. Remarkably they had transformed into their better selves. They were engaged in a series of graceful, stylized maneuvers. I immediately went to the side of the auditorium, took my coat off, and leaned against the wall, looking across the tan planks of wood flooring. The rigor and discipline was breathtaking. One second it seemed to be all about speed and suddenness; the next, the corps was frozen with an emphasis on an isolation of body parts. The flowing movements, the spaghetti straps, and long necks—it was beautiful. Long, mournful notes were interrupted by an exploding call-to-arms from a barrage of horns. I had to admit, I was fascinated by the pointe shoes and pirouettes. Galina nodded toward me as she danced by, punctuating the space with shapeliness, her slender arms and hands moving in adept and inviting ways. I felt guilty, but not guilty enough.

The music came to a dramatic conclusion and the pink tribe dispersed. "You finally made it," Galina said as she walked over, feet splayed at a forty-five degree angle, carriage erect. "We are done with rehearsal. Follow me, I'll take you to a place you can hang out while I change."

She led me down a narrow hallway away from the studio into a drab lounge. I sank deep into an already depressed couch. As I checked my messages, another one of the ballerinas I met at Starbucks glided up and said hello. I couldn't remember her name.

"Can I be a witness too?" she asked rhetorically as she slid by in her pink satin shoes and a dirty smile. I was getting a little too whipped up for my own good. I smiled back with what I hoped was a clean, friendly smile.

"I've got plenty of single friends," I said.

"Bring them to a party. Galina will tell you that we have lots of parties." She disappeared into the girls' locker room (or whatever it was called).

A few minutes later, Galina came out with freshly applied makeup. I stood up as she strutted toward me with jeans so tight they looked like they had been spray-painted on. I felt like I was being pressed between two panes of glass. I had to get a grip. She was a critical witness because she was real, without a criminal record, could put a sentence together, and was locatable. She saw the kiddie killer with gun in hand—fleeing. (Through Galina, I could taste the "Consciousness of Guilt" jury instruction I would ask the judge for at trial.) I knew from years of experience that only half the witnesses showed up for any trial. I took a deep breath, regaining my emotional sobriety.

"I really enjoyed your rehearsal," I said.

"Oh, it's okay. Billy the Kid is not my favorite ballet, perhaps too American, but the audience likes it," Galina said in a language that was not too American.

"I recognized it from high school; I like it," I switched gears and avoided too much eye contact. "I brought the file with me if you want to go over the case here."

"Why don't we go somewhere for coffee and talk?" Galina suggested. I was interviewing Natasha Fatale.

"Good idea, it is too crowded here. Too noisy too. Let's go."

We approached my car. I walked her to the passenger side and opened the door. "Such a gentleman…" Galina's voice trailed off. As she sat into the car, her hand brushed my leg as she reached for the seatbelt. I gently closed her door, took a deep breath, and thought about Kara's light brown eyes. No comparison. We drove to a quiet coffee shop on Florida Avenue near Adams Morgan. I had her statement and the police report from the Slater file. We took our coffees over to a couch in the corner. She lit a cigarette.

I sat far enough away from her, but she shifted her body closer by crossing her left leg over her right leg, her boot practically kissing my calf.

"What brought you to Carver High School that day?"

"Bradford Slater was good friends with Misha, our company director. Many times Slater brought students to watch rehearsal, and Misha promised him that we would go over to Carver to perform a small piece from The Nutcracker." She paused as she took a sip from her coffee.

My eyes walked the line of her slender legs from her black boots to her waist. She adjusted her position and our eyes met. "The performance took place on December 2, 1999. Remember that date. That is why I am here today, to help you refresh your memory so when you take the stand in the courtroom you will know the day."

"Do you have a girlfriend?" she asked. She seemed about as interested in case preparation as half the attorneys in my office.

"No. Yes. I used to date a lot but I just got engaged," I fumbled.

"I hope you are more certain of yourself in the courtroom," she smiled, and continued. "When are you getting married?" Her blonde brow furrowed as she cross-examined me.

"There is no date yet, but I'm sure we'll do it soon." I felt warm around my collar as I tried to swallow the guilt that was building up in the back of my throat.

"Don't you talk to most witnesses by phone?" She smiled.

"No, for an important trial, I talk to the witnesses face-to-face," I said. "Plus it was fun to watch what you do."

"Well, maybe you can watch one of the performances. The upcoming show has three different ballets. They are very different. Billy the Kid is only one of them, thank God." She punched her cigarette out on the bottom of her black boot. "Don't worry. I won't smoke in that nice car of yours," she smiled, knowing I needed to find out more about what she saw on the day of the shooting.

"So on December first you head over to Carver High School. Who went and how did you get there?" I trotted back to the case.

"Misha had rented a small bus. He didn't want us taking the subway because the neighborhood was too dangerous and very few of us have cars. We went there dressed in costume; we knew the bathrooms were going to be disgusting. The dressing rooms in Europe are much better. Anyway, we went to the school and it was scary. We had to go through a metal detector. We did the performances and the students stared at us like we were crazy, but they clapped, cheered, and were very nice. "

I nodded, struggling to keep my eyes from navigating her figure.

"So the performance is over and a couple of girls have to use the restroom before we go. That is when we hear an explosion, a huge explosion. I am just walking out of the restroom and across the hall. I see this guy run out from around a corner. He runs to the left and this other kid, the one with the gun, runs to the right. He almost knocks me over. He is a black kid and he puts the gun in his jeans. I thought it was a bomb until I saw this guy with a gun."

"Describe the first student, then the student with the gun."

"The first guy was tall and thin, but I did not get a good look at him. The second boy was big, very dark-skinned black. He was not short, but not tall either, and fat."

"How did he appear? I mean, what kind of look did he have on his face?"

"I don't know. It happened so quickly. I froze, I couldn't move. I was tired after my performance and scared by the noise. I didn't know if it was terrorists or what," Galina said, adding a little Euro-imagination. Terrorists at Carver High School?

"Here is a piece of paper; do me a favor and draw where you were when you first heard the noise." I handed her a piece of paper on top of a yellow file and a pen. She began making some crude lines for the hallway and I continued to ask her questions. "What else did you see? Who else was in the hallway? Who was near you? Where did the guy with the gun go?"

"Suddenly it was crowded; everyone filled the hallway looking to see what happened. I think maybe one more student came out from around the corner but the hallway filled up. People went below the stage to help Slater and they started screaming. Misha grabbed me and the other girls. I heard someone scream, 'Call an ambulance!'" Galina lit another cigarette, and apologized for her habit.

"No worries," I told her. I could see she was getting a bit stressed by recalling the event. "Do you think you could recognize the kid with the gun if you were shown some photographs?" I asked her.

"Probably. Do you have the pictures now?"

"It wouldn't be me. It would be a detective. I am not allowed to be present during the viewing of photographs because of legal rules."

She cocked her head and pursed her lips. "Then why don't you come see a performance next week?"

"I'm not sure I can do that, but you will be definitely contacted by a detective to show you some pictures."

"Okay, that is fine, but I get free tickets and I will leave one for you at the box office in case you change your mind. Can you please give me a ride home now?"

For a moment, my mind drifted back to Kara; I was worried she would smell Galina's perfume in the car. My paranoia was short lived as Galina quizzed me about the trial.

"This is the way it works," I said, then paused. "Or maybe I should say this is the way I work," I explained as we headed to her apartment in Arlington, Virginia inching our way across the Key Bridge. "First, I get a general idea of how useful and valuable a witness is. Then, I develop questions and go over them with them so we can develop the finer details. After that, I'll pretend to be the defense attorney and cross-examine the witness so they have an idea of what they'll be asked by the other lawyer." I tried to keep my eyes firmly on the road.

"It's like ballet, always preparing. Learn the piece, rehearse, dress rehearsal, and then the show," she said as the windshield wiper added a metronomic squeak.

"But this show is different. It's going to draw a lot of ugly attention and not all the people involved can be trusted. You may be contacted by newspaper and television reporters for stories. You may be contacted by the defense attorney's investigator to gather information to cross-examine you. I can't tell you who to talk to and who not to talk to, but you should be cautious."

"I can keep a secret. Go left." She pointed a slender finger.

"I'll have a detective arrange to show you some photographs," I said as we pulled up to a monolithic apartment building.

"So you'll come to my performance next week?" She leaned across the armrest and ran her fingers through my hair and whispered, "You work too hard. Just come watch me dance and relax."

My heart was pounding and I enjoyed the outline of her long legs, but I just smiled at her, keeping both hands on the wheel.

"Maybe I shouldn't have done that." She said as she got out of the car. "I'll leave you a message about where to pick up your ticket at the box office." I watched as Galina disappeared into the wet darkness. I headed back over the bridge to D.C. to work out.

I found a meter, fed it, and entered the Washington Sports Club to try and untether my mind from Galina's body. I began on the stationary bike to warm up, and noticed how many people were cruising for a hookup. I hit the weights and felt clearer, but I still took a cold shower for good measure. I threw my bag in the trunk and was home in ten minutes.

"I am going to New York next week and the client's paying. Ya gotta like that." Kara was all smiles and kisses. "I'm designing a CD cover for a band, and they want me to hang with them. Possibly do some branding for a restaurant they are buying."

"You're a star. All those graphic artists in Alpha-ville, and they choose a D.C. girl." I wrapped my arms around her. With Kara clinging to me and laughing that deep, body-shaking laugh, I walked to the fridge to get a beer.

# FEBRUARY 25, 2000

"Phil, I think there is a major opportunity here." I had my trustworthy Post friend on the line, trusting it wouldn't be reported. "Hang on, Scott just walked in; I am going to put you on speaker."

My office was a mess with files all over the place. Scott pushed a box aside with his foot to make his way to a chair near my desk.

"Hey Scott, how are you?" Phil asked.

Scott mumbled, "Fine."

"So what's the update, Clay?" Phil dove back into dog-mode.

"I went to talk to the dancer—she was all over me, but I'm not going to do anything to fuck up what I've got. My farewell to all womankind will have to come in some other yet-to-be-determined way," I tried to soften the blow to my posse. You can't please all the people all the time.

"Let's not get too selfish here. Think about your friends. What were the other members of the Kirov like?" Phil asked.

"I didn't forget about you. I was trying to work one for you when I was over there. I was getting a major slut-vibe. They go out a lot and are looking for older guys with money because they are totally broke. For you, I'll have the ballerinas meet us at a bar sometime. I mean, you would do the same for me." I said.

"I don't mind being used, but it's a two-way street, and I'm driving a Carrera on that street. Find out if the one you talked to likes ecstasy. Once I get a little "E" into her, it's a downhill ski."

"When you wrote that story about the hope for peace in the Middle East were you on ecstasy?" Scott asked.

"I never reveal my sources of inspiration," Phil said.

"When Kara gets back from New York, we're going to pick a wedding date and plan a trip. The wedding is going to be small. We'll spend the real money on an exotic trip. I want to take her to one of those huts above the water in Tahiti. Or, maybe Rome—who knows?"

I could sense Phil's tension on the other side of the line. All my relationship talk had excluded Phil, who couldn't care less. What does your honeymoon have to do with me?

I continued, "Phil, you're acting all quiet. Do I have to come over there and change your diapers? Don't worry, we'll do a party or something. We'll have talent—I'll order up a stripper for you and Scott."

"Been there, done that, dated that," Phil said. "I'm interested in the Russian trim."

"We'll figure it out later. I'm glad you're so happy about my engagement," I said and added, "Maybe we oughta do the bachelor party at Phil's apartment. There's a cage there in case things get out of hand and someone needs solitary confinement—KGB style."

"Now you're talking. I've got to jump in a meeting. Keep me posted," Phil said.

# MARCH 3, 2000

Galina called me and told me that my ticket to her show was waiting for me at the box office. I didn't call her back. I called Kara in New York and told her that I was going out and hooking up with Phil for a drink afterward. Lying by omission maybe, but no point in stirring the pot. Besides, this was mostly business—I needed Galina on my side if I was going to win the Slater trial. I put on a black suit and tie and drove down to the show. I parked, picked up my ticket, grabbed a vodka tonic as I walked down the red carpet of the Kennedy Center, and entered the Eisenhower Theatre where Galina was performing. Under the epic ceiling and grand chandeliers, I was strutting my high-society stuff like every other fool in the building.

The program lay open across my lap. I looked at descriptions of the three pieces Galina was going to perform. I was beginning to catch a buzz from my drink. Suddenly the lights went down and horns from the symphony blasted the same music I had heard at the studio, only this was a thousand times more powerful. I was in a trance as the notes tumbled down into a slow, waltz-like rhythm. The dancers entered the stage on their toes. They were dressed similarly and at first I couldn't identify Galina amidst the flock. Another moment passed, and then I saw her.

Her legs, expensive, long-stemmed roses, were moving rapidly while her arms, shoulders, and head rhythmically interpreted the music. It was as though she was conducting the symphony through her movements—or maybe the music was actually radiating from her frame. She would hit a pose, and then hold it for the audience. In the finale, the men lifted the women off into the side of the stage, disappearing. I grabbed another vodka tonic and utilized the backstage pass that she had left for me at the box office. I followed the intricate little treasure map of instructions Galina had provided to get me beyond all the rent-a-cop security.

I waited backstage, wondering if I'd found the right door. After fifteen minutes, I wondered if she had changed her mind and decided to leave. I started to walk away when I heard the squeak of a doorknob. The door slowly opened from the inside, revealing Galina —all black and blonde and shiny. My stomach dropped.

She barely said, "Glad you made it," as she kissed me on the cheek—a little too close to my mouth. "I guess you liked the show," she whispered. "Do you want to go have a glass of wine?"

"The bar is still open, why don't you join me for a drink here?" I asked, nodding toward the drink in my hand.

"Let's not—I don't play where I work," Galina said. "Give me a ride home and we will have a drink at my apartment." She gently rested her hand on my shoulder. "We can talk about my testimony— it is very important, no?"

"Of course it is," I automatically responded.

We briskly walked to my car to avoid the cold. , Her graceful descent into the passenger seat was impeded by remnants of the workday: my briefcase, an empty water bottle, and my video camera. She delicately set the briefcase and bottle in the back seat. "Wouldn't want to break this," she said as she set the camera on her lap.

"Sorry for the mess, I wasn't expecting company tonight." I struggled to keep the conversation platonic.

"Of course not," Galina responded.

The Whitehearst Freeway was empty. I drove way too fast toward Key Bridge, especially after two vodkas.

We arrived at Galina's mammoth northern Virginia high-rise and we walked to the elevator.

"Going up?" Galina teased as she pressed the elevator button. "I'm on fourteen."

The elevator ride seemed to take forever. In those moments, it was impossible not to think about sex. I wanted to leave the temptation behind, but I didn't want to piss her off. My extremely hot and fuckable witness. On the other hand, what was I worried about? I was a new man and as long as Kara was on my mind, I would make myself behave. Besides, Galina might be tall, but she was tiny—a couple of drinks and she'd be knocked out and I could slip out before anyone did anything stupid.

Galina unlocked the door to her apartment. I expected it to be messy—the product of an artistic mind—but I was wrong. It was pristine, almost sterile, with an efficiency kitchen to the left, a living room straight ahead, and a couple of doors off to the right that must have led to a bedroom and a bathroom. She sat me down on an ultra modern metal stool at the bar between the kitchen and the living room. She walked back into the kitchen and poured me a brownish drink from a bottle I didn't recognize. I took a sip—bourbon. I must have looked a little surprised.

"You were expecting vodka?" Galina asked with a wink. "What is the expression? When in Rome..." Her voice trailed off as she poured herself a glass.

I took another drink, and told her I was happy with her testimony. Galina asked about my job, my family, even Kara. She talked about her parents still in Russia and how her dancing basically put food on the table for her entire family. We avoided talking about Slater. Galina chain-smoked and kept the drinks coming as we talked. She complained about ballet politics and her dance contract. I excused myself for a moment to use the bathroom and called Phil to tell him I was too annihilated to meet him. When I returned to the bar, Galina had moved to the leather sofa in the living room.

"I've been on my feet all day. The couch is much more comfortable," she said.

I couldn't remember how much I had to drink, but I had hit the point where I just didn't care anymore. I sat next to her on the couch. "I loved watching you dance tonight. I have to admit, I just loved it," I foolishly said.

"I'm sick of it. Maybe I'll go into the movies—leave Russia for good." She sounded like she was beginning to slur her words. "But it is so fucking lonely in America."

"I don't know, at least you have the other dancers," I lamely offered.

"We don't care about each other. Elena would stab me in the back if she could get a green card out of it." Galina let out a quiet laugh and looked straight at me with a devilish grin. She moved quickly and sat on my lap and started kissing me. Lost in the moment, clothes started to come off. Somehow we managed our way to the closed door by the bathroom. She fumbled with the knob and the door slammed open; we practically fell onto a bed in the cramped room.

I took off her panties and grabbed a condom off the nightstand next to her bed. Her mouth tasted dirty and when I tried to move this way and that way, she whispered that this injury and that injury wouldn't allow movement in that direction. As she had her real or fake orgasm, something felt wrong. I didn't want to finish and my guilt manifested as a horrible headache. I wanted out.

As I propped myself up with my elbow, my attention was drawn to a red flashing light on the nightstand. My neurons were slow to fire, but I eventually realized the red light was emanating from my video camera. I was too drunk to appreciate the irony. She was limp on the bed as I dressed. As I tried to walk toward the nightstand, the floor creaked, awakening Galina; she flopped to her side and clumsily grabbed the camera. I took it from her hands and she mumbled something about this "not being her best work." As she began to fall asleep, I told her this wasn't going to happen again. "It is what it is, I know that," she said. Her eyes were closed.

I barely made it out of the bedroom door before my headache expanded to my stomach. I dropped the video camera to the floor and darted for the bathroom. I vomited but Galina was not disturbed —her snoring drowned out my sounds of discomfort. Once I regained my composure, I picked up the pieces of my broken video camera from the hallway.

I drove home slowly and checked my voicemail. There was a message from Kara. "Hey! So I'm headed up to New York, still searching for a design for the CD cover, when from the window I see this factory lit up perfectly at dusk. Mr. Fiancé, there it was, the CD cover I was looking for. The sky was dark gray like only a moody, polluted New Jersey sky can be. The factory lights were klieg white. There were yellow and blue flames coming out of weird stacks and pipes. I could only take a few shots because the battery in my camera is low. I'll see how the pictures turn out; maybe they're not that good. I just thought I'd share my inspirational moment with you. Miss you. Bye."

I stumbled drunk into the apartment. I'm a fucking idiot, I thought as I scrubbed myself in the shower like I had just gotten off work from a nuclear power plant. The best of myself had drowned in the worst of myself.

# MARCH 10, 2000

"Good luck," the umpteenth person said as I walked down the hall. They were referring to my hearing to determine whether Kevin Ford would be tried as an adult or a juvenile.

"Here ya go, Monster," Annette said, handing me the juvenile waiver hearing report ten minutes before the hearing.

"You do it," I said, pushing the report back toward her. "You've been working here long enough. And when that ultra-liberal judge rules that Kevin Ford should have a little juvenile bench trial and he's sentenced to a youth camp for two years, you can explain it to the reporters too."

Annette pushed it back. "No, baby. You do your job now, that's why they give you that fat paycheck. Get in your office and read it. I'll keep people out."

I flipped through the report and noticed that Kevin Ford had been disciplined at his high school about twenty times. I grabbed a subpoena and yelled for Annette to come back in.

"I'll take you to lunch and Tower Records afterward and buy you whatever you want if you run to Carver High with this subpoena and tell them you want a copy of Ford's school documents. Bring them directly to the courtroom."

"Deal—but it's gonna be CDs and DVDs, Monster."

"Box set, whatever you want," I said and continued reading with my legs crossed and on top of the corner of my desk.

I returned to the report. Who is Kevin Ford? During his interview, he told a bunch of lies, then he lawyered-up and that was the end of communication. This confidential report was prepared by pre-trial services for the court. It took into consideration age, seriousness of the crime, opportunity for rehabilitation, prior record, and special mental and physical conditions. In other words, was the kid just stupid, or stupid and dangerous? If a kid was just stupid, then keeping them in juvenile might be a good thing.

"You better get moving, Clay." Annette opened the door wearing her coat. "Judge Wharton says he wants you in his courtroom now."

"Now? He takes hours to go through his docket!"

"Just head down there and stop complaining. I'm running to Carver High School now."

\*

Briefcase in hand, I was ready to face the most dreaded courtroom in the entire courthouse. The elevator dropped to the bottom floor. There were no windows. Not one.

Outside the courtroom, a cluster of reporters rushed me. "No comment right now. I'm sorry. I know you're under deadline, but I have to get inside."

I made my way toward the prosecutor's table for the first time since I did my tour of duty there five years ago. Just like the red brick of the original Smithsonian building that would never be painted, nothing changed in juvenile court. Judge Wharton's small courtroom was packed with kids, relatives, friends, an occasional parent, and the inevitable grandmother. On this day, however, the press was running in and out, waiting for the Ford case to be called. (Good luck— Wharton would probably call it last to soak up the attention and exercise his God-given right to make the whole wide world wait.) I watched as the seventeen-and-under crowd ambled around, awaiting their fate. These young men were at war with themselves. Outfitted in shiny Bulls, Raiders, and Georgetown jackets, they were filled with unfocused rage, crack, and chaos. Only Judge Wharton had the nerve to enter the maze of hurt and hate and anger. The other judges didn't want to see a juvenile docket. When the judges heard that Judge Wharton was going to his summer home in Maine, they shouted to their secretaries: Call the Assignment Office and make sure I do NOT end up with juvenile court tomorrow. The judges weren't alone in their opinion; the juvenile docket was dreaded by prosecutors too—at least by the ones with ambition.

Alexandra, Scott, and I called it Siberia because you were stuck in a windowless, cold, boring, no man's land where nothing ever happened except an occasional bench trial (a trial to a judge, no jury). The juvenile tour of duty was a requirement to introduce young prosecutors to serious felonies. The young men were between ten and seventeen years old, and they were called respondents, not defendants. If convicted of a serious crime, their penalty was kiddie jail until the age of twenty-one. Of course, the penalties the prosecutors suffered were the endless lectures by Judge Wharton about how he too was a juvenile delinquent before he became a judge (even though everyone knew Wharton grew up in a white, middle-class neighborhood where he was insulated from the true horrors of poverty). It was a cute story, but then something happened during the early nineties: kids starting killing at a phenomenal rate. Suddenly, Judge Wharton had to decide whether to "waive" cases to adult court. The penalties were as different as a match and a hand grenade. A believer in rehabilitation with second and third chances, Judge Wharton rarely waived the teens up to adult court.

I pulled a stack of files off a chair, set them on the floor, and sat down a few feet from the main prosecution desk. Juvenile Chief Gail Baylor and line prosecutor Archie Hill headed toward me. Archie nodded and sat down. Gail, on the other hand, headed right at me, intent on a reunion.

"Long time no see," she greeted me. Gail was a smartly dressed, light-skinned, freckled African American woman in her fifties. Her large, swirling hair contained some type of Motown flip that harkened back to The Supremes or Martha and the Vandellas. She was doing her morning walk-through to make sure her docket was being covered.

"Nice to see you. Judge Wharton ordered me down here and he's not even on the bench. Some things never change," I said and sat back down.

The juvenile unit was a loser unit. Just like Siberia holds political prisoners, the juvenile unit held Gail Baylor and Archie Hill. Gail Baylor was the division chief for life. It was her seventeenth year, and she was essentially retired on the job. She never worked more than a few hours a day. The lion's share of her energy went to selling real estate. She was damn good at it too. The faxes would come rolling out of the machine in small white waves, curl upward then splash down with the latest interest rates (Harrison and Bruce used to Xerox the real estate docs, saying they would blackmail her unless she gave them a good review). "It's a three-bedroom house with a nice view," I used to hear her say as she closed her door. I assumed it was the art of failing upward. She obviously could not try a case, so Tommy Monroe made her a division chief. And the juvenile unit, to the best of my knowledge, was the only place where you could sell real estate.

"Well, best of luck today. I certainly hope Judge Wharton does the right thing and waives this boy up to adult court," she said. (Only an African American could use the word "boy" in our newly politically sensitive courthouse.) "I hope you got the pre-trial services waiver report. They have been running way behind."

"I just got it. Thanks," I said sincerely. I knew she truly meant well.

I walked over and sat next to Archie, who was whispering into his cell phone.

Archie, a black dude who masked his age with Just For Men, had a solid government career ahead of him before his exile to the juvenile division. Archie was once promoted to the lush land of felony jury trials, but he engaged in so many battles with co-workers, judges, and police that he was stuck in a place where he could do little harm. Getting demoted was no easy feat in the Tommy Monroe machine, but when Archie repeatedly failed to provide discoverable evidence to opposing trial lawyers, then lied to judges about it, it was do svidaniya. Two judges walked into Tommy's office, shut the door, and told Tommy that unless action was taken, Archie was going to be locked up for contempt of court. Archie took it in stride, even acted like he was getting a bucket full of frequent flyer miles when he was sent to Siberia. Hell, it was a good match: Archie never wanted to work hard anyway and Wharton had the patience and flexibility for Archie.

"Hey, man, how ya doing?" Archie said.

I extended my hand parallel to the floor, but Archie shifted it to a diagonal, seventies soul-man handshake and squeezed my palm firmly.

"Wharton better waive that little fucker, or I'll kick his goofy ass," Archie said, full of good spirit.

"You're preaching to the choir, Archie," I whispered and started reading.

The report stated that Kevin Ford was seventeen years of age and clearly eligible to be waived to adult court. That was a relief. The next section, entitled "Type of Crime," boldly asserted that homicide was a very serious offense. I was encouraged to see that murder was still taken seriously in D.C. I was hitting gold as I perused the prior record section, but I was interrupted by the "all rise" command and His Honor's entrance.

Judge Wharton, Tsar of Siberia, entered. He looked like a lion with his fantastic mane of brown and silver hair and an equally sage-like brown and silver beard. His manners were impeccable and his speech was clear as a bell. He ascended to the bench, well, when he felt like it, which was usually after he talked to his courthouse family about the snow or fishing conditions in Maine, gardening, running, local D.C. politics, and general gossip. And cooking. Let's not forget he had to talk about his cooking.

"Please be seated. Good morning everyone and welcome to the Juvenile Court Division for Washington, D.C. I am going to go through the docket first," Judge Wharton began. The courtroom was small compared to the courtrooms upstairs. It was incapable of handling all the defendants, cops, probation agents, and freaked-out mothers of both the accused and the victims. (Inevitably, fights would break out between the two due to the close proximity.) Years ago, a speaker system was installed so those people who were unable to find a seat in the courtroom could be informed that their case was up. Between the packed hallway and the crackling speakers, the place had the distinct atmosphere of a bus station. The candy and soda machines in the hallway had massive steel cages around them to prevent further vandalism and theft.

The various stages of Siberian Death-by-Lethargy were: status hearings, guilty pleas, sentencings, waiver hearings, and, finally, the trials themselves. His Honor spotted me and motioned for me to approach the bench using his index finger.

"How are you Mr. District Attorney? Haven't seen you in my courtroom in quite awhile." Judge Wharton gave a warm greeting, thank God. He never particularly cared for me (or Alexandra or Scott) due mostly to the difficulty I had masking my impatience during my brief stint in his division. He once forbade me to read newspapers in his courtroom. (He took so long to move through a docket, I could get through the Post, the Times, and the Wall Street

Journal in a single sitting.) Still, he seemed content to let bygones be bygones; either that, or he was just making nice before horse-fucking me in front of the world. Judges were like that. He told me that he would call the Ford case after he took care of some other matters, and then shifted his gaze toward a juvenile rehabilitation guru.

"How are you Mr. Stillman?" His Honor greeted Stillman like a late night talk show host greeting a bandleader. I drifted back to read and said hello to Stillman on the way.

"Hey, how's it going?" I asked.

"Man, I'm reeling about Bradford Slater. He was a good friend of mine. Needless to say, I ain't letting Kevin in my program—talk to you later," he whispered.

Adrian Stillman was a self-proclaimed "Community Educator" who ran the B.Y.O.S.E. program (as in, Bring Your Own Self-Esteem). His self-invention amused me, as I knew he was little more than a southern, snake oil-peddling preacher. His program, which placed special emphasis on fatherless children, was a creative alternative to standard probation. Whatever else the program accomplished, it put money in his pocket while introducing him to many a single mother.

Archie motioned me over to come sit next to him. I went to his table with my file and began reading. My case was going to be called sooner or later. I might as well man my station.

Kevin Ford's prior record section revealed an arrest for arson. (Fire starting, bedwetting, and hurting animals was the classic children's trio foreboding dangerous behavior.) But it was the twenty disciplinary infractions at high school that would probably be most valuable, and I was hoping Annette would get to court before they called the case. I marked a few of the important infractions with yellow sticky notes.

The public defender, Mary Beth O'Reilly, came over and said, "Hey, Clay. I guess this could go either way since it was an accident." I can't believe this shit! Nonetheless, the expression on her face said that she honestly believed the accident defense. Regardless, she was right about one thing: Wharton was impossible to predict.

"I guess Lincoln, JFK, and Reagan were shot by accident too," I whispered.

Having known me for years, she expected the retort and was unphased. "Are you calling any witnesses?" Mary Beth asked.

"No, I am just going to argue the five factors," I told her.

"Well, I didn't give notice of any witnesses, but I'd like to call a vice-principal and possibly Kevin's father if you don't mind."

"No, that's fine," I spoke softly. "Call anyone you want. Hell, put the kid on and he can explain how he accidentally unlocked the safety switch on the gun so it could fire, and how he accidentally squeezed a trigger that requires ten pounds of pressure."

"Just so you know, a little birdie told me that Wharton isn't going to waive him up," Mary Beth said.

"If that 'little birdie' is Wharton's secretary, she's wrong half the time," I said out of pure fear. Mary Beth and Wharton's secretary Patty were lunch buddies.

I tried to appear confident, but I was getting a little freaked. Wharton hardly ever made up his mind until the hearing was over. Was Stillman spinning me and going to ask the judge to put him in his program? Two years ago a kid grabbed a cop's gun during an arrest and shot him and Wharton did not waive the kid to adult court. He was not afraid to take the editorial heat and the Fraternal Order of Police mudslinging campaign against him.

"What is the status of the Mason, Johnson, Perry, and Shepard cases? Attorneys step forward and tell me what's going on." Wharton was slowly marshaling the cases through. I turned to see if Annette had come back from Carver High with that file. I tried to see if Rodney Ford was in the audience but I couldn't spot Mr. Notorious. Besides, what would he tell the judge? The wrong admission on the record, and he'd open himself up to some low-level firearms felony for allowing his sidearm to get into his son's hands; there was no way he would allow himself to be pulled into the case by taking the stand. A transcript could also be sent to Internal Affairs to suspend him, or, worse, justify some type of independent prosecutorial review.

I continued reading the report. "Opportunity for Rehabilitation." That section explained that since this was Kevin's first major offense there was hope for rehabilitation, but the nature of the crime would not allow such a recommendation. So I guess the arson was not a major offense. Next, I reviewed the section titled "Special Mental and Physical Conditions." Kevin was born in Greensboro, North Carolina. The mother and father divorced when he was a child. The father spent time in the military and went overseas. Social Services removed Kevin from his mother's care after her second drug arrest. At first, Kevin lived with an aunt because his father was out of the country, but a boyfriend shot his aunt during an argument. Next, Kevin was sent to live with his wheelchair-bound grandmother. He'd been shuttled back and forth between a foster home and his father's house ever since. He was given the Bender Gestalt Visual Motor Test, the House-Tree-Person Family Drawing with Story Test, the Wechsler Intelligence Test, the Thematic Apperception Test, the Rorschach Inkblot Test, the Sentence Completion Test, and a clinical interview.

I could hear Wharton talking to some lawyer about the upcoming softball season. I did the softball thing my first year in the office and hated it. The summer heat and humidity, battling the traffic to the field, and drinking with some of the staff that Alexandra, Scott, and I ordinarily had to endure. If I was ever forced to do it again, I would need psychological testing. I kept reading.

"Kevin experiences anxiety due to a chronic lack of nurturing and emotional support … a malevolent non-caring sense of caretakers … appears to have little conscience and exerts his own needs over those of others in a dangerous fashion … sociopathic tendencies…" The language in the waiver report was similar to most homicides, but what caught my eye was his mentioning of Bradford Slater and a girl named Keisha: "Although uninterested in academics, he mentioned an interest in drawing, which, ironically, he learned from the deceased victim in this case. He also mentioned that he especially liked the class because of classmate Keisha [last name unknown]."

I kept reading, hoping to find more clues. "During many of the tests, the respondent would ask, 'What are you supposed to do on this test?' Lastly, he mentioned that he wished the incident never happened, and he wished Keisha was his girlfriend. When the respondent was asked to elaborate on Keisha, he changed the subject." At the end of the report was a signature I couldn't read; below it, "The Eisenhower Institute: Making Children's Lives Brighter."

"One of my kids is sick. I've got to go," Mary Beth whispered. "Rodney Ford is not going to take the stand. I just talked to him. And Carrie is going to do the waiver hearing." Big case, little case, it didn't matter to Mary Beth. Her kids were what mattered, which I admired, but on the other hand, her clients were often left high and dry.

"I hope your kid feels better," I said and looked across the room at the old timers, Carrie Dunst and Tommy Patrick, handling the regular docket. The public defender had exiled them to Siberia as well. The couple lived together in Takoma Park, Maryland, a small burg just over the D.C. line. The town was the equivalent of Berkeley, California and had declared itself a nuclear-free zone. Carrie and

Tommy met at George Washington Law School and were extremely bright, but they were more interested in playing dulcimers and preparing for the next Renaissance Festival than trying cases. Still, they were easy to work with and carried themselves like British barristers.

Just as I was thinking, "Where the hell is Annette—it's been two hours," she appeared avec file. "They said they needed a release from KF's parents," Annette whispered. "I told that lady you don't need no release when you got a subpoena. Fine, you come down and tell Judge Wharton you gonna disobey the subpoena. So then little Miss Huffy gimme the file and you owe me big time, Monster. CDs and DVDs."

"Thanks. Make a reservation for two at Tower Records."

I walked over and whispered in Carrie's ear, "You ready on the Ford waiver hearing?"

Judge Wharton saw me talking to Carrie and asked, "Counsel, are you ready?" We nodded our heads yes.

I gave a quick glance around the courtroom. Still no Rodney Ford.

"I understand we are ready on the Ford matter," Judge Wharton said. "Counsel, remain in the courtroom. I have two pleas and then we will proceed to your matter. Folks in the back of the courtroom, if you need to talk please step outside."

Annette's run to the school was a shot at the buzzer. Teachers had written him up left and right for disciplinary infractions. Carrie Dunst was huddling with several people while Wharton finished his pleas. One of the people in Carrie's little huddle had to be Rodney Ford. He was big, football player big. He wore a black leather jacket, a silver crucifix, and his bronze police badge on a silver chain. Cops often wore their badge on their chain to breeze by security, but today he was trying to remind the judge that he was one of D.C.'s finest.

Our eyes met for a second and he gave me the tough guy look. I turned away in ambivalence, returning my attention to the paperwork. I'd seen that look before. And, based on what Johnny told me, I expected nothing less from Rodney.

"Call the Kevin Ford case," Judge Wharton said, "and tell the marshals to bring him into the courtroom."

"Are you ready Madame Public Defender?" His Honor addressed Carrie.

"Yes and no," Carrie said. "Yes, we're ready, but I am not sure the respondent wishes to be represented by the public defender. His family has hired R. Kenneth Mundy."

My stomach capsized. R. Kenneth Mundy was one of the most famous Washington lawyers to ever step into a courtroom. He was a magician. He'd turned more than one felony into a misdemeanor, including one stemming from the famous videotape of the mayor smoking crack.

"Mr. Mundy has neither informally called my chambers nor has he formally entered his appearance into the case." Wharton sounded pissed. "That said, I'll ask the question again: "Are you ready?" Judge Wharton wanted to show who was in control. The courtroom was packed with media and he would not let things devolve into a circus. He was no judicial clown.

"Yes," Carrie said.

"Thank you. Is the prosecution ready?"

"Yes," I answered.

Kevin Ford, guest of honor, was seated. He was medium height, dark skinned, and overweight—a killer without the bravado.

"Looking at the five factors—seriousness of the crime, threat to society, past record, amenability to treatment and special mental and physical conditions—Mr. Ford should be tried as a juvenile," Carrie began, cleverly deleting the age factor and creating a non-existent threat to society factor. "Think about it, Your Honor: Mr. Ford could end up with life without parole because a gun went off accidentally. There was no intent, and he is not a threat to society. Just because the respondent has been charged with murder, everyone presumes the situation is hopeless. That is simply not true. The respondent is amenable to treatment. In terms of a past record—yes, there was one appearance several years ago, but that's it. The Court may be thinking, 'Hey, he had a gun on school property.' But he never intended to harm anyone. Is it a serious felony? Yes. But it's the type of crime that should be adjudicated as a juvenile. If he is convicted, he will serve many years in juvenile detention. This Honorable Court routinely handles teenagers who have been caught with firearms on school grounds and sentences them appropriately. Judge Wharton, here, there is no motive. Kevin liked Mr. Slater. The evidence will bear that out. I'd like to call one of his vice-principals, very briefly, to give this Court some helpful information."

"You are correct in one respect. It is not a forgone conclusion that I will waive Mr. Ford to adult court just because this is a homicide case," Judge Wharton said. "Still, I don't see any witness endorsement in my file. Mr. District Attorney, were you given notice that the public defender intended to present testimony today?" His Honor asked.

"No, I was just told about this, but I don't object."

"Thank you. Call your witness Ms. Dunst."

"Thank you judge. He is waiting in the hall."

Judge Wharton began talking while we waited for the Carver High School vice-principal. "I understand that there may very well be evidence that this shooting was accidental. I have read the arrest affidavit, and I will, of course, consider that possibility as I weigh the seriousness of the event," Judge Wharton said.

This can't be happening. Did Wharton want to keep this case a juvenile proceeding? A vicious murder had morphed into a mere "event."

"Madame Clerk, swear in the witness," His Honor ordered, and a heavyset black man with a closely trimmed moustache in a 1970s suit took the witness stand. He looked like the quintessential business or academic middle-management type that had never been comfortable in his own skin.

"Good morning Mr. Augman," Carrie began. "Please tell the Court what your position is at Carver High School, and how you know the respondent."

"I am a vice-principal at Carver High School. I know Kevin from school," Augman said nervously. After he spoke, he glanced at Rodney Ford, who was seated in the front row behind his son.

"Based on your contact with the respondent can you tell whether you think he is amenable to treatment?"

"Kevin is a nice kid. He wouldn't really hurt anyone. Sometimes I would see him in the hall clowning around, acting up. Nothing serious though. He liked to draw, and he liked Mr. Slater. I think counseling would help him," Augman told the judge.

Augman threw another nervous look at Rodney Ford. Kevin Ford just stared at the table, motionless.

"Nothing further," Carrie said.

As Carrie ambled back to her seat, I approached the podium and adjusted the microphone, bending it at an angle that would pick up my voice productively.

"Cross." Judge Wharton gave me the green light.

"Mr. Augman, let's back up. Mr. Slater is dead. You and I are in complete agreement that's more than just clowning around, right?"

"Yes."

"You say that the respondent would be amenable to treatment. Does your background include training in psychology?"

"No."

"Psychiatry?"

"No."

"Social work?"

"No."

"Did you testify on the respondent's behalf when he was arrested for arson last time?"

"No, I didn't know him then."

"Well, that was only two years ago. How long have you worked as a vice-principal?"

"Just last year. I was a police officer before that," Augman said.

Thank you for that one, I thought. Wharton raised an eyebrow. He might be slow but he was not stupid. I didn't even need to pursue it. Wharton knew that Augman and Rodney Ford went back.

"You mentioned the respondent did a little acting up, right?"

"Yes."

"What about disciplinary infractions? Did you bring with you today any type of file on the respondent to show Judge Wharton?"

Augman didn't answer. Judge Wharton looked at him and said, "Sir, did you bring the respondent's student file?" Wharton loved to dust off his trial advocacy skills and jump in and do a little cross.

"No."

"Carver has files on students?" I asked.

"Yes."

"And those records are kept in the ordinary course of business."

"I don't keep those records; they are kept in another part of the school," Augman said.

"But as vice-principal you can look at those files if you chose?"

"Yes. But there are also five other vice-principals."

"And all six of you, all six vice-principals can look at Kevin's file?"

"Yes."

"Did you know that last year Kevin Ford committed twelve disciplinary infractions for disrupting class?"

"No, I didn't know that."

"Would you like to review your file?" I said, holding up the file.

"Objection." Carrie was on her feet. "Judge, we have not seen the school file."

"I didn't know they were going to call a faculty member to say that the respondent was a well-behaved student. They opened the door to this line of questioning."

"Madame Public Defender, you pulled the surprise here. The prosecution may continue."

"May I approach the witness Your Honor?" I hadn't planned on getting aggressive, but Wharton had me scared with his unpredictability; if I was going to get this kid to be tried as an adult, I was going to have to earn it.

"You may."

"Mr. Augman, I am handing you what has been marked as prosecution exhibit number one, the Carver file on the respondent. Do you recognize it?"

"Yes, but like I said, I don't keep these files."

"But you have seen student files before?"

"Yes."

"The orange-colored sheets in the file—kindly tell Judge Wharton what they show."

"Discipline actions against the student."

"There are approximately twenty orange sheets in that file. That is more than usual isn't it?"

"Yes, I'd say so."

"A number of those infractions are things like acting in a vulgar fashion, punching female students, refusing to put away a Guns & Ammo magazine when teachers told him to put it away. What steps have you taken to explore psychological treatment?"

"None."

"Do you know of any faculty member that has taken any steps toward treatment?"

"No."

"Do you have with you today any letters of support from teachers or vice-principals agreeing with your position that the respondent is amenable to treatment?"

"No."

"I move to admit prosecution exhibit one into evidence," I said.

"It will be received into evidence," Judge Wharton said. I handed the file to him. He flipped through it quickly. He had seen a million of these files, and he knew exactly what line to look for on the orange sheets. Skip all the charts and checks and times and classrooms and go right to the brief description of the anti-social behavior.

"Nothing further," I said.

"Ms. Dunst, any redirect?"

"No, Your Honor."

Judge Wharton thanked and excused Augman, who couldn't get out of the courtroom fast enough. He refused to so much as look at Kevin or Rodney Ford when he left.

"Mr. District Attorney, I'll hear argument from you. Tell me why the respondent should be tried as an adult. You have the burden of proof to waive him up to adult court, and I'm wondering whether you've met that burden of proof. I can tell you right now that if he is convicted—even as a juvenile—he is going to jail for a long time. Mr. Slater wrote many a letter to this jurist on behalf of his budding artists."

"May it please the Court," I began, knowing that Wharton loved a little serving of formality with a side order of pomp. "As the Court remains on the fence in this matter, perhaps it is best that Your Honor recall Bradford Slater's letters to this Court. I am probably misquoting here, but Thoreau said something like, 'If you make a person breathe a little easier in life you have done something, you've lived a worthwhile life, you've made a contribution.' Your Honor, you help many people, you make them breathe a little easier with Mr. Stillman's program, with your lectures that often help people reset their life and their goals. But this is not a case for leniency. In a nutshell, the waiver report asserts that a series of unfortunate circumstances led the respondent to believe that life lacked significance; that belief, in turn, led to felonious behavior and finally to murder," I paused and continued.

"If Your Honor had never seen the respondent before, that would be one thing. But the respondent is a repeat offender. Arson was merely a stop along the road that eventually led him to kill a man who not only made people breathe easier, but who inspired artists to entertain and enrich our community. We're all sorry it happened, but this hearing isn't about being sorry. The respondent committed a serious crime and he remains a threat to the community. There is a past felony and countless acts of disruption at school to prove it. In terms of age, he's six months away from being an adult. Amenability to treatment? He's been through the system. How many teachers and how many school counselors and how many vice-principals and how many judges and how many probation officers need to intervene before we say that someone is not a good candidate for treatment? There are no special mental or physical conditions that I am aware of except for the usual minor learning disabilities that were mentioned in the report. The statute is designed quite well: when a fifteen-year-old teenager commits arson, there is no way he should be tried as an adult, but when a seventeen-year-old repeat offender is charged with homicide, the legislature clearly intended that the shooter appear in front of a jury so that they can decide how age factors in. The public defender tells you there is no intent, but in the case file there is an arrest affidavit stating that the respondent bragged, 'You hangin' with a murderer.' This statement raises serious doubts regarding the accident theory. I strongly believe I have met my burden of proof to waive the respondent to adult court to be tried for the murder of Bradford Slater."

"Ms. Dunst, anything further?" Wharton quietly asked.

"The only thing I want to mention is that no witness to the remark Mr. Franklin attributed to Kevin Ford has ever been found. It's hearsay through a detective who has since been indicted," Carrie quipped.

"If that bragging remark turns out to be false, the district attorney will have to turn that information over to you. I am sure he will fulfill his ethical duty to turn over exculpatory information. Anything else?" Wharton asked.

Carrie shook her head. Wharton complimented her on her initial argument and thanked her for calling the witness.

"The respondent will stand," Wharton commanded.

Wharton looked at Kevin Ford like he was a ghost. His voice was soft but stern. "Reviewing your file, I noticed that you had an opportunity to make a fresh start with Mr. Stillman years ago, but you walked away from his program. I cannot in good conscience give you another opportunity to walk away from a second chance. The respondent will be tried as an adult. Mr. Marshall, take him away."

I exhaled. Wharton may have believed in people, but, fortunately for me, he could see the difference between bring-your-own-self-esteem and bring-your-daddy's-gun-to-school.

"Way to go, son, way to go," Archie congratulated me.

I grabbed my file and bounded out of the courtroom. Immediately, I was surrounded by reporters. I placed my trial bag on the floor and answered their questions.

"When is the trial date?" a reporter asked.

"No date yet."

"Do you think the indictment of one of your detectives will ruin the case?"

"I can't answer that intelligently because I have not seen the indictment. A different branch of the Department of Justice is handling that. Please call me, and I will follow up on that and try and get you as much information as possible," I said. My dad taught me never to run from a reporter.

"How do you feel about the case?" another reporter asked.

"I can't discuss the details of this or any pending case. Generally, Tommy Monroe and the Slater family are pleased with the outcome of the hearing. Obviously, I don't believe that this is the type of case that should be in the juvenile system. If there are any other questions, here's my card. I'll do everything I can to help you out before your deadlines."

Tommy left me a voicemail telling me he was happy Wharton did the right thing. I called the Slater family and told them the good news. I saved the bad news for Scott and Alexandra: the Ford family had hired R. Kenneth Mundy, D.C.'s Johnny Cochran. Finally, I left a message for Kara telling her I was going to take her out for a killer meal to celebrate.

\*

I opened a beer and called Kara on her cell. Nothing. I turned on the TV to watch the coverage of the waiver hearing so I could get totally prepared for Scott's jokes the next day. On my way to the bathroom, I noticed that Kara's closet was open. Her toiletries were gone out of the bathroom.

Thinking she might have emailed me, I headed into the study to check my messages. Before I could log on, I saw a note on the desk next to my open camera bag.

"I found a video cassette in the bottom of your bag with the broken video camera. I needed a tape for my camcorder and was wondering if the cassette in your video camera was compatible. The tape played just fine in my camcorder, so it turns out it is actually you and I that are not compatible. I can't figure out which is worse: a boring, lifeless husband or an interesting cheat. In the end, it doesn't matter because I can't trust you. Clay, you will never see me again, but I have sent your little videotape to someone who needs to see it. In the end, it will make you a better person. K."

I threw what was left of my Sony video camera so hard against the wall that a chunk of sheet rock fell to the floor.

## Chapter 6

# This is Going to Sting

## MARCH 13, 2000

"You look like shit," Dr. Terry Hanlow said as I walked into his office. (It had been over two months from our first and only session.) It was 7 A.M. and I hadn't slept for what seemed like months. I dug out his number in the middle of the night and left a voicemail asking for the next available opening. I needed to talk to someone, and I wasn't ready to tell Scott and Alexandra that I had fucked everything up.

"Yeah. Thanks for getting me in so quick Terry," I said with a shrug. I sunk into a plush love seat before the doctor could invite me to sit down.

"Right," Terry responded indifferently.

He wasn't going to make this easy. Even shrinks have abandonment issues.

"I need to begin treatment again." I tried my best to fill the awkward silence.

"Again? You never began in the first place." Terry put a cigarette in his mouth and lit it with a chrome-plated Dupont lighter. "I told Tommy Monroe you came to terms with your anger. Isn't that all you wanted?" The doctor continued, "Listen, you were in a jam, and I helped you. Despite your apparent disregard for your own mental health, I think it is better for you to be working. Whether you realize it or not, I am actually here to help you."

I was too tired to bullshit, so I just let it out: "My days with Kara are over. She disappeared."

"Who's Kara?" He scrunched his face in irritation.

"My fiancé."

Terry waited for me to elaborate as he exhaled bluish smoke and ashed his cigarette.

"Former fiancé?" I shrugged my shoulders with my elbows bent and my palms to the ceiling. "I can't live without her. I feel like I want to jump off a bridge."

"I hope you're not serious. Because if you are, I have a legal obligation to report you. "

"I'll be around, at least until after the murder trial," I said. "Hell, if the jury returns a verdict of not guilty that would be a good excuse to whack myself. I don't want people to think I killed myself over a woman." I offered a lame smile to hide my hurt.

"Why?" The doc sounded interested.

"My father—he was a sergeant in the Marine Corps—he used to complain about the soldiers that would shoot themselves after receiving a Dear John letter. My father, he couldn't understand it. He told his troops, 'If you are stupid enough to kill yourself over pussy, I will personally hunt you down in hell and kill you a second time.'"

"Your father sounds like an asshole," Terry said. "On the other hand, there's so much more to life than just the love of your partner, but it would be hard for a young soldier to understand that. After all, that love is the only thing those men might be hanging on to while they're dug in." He cleared his throat, "So tell me about Kara."

"The day I met Kara at the Georgetown Law library years ago; we just connected instantly. We always had something to say to each other. I could show her who I really was and she just got it, you know?"

Terry took a drag from his cigarette. "Go on, tell me more. Have you been with her since law school?"

"No. She was married when I met her. We were friends for years, and I'm not the type of guy to be friends with a woman without getting laid. I'm not into 'coffee-friends.' But Kara, I loved her so much, I took every opportunity I had to be close to her."

"So what happened? How did you move from coffee-friend to fiancé?" Terry asked as he stubbed out his cigarette.

I relayed the whole story, from first kiss to Galina the ballerina. As I told the story of my narcissistic idiocy, my chest tightened and tears welled. "I betrayed her. I can't fucking believe it, but I betrayed her."

"How did she leave? Was there a confrontation?" He seemed genuinely concerned.

"No. She just moved out. All she left behind was a note saying she sent the video somewhere, but didn't tell me where. If that video went to the wrong person, my career is over. Whatever..." My voice trailed off as my thoughts drifted to Kara's smile.

"Go on."

"You know, I didn't even enjoy what I did with the Russian dancer. It was just an exercise, you know? An exercise in stupidity...." I stopped talking and placed my elbows on my knees, crossed my arms, and rested my forehead on my wrists. Gravity sent tears down my forehead instead of my face.

"Go on."

"Gimme a second." I couldn't talk. I thought about going to the movies with Kara—what it felt like to just sit next to her, feeling that deep connection as she crunched the popcorn in the darkness. I couldn't explain it to Scott or Alexandra. They would want to comfort me, and I did not deserve to be comforted. "Shit, I'm falling apart here," I said as I regrouped and grabbed some tissues. I blew my nose, wiped my face, got up, and dropped the small sphere into a short, oval trash basket.

"I would hope so—there would be something seriously wrong with you if you weren't falling apart." Terry looked at me intently.

"Among friends, there are little crimes, big crimes, and war crimes. A video? That was a war crime—you should put my ass on trial at The Hague."

"No need. You have already tried and convicted yourself. You succumbed to a temptation; you made a serious mistake. The trick is focusing on why you made the mistake. Kara has known you for years —she knows your limitations. Don't you think she might come back?"

"Come back? No. With her, when you fuck up, you're finished. Besides, she's just too smart and confident to put up with that type of behavior. She understands loyalty and values. I can't go behind Kara's back like that and expect to ever see her again."

"Who knows what tomorrow will bring? After all, she loved you. She knew your wild side and that was part of the attraction," Terry said. "You are at the beginning of a long process that involves many difficult emotions."

"I understand all that. At work we hand out pamphlets to help families cope with the loss of a loved one that has been murdered. Denial, anger, grief, blah, blah, blah, until the world is an empire of dirt, and everything means nothing."

"Handing out pamphlets and living through an internal crisis are two different things."

"Shit." I shook my head. "What am I going to tell my family?"

"Clay, let's focus on today—worry about your family tomorrow." Terry sat back in his chair and crossed his legs. "I know you don't want to deal with this right now, but you need to think about what Kara did with the tape. Do you think she sent it to your boss?"

"No. Not her style. Plus, Tommy probably wouldn't even fire me. He's such a hound himself, he might think it was a gift."

"She doesn't sound like the kind of person that would seek revenge."

"No. She thinks she's doing me a favor," I said as I grabbed tissues and blew my nose. "I'm supposed to be trying a murder case, and all I want is to find Kara," I said.

"I understand that, but the fact is that Kara is not the only thing in your life. You still have to do your job; it's part of who you are, too. How's the case going?" Terry asked as he shifted his body around his large, well-worn leather chair.

"Are you kidding? The lead detective has been indicted for police corruption and brutality. The key witness is a ticking bomb because I boned her. The defendant's dad is plotting to have my car blown up with me inside."

Terry tapped the side of his pack of cigarettes, shaking one loose.

"Could we do a session tomorrow and I'll tell you more about the case?" I took a deep breath; I felt lightheaded.

"Can I get you a glass of water? You don't look too good." Terry leaned over and reached for a scuffed plastic pitcher.

"Thanks." I took a sip. "And I'd like to get a few sleeping pills to help with my anxiety. That would make me feel better. And could you not smoke?" I felt panicked.

"I'd rather skip the meds," Terry said, putting his cigarette back in the pack. He paused for a moment and then continued, "Normally, I like to do more cognitive therapy—that is, see if we can make things better without medication. "

"Fine," I whispered.

"I'll see you tomorrow." Terry threw me a half-smile, half-look-of-concern.

"Thanks. See you tomorrow." I felt exhausted.

I stepped out on to Connecticut Avenue and walked home. I knew that Terry was right about work, but I also knew myself. I couldn't do my job when my mind was elsewhere. I just needed to find Kara. Where was she? My mind scenario-ed every place on earth and ended up in San Francisco. She loved the place. I had to leave as soon as possible.

Any other day it would have seemed crazy to me, but I felt compelled to see her again. I know she had a friend from Georgetown who lived there, but I could not remember her name. I took a few more steps then remembered. Mary Catherine Foley. Kara knew Mary from the first year of our law school study group and they had kept in touch. Mary was a bit stiff for me, but I always got along fine with her. I guess I would find out what she thought of me once I got to California.

The expectation of seeing Kara again was enough to shift my attention back to Slater and what needed to be done before I left. I couldn't win the Slater trial unless I showed that the shooting was intentional. One witness could help me prove it: Pooh. How am I going to find him?

Tomar will know.

I checked my phone and started scrolling for Tomar's number. As I walked to the entrance of the Metro, I dialed, finding the weight of the wet, dreary, D.C.-in-March day overwhelmingly depressing.

"Yo, dog, what up?" Tomar greeted me.

"I need some help finding some people on the street. The police are not very good at finding people that don't want to be found."

"Yo, five-o could be trippin' over dead bodies and wouldn't know it. Tell me who you want me to find," Tomar said.

I told Tomar that I needed to find Pooh, the kid that Kevin Ford bragged to about the murder. "I can give you his address and a few notes, but be careful."

"Don't even go there. I ain't afraid of five-o or the little street niggas. It's my world G—be good," Tomar said cheerfully and hung up.

I took the escalator down to the subway, marveling at Tomar's invincibility. My admiration waned after a few seconds and I again felt bad about my situation. I drifted through the station and got on the Metro. I walked off the train at Judiciary Square and took the escalator up and into a biting cold and headed into the office.

*

On my way to my desk, I walked by a secretarial station where several women, my office mothers and sisters, were hunched over a catalogue of some type. I flashed a fake smile, waved, and walked to my office.

Annette quietly said, "What up Clay?" then pointed to the catalogue and said, "That's sharp, that looks good." Her voice trailed off as I got closer to my office.

"What are you doing here?" I asked Johnny, who was sitting in front of my computer.

"Surfing for porn," he replied.

"Give me a Rodney update and please get out of my chair," I quietly asked, trying to hide how raw I felt as I took off my winter gear.

"I've been tailing him for a few weeks. It turns out that Rodney likes sixteen-year-old tail." Johnny sat down in the chair opposite my desk, leaned forward, and looked serious.

I knew he wasn't jacking me around. I took out a pad from my desk and began taking notes. "Go on."

"He does a little after-school tutoring session with a sixteen-year-old girl named Keisha."

"Keisha? She was one of Bradford Slater's students. Her name was mentioned in Kevin Ford's juvenile waiver report. There was something about Kevin liking her," I said.

"This girl is way beyond Kevin's reach," Johnny said. "Every boy in that school wants to stick it to her." Given my mood, Johnny's attitude was starting to get on my nerves.

"You think she'd be willing to give a statement? Can we get DNA? Rodney could be in that house for twenty different reasons. We need to know more before we can start making accusations." I held my palm a few inches above the desk to try and get Johnny to slow down and think it through.

"She's sixteen. He's forty-two. That translates into sixteen to thirty-two years in jail." To Johnny, it was as simple as that.

"I don't like this. What's Kevin's motive here? If he liked Bradford, then why would he shoot him? You add Keisha to the mix…"

Johnny cut me off. "You are overthinking this. Kevin bragged about shooting Bradford Slater. This has nothing to do with it. Rodney's affair with Keisha is just something we can hold over Rodney's head when things get rough. Leave it to me; I'll gather the evidence."

"You're right—it's up to the jury," I brushed it off.

"There is an important meeting with the crime scene technicians tomorrow. Annette told me to remind you," Johnny told me as he was leaving.

"I can't be there."

"Clay, you can't miss that meeting. You gotta organize the troops so the evidence doesn't get fucked up," Johnny said as he left, shutting the door behind him.

I was more concerned about my life being fucked up than the evidence. Still, people were going to wonder why I wasn't at the crime scene technicians' meeting. But I had to go to San Francisco. I needed someone to cover that meeting. I tore off the yellow sheets that I had taken notes on and put them in my Slater trial notebook. I grabbed the phone with my left hand and punched Scott's four numbers.

"This is Scott."

"Get in here—I just shaved my balls and I need your opinion." It might have been a lame joke, but it was better than letting my real feelings show through.

"Where have you been?" He hung up and walked over.

"Kara's grandmother died and I have to go to San Francisco for the funeral. Can you cover a meeting with the crime scene techs for the Slater homicide?" Lying to Scott just made me feel worse, but I just was not ready to tell him. I knew he would cancel dinner with his family tonight and glue himself to me to make sure I was okay and to help me work on the case.

"You look terrible." Scott inspected me carefully. "I don't believe you. Something's up, Clay."

"I told you. Funeral for Kara's grandmother, Hiroko," I began my little fiction.

"I still don't believe you. Go online and show me the obituary."

Scott was that smart. That was why he was unbeatable in court.

"She just died. They haven't written an obit yet," I said. Scott just stared at me with his large brown eyes filled with something ranging between pity and disbelief. Mercifully, the phone rang. The Washington Post appeared in the caller-ID screen.

"Hey man, when is the bachelor party?" Phil asked.

I felt repulsed. "Maybe we should skip it. I'm not sure it's appropriate—we're in our thirties now," I said. Scott gave me a weird look. "It wouldn't be inappropriate if we were all in our sixties. You're making no sense," Phil barked on speakerphone. "I want to see the video of this Russian ballerina as I drink some Grey Goose vodka, then we'll bring on the strippers, then we'll burn your black book and send you off to the world of Home Depots and diapers. It's that easy."

There were a lot of words flowing through my head. "Easy" was not one of them. "I changed my mind. The ballerina is a witness in a case. Besides, I couldn't do that to Kara," I said.

"Have you decided to embrace Jesus Christ as your Lord and Savior or something?" Phil asked. "Because if you did, that is front page news."

"I tell you what, we'll do a night in South Beach or Vegas or something—just the guys, I promise." I had to man up a little bit or Phil would never get off the phone.

"Okay, I'll call you later. Have you set a date for the wedding yet?" This phone call was turning into an interrogation.

"No, we'll be doing that soon."

"Let's go out Thursday night—that is, if the other Jesus freaks will let you out of the compound."

"Sure, Thursday sounds good." I suddenly understood the nature of criminal confessions; I would have said anything to get Phil off the phone.

"Let's meet in Georgetown and get Thai food first, so we can stare at the waitresses and get worked up for the evening. That shiny black hair drives me crazy."

"I gotta go," I said, and hung up as fast as I could.

Scott continued to look at me in obvious disbelief.

"Just cover that meeting for me. Scott, please, just tell the crime scene guys they can come by my apartment tomorrow night. I'll be back by then," I told him.

"What is the name of Kara's grandmother again?" Scott asked me.

"Grandma Hiroko, something like that."

He knew I was lying, so he kept staring at me.

"Just cover the meeting. Please, I will explain later."

Scott left. I called a travel agent and left a message asking for the next available flight to San Francisco. Then I started composing an email to Kara:

Dear Kara, my guess is you are in San Francisco. This is my new job, trying to figure out where you have gone and if I can find you. What I did was wrong, but I want to tell you face-to-face. I am getting some therapy. I know it is a cliché, but I am a cliché, right? The guy who wants to shoot a porno right before he begins the Walt Disney script? You won't even return the emails I sent. Has it ever occurred to you that I am worried about you?

I re-read it. Too narcissistic and not contrite enough. I deleted and started over.

Dear Kara, I will never see you again? Is that where it's at? You have pulled out the Japanese sword and cut the bond? I cannot put my arms around that concept. I want you to look me in the eyes and tell me, I want you to sit down and tell me that I was your best friend and I betrayed you and you never want to see me again. I want you to tell me face-to-face. Something in me says you can't do it. I just think you are hurt and confused right now—and I know that I caused it. Can you give me your address in San Francisco? Signed a very sorry fiancé that fucked up very badly (Didn't you once say "Compassion, it's not the name of a perfume?"), with big regrets, and much love, C.

I didn't like it any more than the first email. I knew that I couldn't talk my way out of this mess. All I could hope for was forgiveness. I tried one more time:

Kara, you deserve a face-to-face explanation. I don't deserve it, but you do. Please tell me where you're at. All regrets and love, C.

I hit send and closed down my computer. Annette spotted me as I was packing up to go to the airport.

"You can't leave, Monster. Da whole world lookin' for you," she said. "Tommy wanted to talk to you and I have a pile of these messages you need to return," Annette had a concerned look on her face.

"I know, but I'll be back late tomorrow," I said, squeezing her right forearm in thanks.

"You okay Clay?" she asked.

"Yeah, it's a family matter," I quietly said as I finished packing up.

I waited inside the newly renamed Reagan National Airport, while a small, bird-like woman behind the airlines counter checked into standby availability to San Francisco. I thought of one of my dad's dinner stories about good old Ronnie: Reagan once said, "I saw protestors on the way to this press conference. They were holding signs that said, 'Make Love, Not War,' but didn't look capable of either one." Dad thought Reagan was a dunce, but that joke was funny.

I waited hours for a seat to open up. It was ten o'clock. The night janitor was sweeping the floors. The airport smelled like a spent battery. I was about to fly all night, and I had no idea if I would even see Kara.

My name was finally announced so I approached the counter and got my boarding pass. The tunnel to the plane was cold. I grabbed a pillow and blanket from the overhead bin, squeezed by two people, and settled into my window seat. I eventually fell asleep somewhere over the Meth Belt.

\*

Dawn brought the Pacific Coast. After I stumbled off the plane, I checked my answering machine and cell phone from a bank of shiny pay phones at the San Francisco airport. Nada. Kara hadn't called, and I couldn't call her—she'd cancelled her phone number the day she busted me.

"Hotel Monaco, 501 Geary Street. Thanks," I told the driver. I chose a hotel from Kara's address book on the home computer. If there was a cool hotel in a fun part of town, Kara knew about it. The sun glinted off the steel and glass skyline. My body swayed to and fro as we passed Union Square, trapped in a state that was neither sleep nor waking.

"Here you go," the cabbie said.

The hotel was bright and festive. Big bold stripes and Chinese reds adorned the lobby. Kara would have loved it. Not allowing myself to acknowledge the possibility of failure, I imagined the details of our reconciliation: flowers, dinner, and a night at the hotel. High hopes in a cloudy world.

I checked in, took a shower, and called Mary Catherine at her law firm, Weber & Knight.

"Mary Catherine is out this morning. May I take a message?" An officious-sounding secretary answered. In Tommy's office all you had to do was phone-flirt and offer to buy the secretary a Pepsi, vanilla latte (large), or Yoohoo chocolate drink and they pretty much spilled the beans. This wasn't going to be as easy.

"Do you know what time she will be in?" I asked.

"No, may I ask who is calling?" She was already irritated.

"This is Clay Franklin. I am a prosecutor. I need to speak with her about one of her cases."

"Which office?"

"The U.S. Attorney's Office, San Francisco, Economic Crimes Unit," I lied. "I am sorry to bother you this morning—maybe I could try her cell?" I asked. She gave me the number; I hung up and quickly dialed.

"This is Mary Catherine," she answered.

"Hi, this is Clay. Please don't hang up. I really need to speak with Kara. I think she is in San Francisco. This is an emergency. Can you tell me where she is?"

"You're in San Francisco? Clay, I don't want to be in the middle of this. I'm sorry, but I have to go. I have to take a deposition near the theater district," she said.

"I'm at the Hotel Monaco. We could have coffee before your depo. Please, Mary Catherine, I've always been sweet to you," I pleaded.

"But not so sweet to Kara," she reminded me. "You don't deserve it, but I'll do that much for you. Meet me at Dottie's True Blue Café in a half hour. It's right around the corner from your hotel," she said and hung up.

The city shone with halcyon California light, which then disappeared as banks of clouds quickly rolled in. A brief walk up a hill and I arrived at Dottie's. It was a hip little dive. I spotted Mary Catherine. A thick woman with a lovely face and blue eyes, her light brown hair spilled into the collar of a masculine blue suit.

"Thanks for meeting me." I tried to give Mary Catherine a kiss on the cheek, but she recoiled.

"I don't have much time," she said. "Weber has me hopping."

Talk about strictly business. Mary Catherine billed 2,300 hours a year. She was a vampire workaholic, but she had a heart of gold and loved helping people. Mary Catherine was Kara's friend and a client besides. Kara had designed the firm's website. Kara's web design was about power. It had photographs of a steel spinning wheel on the front of a bank vault, a piece of a facade of an ultra modern building of dark steel and translucent glass, a train traveling so fast it was blurred, the skeleton of a building under construction—formidable images of vigor, speed, and growth surrounded by the simple colors of black, gray, red and white. I remembered just staring at her work and feeling good when I looked at it.

"Listen, Mary Catherine, I love Kara," I said. "Her aunt and uncle live here, you're here, and there's a lot of work in San Francisco for graphic artists. Even if she isn't here, I think you know where she is. I need to speak with her. I want to marry her, to spend my life with her…"

She cut me off. "Kara and I chatted about the video. You have huge problems. Cheating problems. Trust problems. Honesty problems." Mary Catherine itemized away. "Kara's made herself very clear. She doesn't want to see you." My stomach turned.

"Look, I don't know what Kara told you about that video, but it was a drunken mistake. It didn't mean anything, I swear. I was never really into it." As soon as I heard my own words, I realized how ridiculous they sounded.

"You know what Clay? Kara's right. You are scum."

The food came. I drank my coffee but otherwise kept my mouth shut. It was quiet. You could hear the occasional ting of silverware.

"So what do you want to tell me?" Mary Catherine asked.

"You're right," I said. "I'm trying to work through this mess—my mess. That is one of the things I would like to convey to Kara, face-to-face, even a phone call would be a start." I took another sip. Mary Catherine looked perplexed.

"I know there are two sides to every story, but I don't think you realize how offensive your conduct was. If you only knew what Kara went through with her first divorce. "She continued eating her breakfast.

"But I know we can work this out with therapy or something. Marriage and a family—we can still make it happen. I love Kara." I pled with her, "Why don't you just call her? We could meet tonight, have a glass of wine, begin to repair." I cringed at my own words.

"I won't help you, I'm sorry. I believe everything you said, but you have to work this out on your own. Honestly, I doubt Kara will ever see you again.

"Listen, I know you have to go take a depo. I am very grateful that you had breakfast with me. I know you are in Kara's corner, but please try and understand, I have to find her—she needs me just as much as I need her." I wrote my cell phone number down on a napkin and left a twenty-dollar bill on the table.

I took out a copy of Kara's address book that I printed off from the home computer. I hailed a cab and gave the driver directions to the home of Kara's aunt and uncle, whom I had met years ago. I gave Uncle Matsuo a call from the car. He sounded surprised to hear my voice, but welcomed my visit. I thanked him and tried to enjoy the ride. Retrospectively, I couldn't believe all the friends and family we had met on both sides of the fence just by being friends and inviting each other to events—even when I was dating and she was partnered up. I tried to enjoy the hills, views, and architecture but my latte had no effect. I just felt more tired and closed my eyes.

"Here you go man—time to wake up," the cabbie said. I turned my legs to the left so I could reach into my right pocket to fish out money to pay him.

*

I approached the door to a narrow but substantial Beaux-Arts house with a fancy Renaissance dormer and knocked.

"Clay, long time no see," Kara's uncle said and waved me in. "I don't think I've seen you since Kara's graduation from art school. Thanks for calling."

Uncle Matsuo invited me inside for tea. I followed him up a long staircase, wondering how much he knew about me. He knew Kara and I were friends. I was guessing he knew we were engaged, which was probably why he invited me over when I called. We entered a kitchen that spilled onto a deck overlooking the water.

Matsuo was a compact, handsome man with thinning black hair. The kitchen was Architectural Digest-perfect. Mounted atop the custom cabinets were a series of eye-grabbing Chinese red drums.

"Come," he said as he smiled and led the way. "You caught me while I was gardening."

"You've probably heard this a thousand times, but this view is just incredible."

Matsuo began pruning what looked like a ficus tree. I sat down and he poured me a cup of tea.My mind reeled. Why doesn't he ask me what I'm doing in San Francisco? He had to know, and yet he's gracious? If some dude that cheated on my sister had come to my house, I wouldn't be serving that douchebag any tea.

"Matsuo, I don't want to lie to you. Kara and I had a fight. She moved out, and now I'm looking for her." Either the tea acted as a truth serum, or I was too tired to do anything but put my cards on the table. "You were kind enough to invite me over when I called. You deserve the truth. I'm trying to find her to put things back on track," I said, embarrassed but relieved.

"I'm sorry about that," he said. "I have been in the doghouse with my wife on occasion also." He paused and began clipping away, taking a breath as he bent into the stunted tree. "Marriage is hard."

"I will take your word for it, but I would just like to get to the marriage part. Do you know where she is?"

"At this moment, no. I don't know where she is."

I refilled my small cup from a black iron teapot. "At this moment" Uncle Matsuo didn't know where Kara was? Was he a part-time defense attorney? What did "at this moment" mean?

"Kara gives me great joy," he said, carefully pruning.

"Me too."

The mysterious Matsuo said nothing. He would run his "at this moment" smack all day long. Meanwhile my cell phone was vibrating with numbers from the 202 area code.

"Your home is beautiful." I attempted to fill the silence, prattling on like a fool. "I just can't get enough of this view. I bet real estate here costs a fortune."

"Yes, it's practically as expensive as Tokyo. I think I just heard the front door, Clay. I'll be right back."

Matsuo reentered with his wife, Yoshiko. A little surprised, she smiled warmly and greeted me: "Clay, nice to see you. What a surprise to see you here in San Francisco. Thanks so much for stopping by."

Together, Matsuo and Yoshiko gave me a tour of the place. I was introduced to generations of Kara's family through pictures and objects amidst a warm and pristine home. I felt like I was being shown a picture of the life I had just discarded. I desperately wanted to be part of Kara's family, but I was a kid with my nose pressed up to the glass of the pet shop or toy store—and it was closed, permanently. I wasn't going to stick around and wallow in my ruin and defeat, and politely told Matsuo and Yoshiko it was time to get back to the airport.

I tried to fire up the conversation again as Matsuo walked me to the door.

"How long have you been married to Yoshiko?"

"Thirty-six years," he said.

"It was good to see you again. Thanks for having me over for tea. I appreciate it."

"Good to see you, Clay. Hang in there." He patted me on the back.

I didn't really want to leave. I wanted to camp out on his back deck. Do a Ghandi-esque hunger strike until Kara showed. "Thanks," I said. "If you hear from Kara, please tell her I was here for the day and had to fly back to work," I said as I squeezed his hand. Matsuo was a good man. What was he supposed to do? He couldn't throw me out and he couldn't give Kara up. Maybe he'd screwed up at some point in his marriage. I went down the steps and immediately flagged a cab back to the Hotel Monaco.

*

I entered the brightly colored lobby and recognized the same concierge I had seen earlier.

"That was fast," said the man behind the desk. I must have seen him when I arrived but I didn't remember his face.

"Could you tell me when the next flight to D.C. is?" I said, feeling suddenly more exhausted.

"Sure," he said.

"Thanks," I said faintly. I looked down, took a breath, and leaned on the marble countertop.

"There's a flight leaving in about ninety minutes," he said. "I can book it for you now if you'd like."

I dug out my credit card and gave it to him. I couldn't bring this failed trip to an end fast enough.

# MARCH 14, 2000

I reached my apartment around 11 P.M., the jet lag from six thousand miles in forty-eight hours hanging heavy about my neck and shoulders.

There was a knock at the door. I looked through the fisheye and saw a cluster of D.C. cops. I had completely forgotten that I told Scott to send the evidence techs to my apartment.

"C'mon on in guys."

They followed me back and sat at my dining room table.

"I'm Walker. This is Taylor and Johnson," one of them offered.

"I remember your names from the evidence reports. Sorry I couldn't be there today. Thanks for coming by. You guys want a beer? Vodka? Xanax?" I joked.

"I'll take a beer," Walker said. He was a medium-toned African American and thick around the chest, almost NFL-player sized.

"Corona is all I have," I said, thinking it strange that an on-duty officer would take me up on the offer. Taylor and Johnson remained quiet. I noticed no one had any property reports, which evidence techs usually bring.

I sat down. Walker just about chugged the Corona in one swig. As he raised the bottle to his face, his uniform pulled tightly and a button popped off his collar. I looked at the other two and noticed that their gear was mismatched. Taylor had letters tattooed on his knuckles. As Walker set the bottle down on my coffee table, I saw his weapon; some handgun I did not recognize. Definitely not standard issue. Shit. These guys are not cops. My cell phone lay where I'd left it, on the coffee table. I knew I'd never get to it in time.

"I think I remember you guys from some old cases," I lied. I turned to Taylor and said, "Weren't you in on that 7-11 robbery where the guy brought his sawed-off shotgun and his son? Do you remember that one? Two shorties, if you know what I mean?" I smiled.

Taylor smiled, showing a diamond in his tooth. As he crossed his arms, I saw a gang tattoo peek out from his sleeve. Crenshaw Blood —I knew it from my work on gang-related homicides.

"You got a lot of history with cops," Walker took over. "They like you. You like them."

"It's all good. I've never fucked over a cop. Never reported anyone for not going to court," I played along.

"Why you want to fuck over Rodney's son? Maybe you be false-accusing it?" Taylor said and smiled, his arms the size of my thighs. "Maybe you can do something to help a fellow cop out?"

"I thought you were here to talk about the presentation of evidence?"

"You a funny boy. What Rodney call him—the cocky trial dog or some shit like that?"

"So Johnson, which district are you out of?"

Johnson didn't say a word, he just looked at me, all harsh-eyed and unshaven.

"You see, police officers usually wear small brass plaques with their names on them and I don't see yours. Unless you're out of the Crenshaw Blood Gangster District?"

Walker punched me in the face. I blacked out for what must have been three or four seconds. My nose was a faucet of blood. I was on the floor, and the chair was two feet away on its side.

"Would you like another beer, Walker?" I took a swing at him, but, before I could connect, the Johnson-Taylor combination locked me in a Half Nelson. Walker started punching me in the stomach. It was like getting hit by a sledgehammer. They let go, and I dropped to the floor.

"That's right bitch. We CBGs. What you gotta say now?"

I coughed and wiped blood off of my face with my sleeve. "Would you guys like a snack? I think I have some Doritos."

Taylor kicked me. "Shut the fuck up." The dining room light reflected off the diamond in his tooth.

"Get him some paper towels," Walker said.

"I'll get some 409—spray that shit in his eyes," Taylor suggested.

"Just the towels," Walker ordered, clearly in charge.

They sat me up in my chair and watched as I dabbed my face with paper towels. I was covered in blood.

I looked Walker right in the eye. "You know I'm going to have you indicted for this."

"You ain't gonna indict shit. You can't find us. You can't find your witnesses. Only thing you can do is drop the case against Rodney's boy."

I let out a sigh and my best imitation of a chuckle that I could muster in my current condition. "You think I'm going to drop the biggest case in D.C. because Rodney's little bitch tells me to? I don't give a shit about you."

"You're going to cut a deal with the boy—make sure he gets a real short sentence. Counseling and credit for time served and all that shit. You a big shot, you can swing that."

Taylor lit a cigarette.

"This is a non-smoking apartment," I said, trying to stop a new stream of blood that I thought had coagulated.

"You think we kidding? We previewing what we're gonna give you. Next time we gonna ride it into the hook. And after we take care of you, we gonna take care of your girl, Kara." He smiled. "That's right—we know where she is," Walker said.

"And we gonna do a train on her ass," Taylor added.

"You're full of shit." I calculated my move on Taylor.

"First you call me Rodney's bitch, and now I'm a liar," Walker stood up. "Who's laughing now, funny man?"

This was my chance. Between six fists and six legs, I put a forearm into Taylor's nose and he fell backward. Blood ran down over his lips. Then I tried to head-butt Johnson, but I was already down and the two of them were kicking me.

"You understand the score now? We been tailing you and her since day one. You report us—you say one word—and she gets it too." Walker kicked me again in the stomach. I passed out.

When I awoke a few minutes later, I scrambled to the computer and sent a harried warning to Kara. Just in case she wasn't checking email from me, I also called Uncle Matsuo, but there was no answer. Desperate, I called Mary Catherine, but I went straight to voicemail. "It's Clay—Kara's in danger. I know this sounds like bullshit, but it's not. Look, just get her to a police station or something…" My voice trailed off as my head pounded. I could not help Kara if I did not get medical attention. I stumbled to my car and drove down P. Street to the Georgetown Hospital.

*

"A car accident?" The ER doctor wasn't buying it. "I'm sorry, but these injuries are consistent with a fight. I'm obligated to report you," he informed me through a thick Indian accent.

I flashed my D.A.'s badge. "It was a fight with my brother. Haven't you ever been in a family fight? Do you want me to put my brother in jail? Just fix me up, man."

"This is going to sting," the doctor said, dabbing my face with an antiseptic-soaked cotton ball.

"Trust me, it won't."

# MARCH 15, 2000

I tried to cover my wounds with some of Kara's makeup she left behind. Jesus, I look like a domestic violence victim.

"That's funny, I don't remember reading about a plane crash," Scott said when he came into my office.

"I crashed my car."

"You didn't crash your car and Kara's Grandma Hiroshima didn't die. Wait here, I'm going to get Alexandra and you are going to tell us what happened." Scott picked up my phone and dialed her extension. "Get in here. Psycho boy is going to tell us what's going on."

"Annette, hold Clay's calls for ten minutes," Scott said as Alexandra entered.

"Oh, my God, what happened to you?" She hugged me as she examined my wounds.

"You're going to work me over even worse when I tell you what I did."

"Not in a million years," she said softly. "Scott said you were acting weird. I knew something was wrong. Clay Franklin missing in action—that's just not you."

"Present-tee-ism," Scott said (Scott's word for "present but not really working). "Let's go, give it up, no Miranda rights."

"Kara found the video—me and that ballerina. She's gone. I went to San Francisco to find her. She wasn't there," I said.

"Settle down." Scott sounded calm as he placed his hand on my back, right below my neck.

"When I came home last night, I let some cops into my apartment—only they weren't cops. They were gang bangers—CBGs —under orders from Rodney Ford."

"So let's nail these assholes. I'll go get the mug shots," Alexandra said.

"'D.A. Gets Attacked in His Own Apartment.' You'll make the front page of the Post. Damn, Clay, it would be like a new career," Scott said. "Now that you have been beat up, maybe you can get interviewed by Greta Van Susteren."

I blew my nose.

"Sorry man, that wasn't funny," Scott said.

"Don't worry about it," I said. "No, I think they took this as far as they can go. If they kill me, another D.A. will pick up the case—I think they understand that."

Alexandra moved closer. "What do you want to do?"

"Convict Kevin Ford. Work on the case. Fuck these gang bangers. Fuck Rodney Ford. Johnny's got him under surveillance already. He's working up a nice child abuse and statutory rape case. But I need to find Kara. I left her a warning about these goons, but I haven't heard back from her yet."

"I'll do what I can," Alexandra said. "But if you can't find her, chances are Rodney's gangbangers can't find her either. Anyway, let me see what I can do." She patted me gently on my back, and left.

"We'll get you through this. Just turn the volume down inside your head," Scott said.

"Let's go to the evidence locker," Scott suggested. "I know there's a shotgun there from one of my cases. I don't know if those guys would actually come back but we can't rely on the police to protect you. Hell, I dialed 9-1-1 last week at my house 'cause I heard a weird noise and I got a recording."

"Is this your idea?" I grinned. "I don't know who you are, but I like the way you're thinking." Everyone in the homicide unit was forced to become an expert in firearms and ballistics, which included firing off rounds at the FBI range. Never thought it would come in handy.

We took the elevator to the property unit where evidence for cases on appeal was stored. I'd been there before on many occasions. Phil and I had borrowed Ecstasy from the drug stash at least three times. Scott knew about it, of course, but always declined our invitation to partake. He said that Ecstasy might make him enjoy life, and he enjoyed hating life.

Scott located a double-barreled shotgun. Scott's hand slid over the gunstock. "You have to start getting your life together, Clay." He held out the gun to me.

"What life?" I asked.

# MARCH 22, 2000

"Two weeks and not a single phone call or email. Kara knows I went to San Francisco," I told Terry.

"I'm sorry to hear that. How is work?" Terry asked.

"If I lose this case, my career is over. I'm slipping—I can feel it. I missed important meetings. People are wondering."

"What do you think about instead of work?"

"Kara. Why I did what I did." I shut my eyes tight. "What's wrong with me?"

"I think you behaved selfishly and egotistically. You didn't really stop and think how disrespectful your actions were to Kara and to yourself."

"To myself?"

"Yes, by having this affair you were saying that Kara was not enough."

"So I got greedy," I said.

"Yes. Greed comes in many forms. Greed for money, greed for sex."

"So what now?" I asked.

"You need to be kinder to yourself. Accept the mistakes you have made. Self-pity is just as egotistical as having an affair. Try yoga or meditation—something that allows you to think and feel productively."

Yoga and meditation? I don't know if I can take any more of this kumbaya. "Do you think Kara will come back?"

"I wish I could tell you. But coming to terms with your behavior also means coming to terms with the consequences of that behavior. You are going to get spit out on the other side of this and you just might start living meaningfully." Terry gave me both barrels at close range but at least he wasn't smoking.

\*

I flashed through some nasty D.C. traffic, headed to the police department to mend fences with the evidence technicians (the real ones) and to sniff out potential saboteurs.

"Sorry I missed the meeting last week. I had to interview a witness in San Francisco on another murder case," I told Officer Chambers, a small white dude from a redneck Maryland suburb. I distrusted him immediately—but couldn't explain why. Probably spillover paranoia from the last twenty four hours.

"No worries, man," Chambers said. "Akers went through who did what, and your boy Scott took notes."

"Hey, hey. Long time." Clifton, a tall, skinny African American, gave me a warm embrace. Immediately, he began talking about his son's football accomplishments at Cardozo High School.

"Okay, let's do this meeting," I said. "Get out your property reports. I have Scott's notes. I just need to ask a few follow up questions." I lowered my voice, "By the way, how well do you know Rodney Ford?"

"Don't know him, don't want to know him," Clifton said.

"Why?" I glanced over Clifton's shoulder. Football pictures of his kid. A picture of Clifton singing in a Baptist church choir. The group was wearing purple suits and yellow ties, uniquely cool, and totally southern.

"Man's a bad apple, a bad example. He doesn't go near me. He knows I would be on him fast and hard."

Clifton was safe. But I had to check everyone off the list one by one. I flipped through crime scene photos from Clifton's manila file.

"Shit, I was the one who told Rodney Ford to get out of the school that day," Clifton said.

"Rodney Ford was at the school?" I couldn't believe my ears. "You mean, the day Bradford was shot?"

"Yeah, Rodney said he was in the area when he heard about the shooting over the rover."

"Rover?" I hadn't heard that term.

"Police radio." Clifton leaned closer to me. "Rodney said he was in the area, and he heard that his son was the primary suspect. Since there was a family member involved, I told him to leave the crime scene."

"And?"

"He split."

"Can you get me the police dispatch tapes?" I asked. "You bet."

"Thanks, man, I have to get going." I decided to take Terry up on his idea of yoga to help relax. I remember Kim or someone I had dated mentioning a yoga studio called United Woods in the Woodley Park area.

\*

I blasted through traffic and stopped outside Unity Woods Yoga Studio on Connecticut Avenue, NW, near the Duke Ellington Bridge. I went down the steps and there was a short line to get into class. Sign in sheet, curious looks (Who is that six-foot-two guy with no tattoos?). I entered the hot room, determined to sweat the drugs out of my system.

I glanced around the room and gazed upon my fellow yogis. There was a platoon of chicks sporting tailbone do-me tats, and a bevy of survivor women, each with a tortured look on her face that screamed, "My husband left me!" I identified with them and wanted to hug every one of them. I drank some water and noticed a forty-something body builder with bleached blonde hair staring me down. I turned and faced the mirror. To my immediate right was what looked like an uptight Brookings Institute babe that I thought I met at a party a few months back. I remember her mentioning that she was doing yoga to improve her chances of pregnancy. I waved to her and she looked away. Maybe it was not her. To my left was a black woman with a short afro and long legs that I definitely would have gone for in my former life.

"Welcome everyone. My name is Ann. Please drop into child's pose." The instructor ordered us around in a commanding voice.

"First time?" Ann whispered into my ear and helped me make some adjustments. She had that librarian look, which I liked. "Open your knees a bit wider—then you'll be able to drop down lower in front." I felt as though I were praying to Allah with my torso between my thighs and my arms stretched forward. Were we facing Mecca? I composed a shopping list for the Connecticut Avenue Liquor Store—my next stop after yoga.

"Breathe in—first deep breath of the day. Let go. Be present. Untether yourself from everything that happened before you came into this room."

Tall fucking order.

"Exhale. Deep exhale," Ann said. "Let's hear those deep Ujjayi breaths."

The collective exhales sounded like a mythological giant gasping for air while Rodney Ford's goons worked him over in his ancient Greek cave.

"Take a deep breath," Ann commanded again, segueing into "downward dog" and sense-irritation this or that. The language Ann used escaped me. Everyone seemed to know what to do except me.

"Untether yourself from all thoughts except the present," Ann said. "Accept life's groundlessness. Whatever doesn't seem right in life, don't resist it. Accept each moment as if you had chosen it."

What is up with this instructor? Apparently, they were serving up yoga philosophy between poses. I hoped Kool-Aid didn't come at the end. Ann stopped by and helped with a few poses, but I knew how to stretch and could imitate most of the moves.

"Twist into triangle," she said. I was starting to feel like I was auditioning for Cirque du Soleil.

The room got hotter and hotter. Sweat was pouring off me. I began to think about Kara. In one excruciatingly long moment I realized—I would have to live without her. As much as I hated to admit it, the philosophy that came with this twelve-dollar class rang true. I had chosen this moment. My selfishness had sent her packing. My tears mixed with the sweat on my face and the liquids rolled off together, unnoticed.

"Now move from warrior one position to warrior two."

I waited for Ann to announce the cheater's pose. It never came.

I thrust my arms out and tilted diagonally like a jet plane banking into a deep turn. I felt nauseous, as if my drunken pilot was negotiating a serious wind. Was it the heat? Or the simple realization that these yoga freaks were right?

I made it to the end, headed back down Connecticut Avenue (skipping the liquor store) to my apartment, and passed out.

*

I woke at 3:00 A.M. I checked my voicemail and made some coffee.

"How are you doin' Mr. District Attorney? It looks like you and me on this Ford case. And now Judge Stone wants us in the courtroom tomorrow morning bright and early for a status conference. Give me a call."

I took one of those yoga deep breaths and rubbed my temples with my left hand. The voice was R. Kenneth Mundy's. I checked my other voicemails. Mundy was right. Judge Stone's chambers had called. He wanted Kevin Ford back in school or in jail before Labor Day. Stone clearly did not want to delay the proceedings. I had to bear down on the file for the morning status conference to determine the trial schedule.

# MARCH 24, 2000

Mundy and I sat next to each other in the courtroom. Mundy and I had always gotten along. The genial, freckled African American was impossible to dislike. Even when he made his standard motions to dismiss for prosecutorial misconduct, no one took it personally. Rich enough to adorn himself in Versace and Armani gear, Mundy didn't bother. Unpretentious to a fault, he wore old clothes, short-sleeved shirts, cuffless pants, and a signature straw hat with a black band right above the brim. Only Mundy could get away with this type of sartorial unconcern. He was one of those old-time Washington institutions like Katherine Graham, Edward Bennett Williams, Jack Kent Cooke, or Mayor Marion Berry. After Edward Bennett Williams' death, Mundy was T.M.T.S. ("The Man To See") when you were in trouble. He knew how to perform in front of a D.C. jury. Oliver North's attorney, Brendan Sullivan, was brilliant, sure—but perhaps not the guy for the knife and gun club. If I was in trouble for drugs, violence, or both, I'd want R. Kenneth Mundy.

Ford's family had taken a second mortgage out on their house to hire him. For a case like this, Mundy wouldn't enter his appearance for under fifty thousand dollars. Hell, the only reason he was trying this case for fifty was the publicity he'd receive.

"How about the president makin' all these speeches about teen violence? I mean, he won't shut up about this case," Mundy whispered to me.

"Takes people's minds off other issues," I whispered back.

The reporters strained their ears, but we were whispering. Mundy caught me up on the trial bar gossip, and I invited him up to my office afterward. He teased me about being at the D.A.'s office so long.

"It's time to go out and start making some serious money, Clay." Coming up the ladder in the D.A.'s office, Mundy had crushed me almost every time. Big case or small, he was always relaxed. The job was just playing golf for him.

It was 8:25 A.M. We waited in the ceremonial courtroom where the case would be tried. Stone's courtroom was half the size of a football field: it had taken a forest of wood to construct. Great shafts of light poured through the vast windows and ignited the high fluted columns. Behind his bench, two enormous flags stood on a dais—one of the United States, the other of the District of Columbia—

crisscrossed at the top of their flagpoles as if they were getting ready to sword fight. Stone was the only judge who still required The Call of the Docket. At 8:30 A.M. every lawyer who had a matter in His courtroom would have to show up and be interrogated about the status of their cases. He took The Call very seriously. After all, jurors were paid; if a jury was ordered but not used, taxpayer money was wasted.

When I appeared before Judge Stone for the first time, I went to the library to search for biographical information. Stone, one of the District's first African American judges, was born and raised in Virginia's tidewater country. He completed two tours of duty in Vietnam, battling at Tay Ninh, Bien Hoa, Dak To, Da Nang, Hue, She Sanh, Quang Tri, and Pleiku. The exotic names translated into a medal-adorned chest. Prior to ascending the bench, Stone had been a public defender. His clients—murderers and thieves—were afraid to be in the interview room alone with their attorney. I understood the feeling. When he came down the hall at 8:29 A.M., carriage erect, head high, shoulders tossed back, he walked as if he had uncontested, unquestioned ownership of the courthouse.

"All rise," said Karl Tulkinghorn, his handpicked, smartly dressed bailiff. Tulkinghorn always carried the crossword puzzle neatly folded into a small rectangle. As bad as things were going, I was damn lucky to have drawn Stone for the trial. I was going to get my ass kicked, but at least there would be no circus.

"Madame Clerk, call the first case," Judge Stone ordered. His voice contained an ineffable sternness that demanded obedience. It was clearly a voice that had said, "Alpha Company to Baker Company. This is Major Stone; I am ordering an air strike. Here are the coordinates…"

The court clerk announced the first case. A prosecutor and public defender drifted up to the center of the waist-high wooden railing. The railing was sixty feet long and had two sets of squeaky, wooden louver doors at each end for witnesses and lawyers to enter the well of the Court.

A relatively new (and utterly clueless) D.A. named Henry Baker and a defense attorney I did not know had their case called. They waited in front of the louver doors. Stone asked what was going on with the case. Neither spoke.

"Are you deaf?" Stone asked with pure condescension.

"Your Honor, we are not sure if a jury is needed. We're still trying to work it out," Henry Baker explained. Stone found Baker's passivity offensive.

"Sir, you've had plenty of time to work it out. Today is the day of trial. Does your client want the plea offer or not?" Stone asked the defense attorney. Half the room was smiling. Stone was going to atomize both of these lawyers.

"Well, Judge, as it stands now, what my client is interested in..." The defense attorney was swimming the backstroke, but Stone cut him off.

"AS IT STANDS NOW, DOES HE WANT THE OFFER?" Stone had turned the volume up, thereby banishing indecision.

"No," the defense attorney quietly said.

"THAT WASN'T SO HARD, WAS IT? Madame Clerk, order a jury on this case." Judge Stone spoke to the cowering attorneys: "Both of you listen—do not come to the call of the docket not knowing about your case. It is inefficient, selfish, and idiotic. These dockets are packed with jury trials and motions. We have to let the jury commissioner know what to expect, and quickly send out the motions to the judges who are not in trial. Mr. Baker, I am going to call your supervisor, Mr. Monroe. This is the third time you have come in here without a clue—I'm sick of it." By the time Stone was done, Baker looked like he'd been told that he flunked the bar and had a terminal disease on the same day. Stone was wholly unconcerned that the room was packed with reporters (most of them had seen Stone in action before and were unfazed if not amused).

Stone cleared out the rest of the docket and ordered Mundy and I to remain in the courtroom. Mundy had filed over twenty motions when he entered the case.

"Thank you both for coming in. This case is going to require considerable time, effort, and expense. I wanted a status conference and motions update as this case needs to be calendared correctly," Stone began. "First motion." Stone paused and looked at the paperwork. "Motion for impeachment evidence of government witnesses? Mr. Mundy, has the prosecutor supplied you with the criminal records of all the witnesses he intends to call to the stand?"

"Yes and no. He gave me a computer print-out of criminal record checks of all the civilian witnesses, but not the police officers he intends to call to the stand." Mundy intended to leave no stone uncovered.

"Mr. District Attorney, you are hereby ordered to produce that information to Mr. Mundy's office one week from today," His Honor commanded. Stone's face looked disgusted. The first time a defense attorney requested a record check on a police officer, he told the attorney it was absurd. Problem was, the office had prosecuted so many of the boys in blue that Stone could no longer ignore dirty cops and their criminal records.

"Next motion: motion for expert witnesses. Has the district attorney provided you with the results of all scientific tests, and who their experts will be?"

"Yes," Mundy said.

Next motion: motion for release of grand jury testimony. Next motion: motion for Mr. Ford's prior acts of misconduct. Next motion, next motion, next motion... And so it went for the next hour and a half. Twenty-seven pre-trial motions were filed, but not much case law was argued. Stone only granted Mundy what he was entitled to. He loved to show off his encyclopedic knowledge of D.C. case law.

"I'll see you gentlemen on August seventh for jury trial. If you want to litigate more motions, call my chambers and set a date." Stone dismissed us.

A young reporter called out, "May I address the Court about the upcoming murder trial?"

The room went silent. Karl Tulkinghorn looked up from his crossword puzzle in amazement. Stone actually kept pretty cool.

"Absolutely not. I do not give press conferences," he said, and descended the bench.

Mundy left, graciously declining to come up to my office, but promising to stop by next time. Mundy told reporters that he intended to argue that the gun went off accidentally. Then it was my turn.

"Listen guys, I want to help you, but Mr. Monroe does not want me to comment on witnesses or details of the case until after the trial." The reporters peppered me with questions about the trial anyway.

"Rest assured, Mr. Monroe is both sad and angry that teenagers do not feel safe in their own schools. It is his intention that our office prosecute this case to the utmost of our ability." The reporters flashed looks of impatience with my boring, worthless quote, and shot toward the hallway.

I packed up my briefcase and ran my fingers through my hair as the crowd dissipated. My thoughts returned to Kara and the danger my work had put her in. I hoped that Alexandra was right: if I couldn't find Kara, neither could Rodney's thugs.

## Chapter 7

# Trial by Stone

## AUGUST 1, 2000

I was awakened by the electric thring of a doorbell somewhere in the building, perhaps the apartment below. It was the summer of my discontent and a full night's sleep was still a rare commodity. I lumbered out of bed, put on some music, and grabbed a cup of coffee. It was 3:30 A.M. I couldn't sleep. My mind was racing to the same crawl: Where was Kara? Was she safe? Deciding I might as well take a stab at productivity, I put in a tape of Bradford Slater (Annette had given me a handful of unedited classroom videos from the school). I needed to know him. I had to breathe life into him before the jurors' eyes. Most importantly, I needed a break from my pining.

"Look at that picture—what do you see?" Bradford asked a packed classroom. His deep voice grabbed me, silky-smooth and self-reliant. Bradford was not a big guy. He was probably around five-nine, slender, and dressed in an unassuming fashion. Fashionable tan pants (not Dockers) with a stylish silver buckle, and a neatly pressed plaid shirt of various blues. The students were quiet and still.

"The picture in this slide is called Coronation of the Virgin. It was painted in the year 1414 by an artist named Lorenzo Monaco."

"There's some black dudes in that picture," a young student observed. "I told you Jesus Christ was a nigga." Another student told him to shut up.

"This painting is housed in Florence, Italy in the Uffizi gallery. The next slide is a painting by Piero di Cosimo from 1510 located in the same gallery, the Uffizi. It shows the slaying of the dragon. We have seen this theme before—who can tell me where?" Bradford asked.

"From the Chinese art you showed us," a female student said.

"Here as there, the dragon symbolizes a malignant force, separating you from the vitality of your experience. The dragon might represent greed, or it might represent obstacles," Bradford said.

"This next slide deals with temptation—a common theme. Here, Christ is tempted, but we have seen this imagery applied to Buddha and Mohammed too. They all had temptations— just like we have them in our community. Drugs, alcohol, crime, and violence. But what is the source? Where do the dragons, the temptations come from? Your assignment is to pick a medium, either photography or painting, and show me your dragon, your temptation. Like the slides we have been looking at, your work should tell a story."

"What if I took photos for one side of the picture and painted on the other? Can I combine them?" a student asked with hesitant teenage awkwardness.

"Do it. Be vital in your work. Nourish your creative imagination." Bradford clicked over to the next slide. "There are no boundaries, but there are deadlines. Your projects will be due next Thursday."

Bradford whipped through slides like a top-shelf art historian. His facts segued into the mythical aspects of the pictures. "Look at the size of this painting. The artist took three years to paint the wall of this church. You know that artists can be heroes, right? After all, a hero is only someone that gives his or her life to something bigger than themselves." He infused his explanations about the sculptures and paintings with expressions like "the soul's high adventure." He encouraged his students to view their lives through mythology. When caught in difficult situations, he instructed them to choose the right path, discover their higher nature rather than the lower. It was as if he was telling his students—all his students, regardless of their creative abilities—that just being alive was rapture.

I sipped my coffee, watched, and listened. I let the tape roll as I went to the bathroom. As I walked back, I saw Bradford pointing to a painting of stylized human and demonic forms with tortured expressions as they were enveloped by fiery tentacles. Identifying the work as a Byzantine representation of Hell, Bradford's voice turned slightly somber, "It is only by going down into the abyss that we recover the treasures of life." I stopped the videotape. In Bradford's death, the hopeless had lost a beacon, a Virgil to guide them through their Inferno.

With the importance of the case clear in my mind, I decided that I finally had to let go of Kara. I was barely sleeping, hoping some 3:00 A.M. buzzer at the door would be her. Across the room, the computer monitor glowed brightly. I knelt before it, timidly pressing down on the keys.

Dear Kara,

I love you. I never deserved you. Wish you were here.

Wherever you are, good luck.

Love, Clay

# August 6, 2000

It was Sunday, 6:30 A.M. I couldn't believe the heat at dawn. The night had failed to cool the humid boil that defines August in D.C. A filament of a partially visible spider web got into my right eye. I stumbled forward a few steps, and another spider web crossed my lips. By the time I reached my car, I was spitting, sweating, and swatting bugs away.

Driving toward Terry's office, I turned on the radio. The case had been out of the news for quite some time, but now, since the jury trial was fast approaching and August is traditionally a slow news month, the case was again an item. "Our educators, like Bradford Slater, must be safe in school," said the president. I wondered which handler told him to use the word "educator" rather than teacher. Terry planned to spend the rest of the month in Martha's Vineyard. He'd given a select group of clients the option of scheduling a weekend session before he left. As I approached the door, I heard Terry playing his cello. I knocked. The music stopped and he opened the door.

"Thanks for meeting on a Sunday," I said. The brass door handle felt cold from the air conditioning.

"I like weekend sessions—things are just calmer."

"The piece you were playing; I liked it."

"Thanks." Terry leaned the cello against the wall before turning back to me.

"What was it?"

"A feeble attempt at one of Bach's cello suites. Grabbed you, huh?"

"Yeah, three hundred years old but sounds fresh," I said as I settled into my chair and grabbed a tissue to wipe the sweat from my brow.

"Bach was orphaned at ten, married his cousin, and had four kids. Then his cousin died, so he remarried, and had five more kids. He lost something like eight children in their infancy, which happened back then. Lots of ups and downs with the church, politics, and life, but he cranked out some tunes didn't he?" Terry smiled, then changed gears. "How are you feeling about the trial?"

"Fine. Ready to go, ready to lose. I've become well-versed in loss over the past few months," I said as I shrugged my shoulders.

"I read that trial lawyers don't win or lose cases, they just try them," Terry said.

"That's like saying NFL quarterbacks don't care about touchdowns. Trust me: trial lawyers are like salesmen. If you don't make the sale, you're out of a job."

"Tommy would never fire you."

"No. At the D.A.'s office you fail by getting demoted to juvenile or promoted to the head of grand jury—bullshit like that."

"I have a feeling you are going to be just fine, Clay. Maybe even better than you think." Terry shifted his weight and crossed his legs.

"Maybe—but I am still angry." I looked at a stain in the worn-out beige carpet.

"Angry about what?"

"Being an asshole and losing Kara."

"Is that all?"

I closed my eyes, took a deep breath, and organized my thoughts. I had learned to let myself feel the pain and the fury. "I'm pissed off at her for her no-contact attitude, like it was a court order or something. I think it's immature on her part. I hate that my dad was cruel when he was drunk—not only to me but my siblings. He demanded that we be macho, and he wasn't really there for us." I paused. "Then again, I'm pissed at myself for blaming him. Push comes to shove, the things I have done, I can't blame anyone but me."

"I don't want to oversimplify it, but many guys from your father's generation didn't conduct much of a character education," Terry said. "I've cut way back on my smoking but do you mind?" He reached for a pack of butts.

"Go ahead. What did you mean by that last comment?"

"Neither my father nor yours spent too much time teaching us to value other people and to empathize. It was all about being John Wayne, about being tough." Terry leaned back in his chair and took a drag. "Generalizations about child rearing aside, how do you feel about your dad in this moment?"

"I know I care about him, but it doesn't feel that way. It's confusing."

Terry nodded and waited.

"And I feel embarrassed about losing Kara. I fucked up, and now he can't have grandchildren. I hate the thought of him looking at me like I did something wrong. "

"As a father myself, I can tell you that there were years I didn't talk to my son. After my divorce went through, he never called. Wouldn't return my calls either," Terry said. "He was angry at me for my selfishness, for running off with another woman, for getting remarried. Eventually, he forgave me, and I forgave myself. I couldn't get along with his mom for ten minutes. It was the right thing to do for me and for him, but he will always view it as a mistake. Still, to avoid mistakes entirely would involve me never leaving the room."

I said nothing and let the conflicting feelings swirl. After a few minutes, I returned to the conversation. "I've been lying awake most nights, reviewing my ESPN highlights. Here's a recent favorite: A couple of years ago I was doing an economic crimes case. Husband/wife defendants. Embezzlement. Three kids—one had a learning disability. Big suburban McMansion in Virginia with a pool and two S.U.V.s. Anyway, mommy and daddy are so fuckin' upside down financially they should be taking dramamine instead of prozac. They are both selling houses. They stumble and reach into the RE/MAX cookie jar. They would not accept my plea bargain so I slammed them hard. They didn't do much time, but I separated them from their kids. I wish I had been more empathetic. I probably fucked up that family forever." I concluded.

"I hope you realize that finding empathy is an important step for you. But you might want to apply that to your personal life, too. Any other late night thoughts?"

"That's only the tip of the iceberg, but I do want to reconnect with Dad-zilla."

"What's the worst that can happen after what you've been through? Even if you cuss him out, it's a start. I don't encourage you to trim the edges off the truth. If you feel like you'd like to talk to him —go talk to him."

"He could help me through this trial. There might be some support there. Plus, once this missing tape surfaces, he can help diffuse the headlines when they read, 'Prosecutor Caught in Love Nest with Star Witness.' That's a little selfish, but I might need his help."

"And that, my friend, is self-love," Terry punched out his cigarette. "That's not selfish, it's using the support around you to help you. He's your father. Even if you dont feel it, you are still his responsibility. That never changes." Terry looked somewhat pleased with himself as he picked up some pages of black and white sheet music.

"Fair enough. I'm going to grab some coffee, then take a drive into the past. I might as well go clean up all the loose ends in my life. When I lose this trial it is going to be the end of my career."

"Or the beginning of something new."

"Yeah. Maybe. See ya."

"By the way, how much time did the embezzlers get?" Terry asked as I was leaving.

"A year but served nine months."

"They deserved it."

*

After my session with Terry, I bought a coffee and read the paper. My dad had a guest column under "Ombudsmen." I didn't read it. There was a profile on the Slater case, of course, with accompanying profiles of R. Kenneth Mundy and myself. I skipped it, threw the papers into a recycle bin, and sped to confront my father.

I parked my Beemer in the driveway behind my dad's Cherokee ("Always buy American," he would say.). I pounded on the door, half-nauseous from the heat. It was 10:30 A.M. and already in the nineties, which meant it would easily hit a hundred by noon.

My dad was wearing his bathrobe when he opened the door. I followed him down the hall. He held his side as he walked.

"Well, well, well... What brings the Roman warrior to my castle on the eve of battle?"

"You left fifty messages. I figured you had something to say," I said.

I followed him into the den. There were stacks of newspapers, a few highbrow mags, and an old movie in the background. I recognized Gregory Peck and Ava Gardner—it must have been The Snows of Kilimanjaro. Alexandra adored Ava. Scott and I concurred.

"Good guest column in the Post today," I guessed, trying to break the ice.

"Nice piece on you too. Why don't you get yourself a drink? There's OJ in the kitchen, vodka in the den." He sat heavily in his brown leather chair and matching ottoman.

I asked, "Why are you drinking? Where is Mom?" I sat on the couch.

"Your mother is down at the eastern shore. And I am drinking because if she were here she wouldn't let me drink."

"Why? You've always had the run of the castle."

"I am sick." He picked up the remote and muted the television.

"With what?"

"Different things—I can't remember them all. Low this, high that."

"Bullshit, something is wrong," I said.

"Okay," Dad took a long drink from his glass. "I have cancer—had cancer. The doctors removed a tiny little piece of my colon."

"Are you fucking kidding me? You should have told me." I paused. "I mean, how are you doing?" I felt winded by the news.

"I'll gut it out. Only…why haven't you called? " Dad looked me right in the eye. For the first time, I noticed the deep bags under his eyes. I panned downward—his skin looked pale and puffy.

"When did this turn into a Lifetime Movie of the Week? You've never cared if I called. I leaned toward him, elbows on my thighs."

"That is just not true," Dad said and shook his head, still unable to say he cared. "Why don't you rewrite that story—include a chapter where you start acting like a grown man?"

I glared at him.

"I just can't believe you never told me you were sick." I dropped it down a notch, and leaned back on the couch.

Dad shook his head and changed course. "Clay, I'm concerned about you and Kara."

Silence. Dad tilted back his glass and finished his drink. How could he have found out?

"Come with me." He stood up, grabbed his side again and winced, but quickly shrugged it off as he sensed my anxiety. "It only hurts when I laugh."

"Dad, let me help you," I said, stepping toward him.

"I'm serious, it is not as bad as you think. Come with me. Believe it or not, I'm glad to see you."

I followed my dad down the steps into the basement. Next to the pool table was an old gun safe. An All the President's Men poster hung on the heavily knotted wood paneling. (Having discovered Bob Woodward's talent and being part of the core Watergate story team, Dad was a consultant to the film.) A few feet away, a U.S. Marine Corps flag hung against the wall. Upon the flag, a coiled rattlesnake lay poised above the words "Don't Tread On Me." Semper Fidelis was embroidered at the bottom of the flag. He opened the safe, pulled out a small videotape, and tossed it on the pool table.

"Kara sent this to me."

"Holy shit." I exhaled. The morning had started off well with some solid therapy, but things were rapidly deteriorating—first cancer and now my Dad knew I was a cheater with a recording fetish. I stared in disbelief. My heart hammered at my ribs. He was the last person I had imagined that she would send the tape to—and I had imagined plenty.

"I took a quick look at it on a video camera. It's been in the safe ever since." Dad closed the door to the safe and spun the dial. "You haven't seen Kara?"

"No. Disappeared into thin air." I leaned on the side of the pool table, and ran my fingers along the green felt. I stared at the tape a few feet from me on the rail of the table.

"I'm sorry, Clay." My dad's whole manner proclaimed him to be the type of guy that had seen it all.

"I was engaged to her, and now she's gone."

Dad just looked at me, steady at the helm. His stoicism grated on me.

"I never fully appreciated my relationship with Kara because you never set an example," I picked up the tape and tossed it on the hard linoleum floor; when it stopped moving I crushed it with my foot. "You were such a prick to us," I grumbled.

"I plead guilty to being a prick, but I did teach you to respect and appreciate people, so fuck you on that one. Maybe I was harsh...." He shook his head and looked down.

"Harsh? You ran this house like a dictator," I said, raising my voice at him. "You had to be the Marine Corps captain of Spring Valley—always in charge, always right."

He bent over gingerly, picked up the smashed tape, looked at me and added, "I guess you've never made a mistake." He threw the tape in the trashcan.

I said nothing. He looked at me and sighed heavily. For what it was worth, I felt better. Did he actually understand where I was coming from? Or maybe he just looked at me as a three-year-old throwing a temper tantrum.

Then Dad's demeanor softened. "I'm sorry, Son, sorry for being a prick. But I tell you what— you have made me prouder than you can imagine," he said as he took a few steps toward a wooden chair covered with a thick cushion and sat down. "There's nothing I can do about the past, but I want to do what I can about the now. Tell me what you need."

This was more than I ever thought I would get from him. I eased up a bit. "Dad, I wish I knew." I quietly rolled a ball on the slate bed of the pool table and watched it traverse the bright green felt.

"I know you were nuts about Kara."

"Still am," I said.

"You think you invented infidelity? You think temptation wasn't around before the invention of the video camera? I cheated on your mom once with a Post typesetter. It was many years ago, before you were born."

I had already heard that urban myth, but I tried to act surprised. "And that's supposed to make me feel better?"

"Clay, bad things happen. Horrible things happen. I don't approve of what you did to Kara, but you don't need my approval— you never did."

"Maybe I do," I said.

"Return a goddamn phone call and it will be there for you. Now, let's go upstairs and fix ourselves a drink before your mother gets home," he said.

"Does Mom know about the tape?" I asked.

"Of course not." He ambled toward the steps and added, "I take it you don't have feelings for the woman on the tape?"

I looked at my dad and shook my head slowly.

"I didn't think so," he said.

We went upstairs and set up lunch.

"I know a private detective," Dad offered, as we unwrapped barbecue chicken, tomatoes, and corn on the cob that had been wrapped in tin foil. "I've used him before on a couple of discreet issues. I bet a private eye could find Kara."

"Maybe. Let me think about that," I said and we sat down and began to eat. "I meant to ask you, was there a note? Did she send anything with the tape?"

"No . She just sent the tape to the house, addressed to me, with your apartment as the return address. No note."

"Why didn't you call me?" I asked.

"I did. Fifty times," he said and took a long sip of water.

"I know," I said, reloading my plate. "I am going to try and move on." I looked at my dad and nodded slowly.

"Son, you have to focus on your trial tomorrow. Then when it's over we'll pick up the dialogue on this and we'll find Kara."

Dad headed back to the den. I stacked the dishes, said goodbye, and left.

\*

It was 8 P.M. I was putting my trial notebooks into boxes when my cell went off.

"Yo, Clay. I wanted to come by and wish you good luck on your case tomorrow. Gotta little something for ya too," Tomar said.

"Great, I'd like to smoke crack the night before trial. I'm going to get my ass kicked anyway."

"Why you gotta be like that? No man, it ain't that," Tomar said. "Just give me your address and I'll take it from there, Holmes." I gave him the info and continued preparing for trial.

Twenty minutes later Tomar called back.

"Why don't you come down to your parking lot on P Street?" he asked.

"I'm on my way."

I saw a large Cadillac Escalade on one side of the parking lot, its tricked-out rims still spinning. As I walked toward it, I noticed two guys and a girl reclining inside. The door opened and Tomar smiled. The girl was young and way sexy. It had to be Tomar's girlfriend or his buddy's. I leaned inside the mac daddy rig and shook Tomar's hand and banged fists.

"This is my friend, Life," Tomar said. "He a rapper."

"'Life,' huh? How do you spell that?" I asked.

"L-y-p-h-e," said the young, heavy-set brother wearing some bling and a FUBU jersey.

"What does Lyphe stand for?" I asked, looking at Tomar's friend.

"Let young people hear everything," he informed me.

"Don't listen to Lyphe; dat nigga change his name every other motherfuckin' day," Tomar jumped in.

"Back off dog, I'm previewing it with your friend," Lyphe said.

"The same friend that might put your fat ass in jail some day," Tomar said.

"D.A.-ing is coming to an end. Some days I'm thinking of doing the defense attorney thing," I responded.

"My nigga, making me proud. We upgrade your ass to a BMW 745i, and I'll get you all the clients you want."

I wasn't sure I wanted the clientele Tomar had in mind. "I'm not sure what I'm going to do. I'm sick of the office politics, my family's a mess. The world just feels...empty."

"That's deep water dog, that's deep water. C'mon down to my church anytime. I pray to my higher power every day. I ask him to take care of my baby's mother and stop me from making any stupid moves."

"You still make stupid moves Tomar," Lyphe said as the young girl in the backseat played with the braids in her hair.

"Hangin' around you is stupid. I gotta change dat shit," Tomar retorted.

"Are you going to introduce me to this lovely young lady?" I asked.

"Oh, yeah, sorry. That's Keisha."

"Shit, man, when were you going to tell me?" There she was in all her under-age splendor—Rodney Ford's girlfriend. Kryptonite delivered in a Cadillac Escalade.

Tomar and Lyphe started laughing, and she smiled. I jumped in the backseat of the SUV.

"Are you willing to make a statement right now?" I asked her. She nodded. I decided to push my luck a little farther. "Is it okay if I videotape it?" She nodded again.

I called Johnny LeGray and told him to meet us at my apartment and bring a video camera. I explained that mine had accidentally exploded.

"Keisha, come on up to my apartment." I helped her out of the S.U.V.

"C'mon on up too," I said, looking at Tomar and Lyphe.

"No, we getting something to eat. Just hit my cell when you're done," Tomar said.

*

"Okay, darling, I'll ask the questions. All you have to do is answer." Johnny bonded with Keisha quickly. He told her he would take a bullet for her and promised that nothing would happen to her —ever. Classic Johnny.

"How old are you?"

"I just turned 16."

"Who is Kevin Ford?"

"He a boy I go to school with," she said.

"Do you know his father, Rodney Ford? If so, how do you know him?" Johnny asked.

And so it went for over an hour. Theirs was a typical underage affair. It was difficult to tell who seduced who, but one thing was certain: Keisha was fifteen when the affair started. That was that. (Fifteen used to get you twenty; now it entailed longer sentences and a lifetime of sex offender registration—a suicide-inducing nightmare that included instant prison for the most minor probation infractions.)

When Johnny asked about the murder of Bradford Slater he struck out at first, but then Keisha revealed that she had gone to Slater to ask for help ending the affair. Apparently Keisha was one of Slater's good works, and he had been encouraging her artistic development. Keisha said she didn't know whether Rodney knew that she was seeking help from the teacher.

Once her initial curiosity about sex (and, to a lesser extent, Rodney Ford) ended, she tried to stop seeing him. Only Rodney wouldn't call off the affair. Instead, he threatened her, saying bad things would happen to her family if she refused to play. They saw one another less frequently now, but Rodney still pressured her into seeing him from time to time. Keisha's mom was in jail, and Rodney kept saying he would influence the parole board to make sure she never got out.

"Last question, Keisha. I apologize for having to ask this: do you have any clothes or underwear that might have Rodney Ford's semen on them?"

"Maybe. I'm not sure, but there might be some on my Lucky jeans in the dirty laundry basket," she said.

Johnny turned the video camera off, and told Keisha he was going to put her up at a friend's house in Prince George's County, Maryland, for her safety. "But before we leave the city, we need to pick up those Lucky jeans."

Johnny and I looked at each other. We said nothing, but we were thinking the same thing: Rodney Ford was finished as a police officer, and—perhaps more importantly—there was a new suspect in the Bradford Slater case, a suspect with a solid motive.

"Johnny, before you go, can I talk to you in the hall for a minute?"

I waited until the door was shut completely before I spoke. "I have a police witness, willing to testify that Rodney Ford was at the school within minutes of the shooting."

"We'll see which way the case turns. There were a hundred cops at the school that day, Clay. You can't prove Rodney shot Bradford

Slater just because he was at the scene. You want my advice? Pick a jury, try the case, and see if that forces Rodney's hand."

"That's all well and good except for one minor thing: what if Kevin Ford is innocent? What if Rodney shot Bradford Slater and Kevin winds up doing his prison time?" I looked at Johnny incredulously.

"You're running out of options, Clay. Sure, you could dismiss the case, but you don't have enough evidence to indict Rodney for murder. You have to have some faith, my boy. Like it or not, right now, Kevin Ford shot Bradford. After all, he confessed to it."

"I have faith in something else," I said.

"What?"

"R. Kenneth Mundy." I could tell my answer startled Johnny. "Mundy isn't about to let an innocent person go to jail. He'll figure out a way to get Kevin to testify—even if it means giving up daddy," I said.

# AUGUST 7, 2000

An hour before jury selection was slated to begin, half of the large, ceremonial courtroom was already packed. The other half was empty, reserved for potential jurors. The judge was not on the bench so the room was filled with a hundred conversations bouncing off the marble floor, tall ceiling, and long, fluted wood columns along the front wall surrounding the bench. Karl Tulkinghorn walked toward me through the small wooden gate in the middle of a fence made up of balustrades that separated the galley from the proceedings. As I was setting up, he came to me and whispered, "R. Kenneth Mundy? Boy, you got your work cut out for you."

"Is that a polite way of saying I'm going to get my ass kicked six ways to Sunday?"

"You said it, not me." Karl looked me dead in the eyes, super serious for a moment, but only a moment. He smiled and said, "Maybe I'm a fool, but I put money on you." It was common knowledge that the bailiffs gambled on big cases, and the Post reporters left it alone because the bailiffs were valuable sources.

"There are horses in the race you don't even know about," I whispered back.

"Sure gonna be interesting. Might be I leave my crossword puzzle at home," he said.

R. Kenneth Mundy came over and shook my hand. "Good luck, Clay," he said. You had to give it to Mundy—when he said "good luck," he actually meant it.

"ALL RISE," Tulkinghorn boomed. Hundreds of feet shuffled in unison.

Stone paused and scanned the gallery briefly, perhaps to see if everyone was standing, then sat down.

"Enter your appearances," Judge Stone ordered as he sat down on the bench.

"Good morning, Your Honor. R. Kenneth Mundy for the defense." Mundy stood when he spoke and sat down quickly.

"Good morning. Clay Franklin for the government, Your Honor," I said.

Behind me in the first row of spectators, I could hear the quiet scratching of pencils as two courtroom artists began their renderings on large swatches of brown paper.

"Good morning counsels. I have ordered the jury commissioner to send the prospective jurors in. I trust that we can proceed without objection?" Judge Stone asked. Typical Stone, he might as well have said, There is no stopping this trial or changing the way I am going to run it.

"Let the record reflect silence, indicating that we are ready to proceed." His Honor added this type of "official" signature for appellate purposes. Such anal retentive attention to detail clearly worked as he was rarely reversed on appeal.

Tulkinghorn escorted the jurors into the courtroom.

"Good morning, members of the jury pool; my name is Judge Stone," he announced, delighted that day one was his day. I thought it appropriate that D.C.'s best teacher would have D.C.'s best trial judge oversee the story of his tragic demise. I scanned the audience, foolishly hoping I might see Kara sitting among the assembled throng.

"Members of the jury pool, welcome to my courtroom, and thank you for performing your civic duty. We have a lot of hard work to do today, deciding who will go and who will stay. Rest assured, we will get through this difficult process together and in one piece.

"Next, the bailiff, Mr. Tulkinghorn, will call out a series of numbers and ask you to step into the jury box. Before we begin, allow me to give you some friendly advice: when you are excused, do not take it personally. For many of you, jury service is not a good fit. This is a highly emotional murder case, and we need jurors that are going to be fair and impartial. Of course, you may be excused for any number of reasons that have nothing to do with fairness. One of the lawyers may excuse you because, for instance, you are a member of an organization that gives the appearance of being pro- or anti-law enforcement. Do you understand?" Judge Stone paused like a talk show host just to see what kind of response he would get.

A few jurors collectively said, "Yes."

"Thank you for answering. I appreciate it. This is my opportunity to help you through this process. Some of the questions I will ask are more personal and will require you to raise your hands like you are back in school. My job is to make your stay here in the courthouse as comfortable as possible," Judge Stone said, like a compassionate general visiting the troops.

Tulkinghorn filled the jury box with potential jurors and Judge Stone began reading the typical juror selection questions.

"Is there anyone here that is no longer a resident of Washington, D.C.?" No one raised a hand.

"I bet a few people raise their hands on the next question," Judge Stone said. "Have you or any member of your family been a victim of a crime or had any contact with law enforcement officials, including members of any federal law enforcement agencies?"

Hands shot up across a jury pool of hundreds.

"I told you I would get your hands up," His Honor quipped.

Laughter was accompanied by collective exhales and the shuffling of feet.

"I don't mean to make light of such a serious question, but it is essential that you relax so we can talk openly. Many of you may not want to express your answer in public. If that is the case, you are invited to approach the bench to discuss your answers privately. All you have to do is say, 'Your Honor, may I approach to answer?'

"I will go around the room and ask some questions to each person who raised their hand. Again, if you want to step out of the spotlight and come up here, just indicate that is so. I will move from left to right, starting with you, sir." Judge Stone pointed toward the man seated to his immediate left. "State your juror number before speaking. You do not have to use your name."

"Your Honor, I am juror 841, and my son works at the F.B.I."

"Sir, based on that fact do you think you could still be a fair and impartial juror? Can you sit on this jury in an unbiased manner?"

"Yes, Your Honor."

"Next. Ma'am," His Honor indicated.

"I need to approach," she said.

"Yes, come up here. Counsel, please approach." Mundy and I stood on the decorative molding that united the floor with the judge's large, rectangular bench. Most of the jurors were at least forty feet away when they came up to discuss their situations confidentially.

"My son was shot over a drug deal and these cases are too much for me. Plus, my daughter went to Carver High School, and my family knows all about Mr. Slater, the teacher." She started crying. Judge Stone offered her a tissue as we all huddled together at the judge's bench. The lady took the tissue. "Thank you, Your Honor," she quietly said, as she dabbed her eyes. Mundy and I glanced at each other for a moment, and wished we were not just inches from this poor woman and her searing grief.

"Ma'am, thank you for sharing that. You may be excused," Judge Stone told her, before looking to the jury and calling, "Next."

"I'm juror 298; may I approach?" an elderly woman asked and ambled her way to the bench.

"Yes." Then Stone added in a softer voice, "Gentlemen, you might as well stay here. There's no need to go back to counsels' table."

"Yes, good morning. I have prayed on this matter and God has told me this young man is guilty, but I do not want to sit in judgment," she said.

"Not exactly responsive to my original question, but I'm sure you gentlemen don't object to me sending her home," Stone quietly said to us, then told the woman, "Ma'am you may return to the main jury room, thank you."

As soon as she was out of earshot, Stone whispered, "I don't want this case reversed because we failed to screen out lunatics that can predict the future." Mundy and I shook our heads in agreement.

"Let the record reflect that there is no objection to my sending that last juror back to the jury room," Judge Stone said, as he looked at the court reporter.

"You gotta love this job," Mundy whispered to me. "I bet that woman could give me stock tips directly from the Lord." I stifled a laugh.

"Next," His Honor commanded.

Stone rocked through the room for almost three hours. Parents with children in jail, ACLU members that hated the police, diabetics that couldn't concentrate when their blood sugar got too low, folks that knew Bradford, and a Buddhist that said finding Kevin Ford guilty would lead to violence against Kevin in jail.

Finally, Judge Stone gave Tulkinghorn a series of numbers.

"I am going to have Mr. Tulkinghorn seat the following people in the jury box." Tulkinghorn herded them in like cattle.

"I want each juror to answer several basic questions about your occupation, family status, radio and television preferences, organizational affiliations, number of children, and so forth and so on. You don't have to memorize the questions. Just look at the large easel to my left and the basic questions are right in front of you. Kindly go down the list and answer the questions so the attorneys can learn more about you." Stone pointed with his outstretched left hand to the list of questions in large bold letters.

As the jurors recited their answers, Mundy and I furiously took notes.

"The time has come that you will be asked to leave as each attorney exercises their legal right to excuse you. Again, don't take it personally. This too is part of the process," Stone explained. "Mr. Mundy, the first strike is yours."

"Please thank and excuse juror number 24," Mundy said, excusing a woman who was treasurer of the local Mothers Against Drunk Driving group (even the acronym scared defense attorneys: MADD, as in, I want to get even and convict).

"The prosecution will now exercise its strike."

"Please thank and excuse juror number 387," I said, booting a white physician that listened to NPR all the time, belonged to Doctors Without Borders and made a charitable contribution to Human Rights Watch. Perhaps his heart was in the right place but I wanted him gone.

Mundy booted off someone that hesitated about being "fair and impartial." I booted off two women that complimented Mundy on his defense of Mayor Marion Berry. Groupies! They were looking at him with pure lust. Over the next hour and a half, we continued the selection process, whittling down the pool through our strikes.

"Gentlemen, please approach," His Honor commanded. We scooted up to the bench like dogs. "Both of you are out of strikes and I think we are good to go. Does anyone want to make a record?" We shook our heads no.

"Okay, we have a jury. Mr. Tulkinghorn, please swear them in," His Honor commanded. "The rest of the jurors can return to the jury lounge." Stone paused as the jurors rose from their seats. "We will break for lunch. I am sorry this took so long. Tomorrow we will eat lunch closer to twelve than 1 P.M., but we were so close to having a jury I just wanted to get us there. My apologies if you are exceedingly hungry. When we return, Mr. Franklin will give his opening statement, followed by Mr. Mundy. Opening statements are not arguments and they are not evidence. They are an outline of how each side thinks the evidence will unfold. This case has garnered a lot of media attention, but you must not talk to the media during the case. After the case, you can go on Oprah, write a book, anything—I don't care." Judge Stone smiled, and the jurors laughed. Then Stone's face became grave as he added, "You will not talk to anyone about this case, not even your family, during these proceedings. That is Judge Stone's law, and I expect you to follow it. I will see you after lunch."

"All rise for the jury," said Tulkinghorn. Everyone rose, including Judge Stone. Stone didn't even ask us if we were ready or needed anything. The train had left the station as far as he was concerned. They might take three months to do a murder trial in L.A., but Stone did them in three days, period. The twelve jurors and one alternate stood and slowly navigated the tight spaces of the jury box, exiting through the wooden door five feet to the left of the judge's bench, orderly as kindergarteners on the first day of school.

\*

I ate lunch at my desk. It wasn't the press I was trying to avoid—it was the heat. Ninety-nine degrees and humid. The door opened slowly and Annette peaked in. "How's it going player?"

"I'm not a player anymore. I haven't gotten laid in six months," I mumbled.

"Avocado sandwich? That ain't no real sandwich," Annette said, mercifully leaving the Kara topic alone.

"Why do you have to pick on me when you're nervous?" I asked her.

Scott and Alexandra walked in.

"It helps me relax," Annette said. "Now, you go lawyer it up with your homies. I'll hold down the fort out here."

"Please put a 'Do Not Disturb' yellow sticky on the door," I told Annette as she left.

A minute later, I heard a thud against the door and Annette's muffled voice. "There you go Monster."

"So, how's the jury looking?" Alexandra asked me.

"Black and in love with Mundy," I said and added, "I'm sorry, I forgot to mention, there are two white folks on the jury."

"The kid killed a teacher. You have to trust that the jurors will do the right thing," Scott said.

"Easy for you to say, my brutha," I looked at Scott.

"Bradford Slater was black too, you looking-for-an-excuse-to-lose motherfucker," Scott appropriately fired back.

I shook my head. "Thanks for your support."

The door opened.

"You gonna get a conviction?" Tommy Monroe ignored the "Do Not Disturb" sign posted on the door.

"I will get you a conviction—I'm just not sure who I'm going to convict yet." I joked despite shifting moments of doubt.

"I will ignore the latter part of that sentence. Just keep me informed and get me ready for that press conference," Tommy said and bolted.

"I can't wait until I run the office, and all I have to worry about is what I wear," Scott said, mocking Tommy.

"Or which women to seduce," Alexandra added.

I rubbed my temples for a moment, then picked up some messages and put them in my briefcase.

"Let's go," Alexandra said. She began gathering up the few things I needed and stuffing them into my briefcase.

Scott and Alexandra flanked me as I headed back to the courtroom. I avoided making eye contact with anyone during high-profile trials. I didn't mind the reporters yelling out questions (besides, most of the reporters knew I wouldn't say anything until after the trial, or, if I did leak news, it would be to Phil); no, it was the constant stream of officemates and courthouse staff wishing me good luck that drove me a little crazy. I wanted to be polite and talk to them but there wasn't time, especially with the Stone marching forward.

*

"Members of the jury, welcome back. I hope you had a nice lunch," Judge Stone greeted them warmly. "The time has come for opening statements. Mr. Tulkinghorn, please lock the doors, I don't want anyone coming or going, thank you."

Tulkinghorn stood up, placed his neatly folded crossword puzzle where he had been seated, and followed the Court's instructions as Stone resumed speaking.

"Members of the jury, notice I said statements, not arguments. The lawyers are not allowed to argue now, but may only present a road map. Remember, though, what they say is not evidence. The prosecution will now proceed," Stone announced and nodded at me to proceed.

I hoped to summon up the right combination of energy, character, and dignity—not the usual lawyer self-importance. I walked in front of the jury box and immediately got in the water.

"Bradford Slater went down to the basement of Carver High School to grab electrical equipment for a show set to take place later that day. He never left. That was where he was killed on Wednesday, December first, last winter. Ironic that he died while he was helping to produce a show for high school students. Bradford was a true showman— he was a dazzling teacher and lecturer. He brought art to life in all of its forms. The evidence will show that for almost twenty years, Bradford Slater forged meaningful relationships with his students, including the defendant, Kevin Ford.

"Yes, many children came to him with their personal problems. And Bradford Slater helped solve those problems by connecting teenagers to art and to each other through the beauty of performance. He would encourage the kids to connect with their talent, their humanity. He helped them perform or paint so that they could connect with an audience.

"Only this young man shot and killed Bradford Slater..." I walked over and pointed my finger toward Kevin Ford's face. "Gunshot residue, found on Bradford Slater's body, shows that the shooter was about three feet away when he pulled the trigger. You jurors will hear testimony that Kevin Ford's own statement places him in the basement with Bradford Slater."

"It's tempting to have sympathy for a young defendant in a murder case, but you will receive a jury instruction at the end of this case to deliberate without sympathy, bias, or prejudice. You will be the trier of facts. You will all wear invisible black robes. You will decide the outcome. The day Bradford Slater was killed, the facts are clear. He was running a dance performance at the high school. At 2:20 P.M., he went to the basement below the auditorium to grab some electrical equipment. The defendant followed Bradford Slater downstairs where he shot and killed him. Afterward, the defendant ran out of the school without offering assistance of any kind.

"You may hear the defense argue that the shooting was an accident. An accident? The defendant had a gun. In school. Even if the gun went off accidentally—which it did not—the facts will show that the defendant never called 9-1-1." I placed a copy of the school's floor plan on a large easel and drew in the escape route Kevin used to leave the school. The squeak of the magic marker pierced the room. "The defendant even tried to get rid of the gun. You'll hear testimony from David Triplett, whose nickname is Shoeboot. David Triplett will testify that the defendant gave the gun to him. Make no mistake: a gun is a murder weapon—not an accident weapon. You'll hear evidence from a gun expert that it takes nine pounds of pressure to squeeze the trigger—too much for an accident. You'll also hear evidence that after Kevin Ford intentionally killed Bradford, he bragged about it, telling his friends, 'You hangin' with a murderer.' That is not the language of accident."

I let the echo of those words sink in. I paused, looked at the jury, nodded, and very softly said, "'You hangin' with a murderer'—those were his words."

"Now what?" I brought my voice up. "The community wants to call 9-1-1 for all its grieving students, the students that grieve with Bradford Slater's family, but it's too late to dial that number. Healing begins when justice is done, and that is what this trial is about. The evidence will show that the defendant is guilty of murder. On behalf of the community, you are being asked to convict the defendant of murder. Thank you."

Judge Stone looked unfazed. "Mr. Mundy, does the defense wish to give an opening statement?"

Kevin Ford, who wore an oversized suit to make him look even younger than he was, sat next to Mundy. Kevin Ford looked lost, unsure what Mundy's answer would be. The jury looked toward the defense table, but they looked less star-struck than during jury selection. They looked like they wanted an answer more than anything else. Several of the jurors crossed their arms.

"Yes. Thank you, Your Honor. Well, it's that time—time to tell you why my client, the young Kevin Ford, should be found not guilty." R. Kenneth Mundy smiled a fatherly smile, and the jury responded with smiles in return. This was Mundy's courthouse as much as it was mine.

"Folks, let me be straight with you. Was Kevin Ford in the basement of the school? Yes. Is his father a police officer? Yes. A highly decorated police officer? Yes. But Kevin Ford's father is not all knowing. He had no idea that his teenage son took his gun to school to sell. What parent can predict how his teenage son will act? Unfortunately, Kevin Ford got into an argument with Bradford Slater because Slater, who was single and unmarried, acted in an inappropriate way toward young Kevin. The evidence will show that the gun went off accidentally. An accident is not a crime."

Mundy was playing the molestation card. I expected as much. Mundy was famous for fiction. If there was one bullet casing that was unaccounted for on a crime scene, Mundy would conjure a hidden assassin. That was his modus operandi. Mundy had melody and tempo. That, along with the accident theory, could add up to a not guilty. But then something occurred to me: Bradford Slater was dead, and Mundy just put a gun in Kevin Ford's hand... at school. That visual helped my case.

"And the one thing we can never take our eyes off is the burden of proof. It is just like His Honor said, 'We have no burden of proof.' We don't have to call a single witness. We don't have to ask a single question. The beauty of our criminal justice system, our Constitution, is that we are innocent until proven guilty," Mundy said.

I took notes as Mundy spoke. Like me, he was doing some arguing, knowing Judge Stone would allow some argument—so long as it wasn't excessive.

"Please take into account all the circumstances surrounding this tragic situation. Bradford Slater was a teacher, yes; but he was also human. Kevin Ford, like so many young men in our community, was the product of a difficult divorce. He was a very confused and lost young man."

"Mr. Mundy, please stick with the facts of the case and do not argue. There are no psychologists testifying in this case. The plight of other young men in our community has no bearing on this case," Judge Stone said.

I was wrong about what Stone was going to let slide. I shot a look over to Tulkinghorn. He smirked.

"Yes, Your Honor. I'll move on. Remember folks, don't rush to judgment until you have heard our side of the story, until all the facts are in. Because the prosecution goes first, it is easy to get swept up in its case. But the prosecution goes first because their argument is just an allegation, a charge, nothing more, and nothing less. Thank you, folks," Mundy said.

Three jurors said, "You're welcome" out loud. They loved the guy. What's not to love in his blue suit, red-striped tie, and '60's tie-clip?

"Call your first witness," Judge Stone ordered me, showing neither irritation nor pleasure with our drama-mama opening statements.

"The prosecution calls the forensic pathologist, Dr. Sandra Schoenfeld," I announced. Tulkinghorn unlocked the courtroom door and went outside to fetch her. The jurors already knew who Bradford Slater was, now they could look at pictures of his dead body. Besides, it was late in the afternoon, people were tired, and I didn't want to introduce any questionable witnesses on the first day. (Galina? I might as well put on an orange jumpsuit and get ready to be held in contempt of court after her testimony.)

Tulkinghorn escorted Dr. Schoenfeld through the sold-out courtroom, holding the wooden gate open while he placed a soft hand on the small of her back. Dr. Schoenfeld had been through the drill before. She was the quintessential handsome woman, strong with a prominent mane of thick black hair (Tommy referred to her as "Dr. Stacked."). Mundy was an expert at crossing experts, but even he would have his hands full with Schoenfeld.

The clerk approached the witness and said, "Good afternoon, Dr. Schoenfeld. Kindly raise your right hand and face me." Dr. Schoenfeld obeyed and the clerk continued, "Do you swear to tell the truth, the whole truth, and nothing but the truth, so help you God?"

"Yes, I do," Dr. Schoenfeld said, grasping a well organized, yellow manila file in her left hand. I could see the little red Post-its attached to her key documents.

"State your name for the record, spelling your last name for the court reporter, and tell us where you work," I began.

"My name is Dr. Sandra Schoenfeld, S-c-h-o-e-n-f-e-l-d. I work at the D.C. Medical Examiner's Office as a forensic pathologist; similar to the ones you see on Law & Order and other television shows. My job is to determine the manner and cause of death."

The jurors took notes and their faces revealed a sense of empowerment. Like all jurors in a murder case, they were swept away by the gravity of the situation. I proceeded with the next formality—expert witness qualification—something I could do in my sleep.

"What college did you go to? What medical school? Where did you do your residency? Have you published or taught in the areas of forensic pathology? How many autopsies have you performed over the course of your career? What are the various manners and causes of death?

How many times have you testified for the prosecution? For the defense? How much do you get paid? Did there come a time when you examined the body of Bradford Slater? When? Did you do a report on it? Would looking at that report refresh your recollection? Go ahead and open up your report." The doc blasted through the questions with a blowtorch.

"At this time, Your Honor, I move to qualify Dr. Schoenfeld as an expert in forensic pathology," I said.

"I stipulate," Mundy quickly said.

"The Court will receive her as such. You may proceed counsel," said His Honor.

"For those of us who don't watch Law & Order, perhaps you can tell us what a forensic pathologist is in greater detail," I said, and got some laughs. Even the stoic Stone smiled.

"A forensic pathologist is someone that determines the manner and cause of death based on an analysis of the body. We generally divide causes of death into five categories: natural, suicide, homicide, undetermined, and accidental. Forensic pathologists possess specialized knowledge that allows us to distinguish between the various manners and causes of death. Generally, that determination is made by examining the exterior of the body for what we refer to as pattern evidence—things like gunshot or stab wounds. After we analyze the exterior of the body visually, we begin working our way into the body so that we can examine what we refer to as microscopics."

"What are microscopics?" I occasionally had to ask a question, so it didn't look like she was on remote control (although, of course, she was).

"Microscopics are minute sections of tissue that we examine under a microscope for disease processes and additional information. Microscopics also include examination of bodily fluids even though they are not always done under a microscope."

"Can you give the jury an example?" I asked.

"In this particular case, microscopics were run on Mr. Slater's blood, urine, and liver to check for poison or drug use. Although the manner and cause of death is clear—gunshot wound to the chest—it is the forensic pathologist's duty to rule out other potential causes."

Schoenfeld laid down the medical due diligence rules in clear, albeit somewhat antiseptic terms. What she really meant was, we want to be really sure before we fry somebody.

"Thank you for those definitions. Were you able to determine—within a reasonable degree of medical and scientific certainty—the manner and cause of death in this case?"

"Yes, the manner of death was homicide caused by a gunshot wound to the chest."

"What is the basis of that opinion? That is, can you walk us through your analysis step-by-step?" I inquired.

"Your Honor, the defense stipulates that the manner and cause of death was gunshot wound to the chest," Mundy said. "The gun went off accidentally. I don't think autopsy pictures are relevant."

"Does the prosecution accept that stipulation?" Judge Stone asked in a loud voice.

"No, Your Honor," I said.

"I didn't think so." Stone directed his attention to Mundy. "Mr. Mundy, the Court does not accept your proposed unilateral stipulation nor will it tolerate your speeches about whether this homicide was intentional or accidental. I already ruled at motions that the autopsy pictures are coming into evidence. Just because something is unpleasant to look at doesn't mean it will be excluded from evidence."

His Honor made no attempt to hide the irritation in his voice. Mundy only nodded.

"The prosecution may proceed."

"Dr. Schoenfeld, with the Court's permission, I'd like you to step down from the stand and show us where the bullet entered Mr. Slater's body," I resumed.

"Permission granted. You may step down, Doctor," Judge Stone granted her the right to move, to breathe, to explain. I had her approach the large tablet of vibrantly colored Gray's Anatomy-style diagrams of the human body that I used for all my homicides. Each drawing had a plastic sheet over it so that medical examiners could illustrate the path of destruction. It was low tech, but it gave the jurors a solid visual of how a TEC-9 bullet ripped through skin and tissue.

"Would you be kind enough to give us a step-by-step explanation of how you came to determine the manner and cause of death was a gunshot wound to the chest?" I asked.

"After Bradford Slater's body was transferred from D.C. Hospital to the morgue, I immediately began reviewing the medical charts so that I could rule out other causes of death. Of course, I reviewed all the information that accompanied Mr. Slater's body, but the medical conclusions I reached are based primarily on my own investigation of the corpse," she said as she pointed to the large chart.

Schoenfeld was a pro at eliminating the typical defense attorney allegations (the victim had a heart attack five seconds before being bludgeoned to death with a baseball bat).

"Dr. Schoenfeld, did a detective accompany the deceased, and, if so, did you gather information from him or her?"

"Yes, for chain of custody purposes, there is usually a detective there. In this case, the detective told me about the shooting at the high school."

"Objection—hearsay," Mundy said.

"Overruled, Mr. Mundy. There is an exception to the hearsay rule for information gathered for medical purposes." Judge Stone proceeded to spend the next three minutes explaining the hearsay rule and its exceptions to the jury. He then ordered me to continue.

"Dr. Schoenfeld, you were saying," I relit the fire.

"Yes, there was a detective on hand when the body arrived. However, my focus is the body itself. Although I have great respect for law enforcement, I don't take their information into account when I make my conclusion. I don't know how to investigate crimes, and they don't understand pathology. At any rate, the cause of death here was a bullet that entered this area of Mr. Slater's body and severed the artery to the heart..."

She went on to explain how the bullet tore through Bradford Slater's heart and lodged in his back. She described the loss of blood, the loss of consciousness, and, finally, loss of life.

"Did you remove a nine millimeter caliber bullet from Mr. Slater's body?" I asked.

"Yes."

"Your Honor, may I have the Court's permission to approach the witness with that bullet?" Courtroom formality was a crisp military uniform to Stone, it was marching in step, it was saluting the flag.

"You may."

"Dr. Schoenfeld, I am showing you what has been marked as prosecution exhibit number seven, for purposes of identification only. Can you tell us what it is?"

"That is the bullet I removed from the anterior—the rear area— of Mr. Slater's body."

"How do you know that it is the same bullet?" I asked, knowing that Mundy wasn't really going to waste any time arguing it was the wrong bullet—unless, of course, I forgot to mention it.

"During the autopsy, I put this bullet in a stainless steel pan. After the examination was over the officer who brought Mr. Slater's body to the morgue placed the bullet in this plastic bag. Agent Sakar placed his signature on the bag and so did I—actually our initials," she said.

"Are those your initials on this yellow evidence tag?"

"Yes."

"Your Honor, I offer prosecution exhibit seven to be received into evidence." I held up the plastic bag. Several jurors looked at the bag and took notes, as if they were sketching the bag for one of Bradford's art classes.

"Any objection, Mr. Mundy?"

"No," Mundy said.

"Exhibit number seven will be received into evidence," Stone stated, making some notes of his own.

"Dr. Schoenfeld, did you or the hospital discover that Bradford Slater had any preexisting medical conditions?"

"Bradford Slater was en route to the hospital when he died. I made inquiries into the handling of the body as well as the emergency treatment provided by the paramedics. I determined that the paramedics had nothing to do with the manner and cause of death. This conclusion is supported by a panel of microscopic tests that I ran on Mr. Slater's vital organs to check for cancer and other diseases. Those screens and tests also check for drugs and alcohol use, of which there were none. The manner and cause of death was a gunshot wound to the heart. In my professional opinion, Mr. Slater's death was a homicide."

"Do you hold that opinion to a reasonable degree of medical and scientific certainty?"

"Yes."

"Nothing further, doctor. Thank you," I said and sat down.

"Mr. Mundy, your cross-examination?" Judge Stone said, attempting to barrel on hard and fast without giving the jurors a break.

"Dr. Schoenfeld, good afternoon. And a long day it's been for all of us," Mundy began. The jurors grinned, immediately connecting with the general feeling that the combination of first-day nerves and brain-boiling heat outside had wrung everyone out. Schoenfeld, who normally delighted in giving defense attorneys the business end of her I.Q., gave him a smile.

"You said the manner and cause of death was a gunshot wound?" Mundy asked.

"Yes."

"A gunshot wound to the heart?

"Yes."

"You cannot say who killed Bradford Slater?"

"No, that is not my job."

"That is up to the jury, correct?"

"Yes, Mr. Mundy," Dr. Schoenfeld said, fighting her boredom with non-medical facts.

"And you're good with that? You're okay that it's up to the jury?"

"Absolutely."

"Objection," I said, a millisecond after the doctor answered.

"Objection sustained. Move on, Mr. Mundy. These questions have nothing to do with the analysis of the body," Judge Stone said quietly but firmly.

"Dr. Schoenfeld, generally speaking, there is more than one possible cause of death?" Mundy asked quickly, skimming over the objection like a small, flat rock over a rippleless pond. "Natural causes, for example. Someone can die of natural causes, like old age or disease?"

"Yes."

"Suicide, that is a cause of death?"

"Yes."

"And sometimes a person can die of unknown causes—you can't always tell what happened?"

"Correct." Schoenfeld politely agreed with him. I was down with giving Mundy respect, provided he didn't go too far.

"There is also an accidental cause of death, correct?" Mundy asked.

"Yes," the doctor said, knowing which way the train was moving but powerless to stop it.

"There is a box on the official examiner's form marked 'accidental,' is there not?"

"Yes."

"You don't know if the gun went off accidentally or not, do you?" Mundy took his money shot.

"No, I don't."

"But you decided to check the box marked 'homicide,' not the box marked 'accidental death'?"

"That is correct," the doctor quickly rebooted and held her ground.

"Earlier you agreed that the determination should be left to the jury—in light of that fact, do you feel you rushed to judgment?" Mundy underscored his point a bit too theatrically.

"Objection," I said quietly.

"Sustained," Judge Stone said.

"Nothing further," Mundy said.

Mundy knew what he was doing. He empowered the jury.

"Does the prosecution have any redirect?" Stone asked.

"No thank you, Your Honor."

"Members of the jury, it is ten minutes to five and this is as good a place as any to stop," Stone said. "But before you leave, I am going to repeat my admonitions. You can't talk to the press about this case. You are not to watch television or listen to radio coverage of the case. You can't talk to your family about the case, and you can't conduct Internet research on the case. That said, I can't follow you to your houses. I must trust you. Which is why I ask that you trust me—this is the fairest way to do things." Stone owned them. "Does anyone have a problem with what I'm saying about fairness? Are we all going to be fair?"

"Yes," the jurors said in unison and smiled. All thirteen of them.

"Okay, have a wonderful evening and we'll see you all tomorrow morning at 8:30 A.M. sharp. Mr. Tulkinghorn, please escort these folks back to the jury room so they can get their belongings. Remember, 8:30 sharp. Thank you."

After the jury left, Stone spoke with us privately. This time, he skipped the sweetness. "Okay, counsel. I intend to keep this trial moving forward, and I don't want any monkey business from either of you. I'll see you in the morning." Mundy, God of the trial bar, rolled his eyes ever so slightly. No monkey business. I was inwardly smiling.

I went back to my office and worked the phone for over two hours, arranging and rearranging schedules. Then I grabbed some Italian carryout at a little joint on P. Street. The chef, whom I had met before, came out from the kitchen. He wanted to know whether some petty traffic offenses in Virginia would affect his immigration status. I enjoyed the distraction. I explained the potential consequences, with the caveat that I had not prosecuted traffic offenses for years, as he loaded up the bag with extra bread sticks and a tiny container of olive oil.

\*

I drove a few blocks to my parking lot. I stopped on the edge of the lot next to a wooded area. It was around 9 P.M. as I got out of the car. I was exhausted. I had left my trial notebooks back at the office so I wouldn't be tempted to tinker with them. I twisted the key to the car's trunk to grab my briefcase, my mind intent on getting my tie off and taking a shower.

"That was a real dramatic opening statement, Counsel. But it's time to end this case." Rodney Ford stepped out from the shadows of Rock Creek Park. I had always said to myself that anyone that parked on the edge of the lot overlooking the woods could be mugged. The apartment owners recognized user vulnerability and added some nighttime lighting that lit Ford up. He was bigger than I thought he'd be, and leaner and more athletic than his son.

"I didn't think you had the balls to face me alone," I said, throwing my briefcase back in the trunk. Rodney Ford stood before me in all of his authoritarian glory, out of uniform but gun and badge prominently displayed.

"You should have grabbed your tire iron when you opened up your trunk. I could have put you out of your misery," Rodney said, smiling and touching his gun lightly, as he took another step toward me.

"What do you want? I need to get some rest. I'm in the middle of a jury trial, busy trying to put your son in prison."

"Unless you plea out to manslaughter with a light sentence, I'm gonna tell the Post all about Ray, the guy you sucker punched at the bar on Georgia Avenue. Ray's gonna tell the world how you badged your way into his bar."

I said nothing at first. "I'll kick Ray's ass again on cross-examination and win on self-defense," I bluffed, trying to soak in the new twist on an old and rather unpleasant set of facts.

"Can't wait to watch that trial. Cherry, the waitress who watched you attack the victim, you gonna cross-examine her too?" Rodney smiled, the picture of pure cockiness.

"Whatever, whatever, whatever. The show goes on tomorrow. Every hour it gets uglier for your son." I tried to stare straight through his eyes to the back of his skull.

Rodney lit a cigarette and tossed the match at my feet. "'D.A. prosecuted in bar room brawl—sounds like a story CNN might like," Rodney said, already celebrating. "Judge Stone would have to declare a mistrial. Conflict of interest or something, you know, your office prosecuting you. You can't prosecute while your office is prosecuting you."

"You're probably right, but then they would put another D.A. on the case. Sooner or later they'll start the trial again, only you won't be there to watch it."

"What the fuck you talking about?"

"You'll be locked up as a sex offender pending your trial. Release bar fight details and I'll have you indicted for statutory rape within the hour. I've got Keisha's personal statement on record—hell, I've got enough evidence to put anyone, even a cop, in jail. Bet CNN would like that one too. And NPR? Hell, they love any kind of corruption in government—they'll run your story every hour on the hour." I pronounced it Eh-Ree, just like Tomar taught me.

"Her word against mine. I'm a police officer. She's just a teenage ho." Rodney shifted his weight and smiled, but he was rattled.

"You're right—only we don't have to rely on Keisha's testimony. We got DNA," I told him.

"Bullshit."

"Your sperm on her Lucky jeans."

"Bullshit."

I began walking away. "Take your bar room brawl shit, make a movie with Ray and Cherry, and give it to fucking Blockbuster—I don't give a fuck."

"Wait. Ain't no need to do nothing rash." Rodney's boldness waned.

"What's there to talk about?"

"A way to do this that won't ruin your career," Rodney said as he shifted his weight again and crossed his arms.

"Don't get civilized on me, now." I was pretending not to be curious, but I was wondering what card he would play next.

"You'll be hearing from my lawyer," Rodney Ford called back as he walked away. "Don't you do nothing rash Counsel, or the whole world will be hearing about your bar room violence, how you attack witnesses in cases." Ford walked up the driveway and laughed as he hurled a couple more taunts my way and disappeared into the summer night. "Don't do anything stupid 'til you hear from my counsel. Okay fighter, try and stay out of trouble tonight." He was still too confident for my comfort.

I got my briefcase and food out of the car, headed upstairs, and decided to call Johnny in case the détente with Rodney was just another ploy. I put everything down by the front door of my apartment and called.

"Where you been?" I asked. The sound of wind distorted the line.

"You sound worse than my wife and my girlfriend put together," Johnny said. "What are you melting down about now?"

I told him about Rodney and then complained about the trial. "I promised the jury in my opening statement that I would produce a witness who could tell them that Kevin Ford bragged about the murder. I have nothing."

"Cheer up, Clay. You're over-thinking, over-worrying," Johnny said. "Maybe this will cheer you up—Pooh, say hello to Clay."

"Yo," a small voice uttered.

"Johnny, don't play with me—who was that really?"

"That's really Pooh. I found him at his grandparents' house in North Carolina. I told him there was a warrant issued for his arrest."

"A warrant? But you'd need a court order for that." I exhaled. "How'd you get him in the car?"

Johnny whispered, "I showed him a lease for one of my beach rental properties in Ocean City and told him it was a court order. Sue me."

"Mother fucker."

"Get some rest, Clay. Big day tomorrow. I'll be in D.C. in a few hours," Johnny said.

"I owe you one."

*

I was climbing into bed when my cell phone went off again. Typical, right before trial everyone freaking out about everything, from being killed to missing work. Whatever—I'm not sleeping anyway.

"Hello?" I said with a hint of fatigued irritation.

A cold Russian accent greeted me. "This is Galina."

What the fuck does she want? I took a deep breath and tried to calm down. "Hi, did you get the subpoena our office served you for the trial?" Of course, I knew she had been served.

"I'm not coming to the trial unless you get me a green card." Galina took a drag from a cigarette. "I'll tell everyone what happened."

"A green card?" I spit back. "What the hell are you talking about?"

"Don't fuck with me." Galina's voice seemed to shake—she was nervous. "I'm not going back to Russia."

I wanted to hang up on her, hang up on my past, but the trial was too important. I spoke slowly and confidently. "Galina, you don't want to play these games. First off, without the tape no one is going to believe you. Second of all, if you needed help with your immigration issues, all you had to do was ask. Threatening me doesn't change a thing—it just pisses me off." I tried to explain the situation rationally but my anger still threatened to cloud my judgment. "You think just because I work at the Department of Justice I can demand that the I.N.S. give you a green card? It doesn't work that way. Concerning Bradford's trial, you are subpoenaed, and you will testify. If you want my help, I will see you at the courthouse tomorrow morning."

No response. I hung up, turned my cell phone off and tossed it on top of the nightstand. I opened a drawer and fished out a bottle of old sleeping pills. Tomorrow was too important to risk a fitful night's sleep.

## Chapter 8

# August and Everything After

## AUGUST 8, 2000

The sun was just coming up, and I was already in the office. Day two of any trial was usually easier, but not this time. Knowing that Rodney had the means to kill the case along with my career, I felt wired to detonate. I sipped my coffee and waited in the witness room near the front of the office. I greeted the various police officers as they sat down.

"Good morning, I'm going through the witness line-up today and trying to figure out who testifies when—thanks for coming in," I said to each officer, some lumbering in heavily after an all-night shift.

I looked down at my notes scratched in black on my yellow pad, but I was thinking about Rodney and his next move. What difference does it make? I already lost Kara. What did I care if Rodney had a statement from Ray claiming prosecutor brutality and how he was going to sue me and the D.C. government? What's the worst that could happen? Tommy would probably stick me down in the juvenile unit until the smoke cleared.

As my eyes wandered from my notes to a side table next to my chair, I caught a glimpse of the Post headline: "Justice for Fallen Teacher?" Those words violently pulled me from my narcissistic state. I needed to win the case. As for Rodney—forget him—he knew his DNA was on those Lucky jeans and he wouldn't test me in this game of chicken. I loudly called out the names of two officers and told them to follow me back to my office.

"Hey guys, thanks for coming in," I said as Officers Clifton and Akers entered my office. "Okay, we don't have much time, so let's get started. Akers, do you have the murder weapon?"

"Yeah," Akers, short and white, with thick brown hair matted down by a healthy dose of gel, held up the gun. It was in a plastic bag with a yellow evidence sticker.

"I am going to put the F.B.I. gun expert on first. Normally, we'd try to present the case chronologically, but he's got a scheduling conflict." I turned to Akers. "You don't have a scheduling problem do you?" I asked.

"No worries," Officer Akers said.

"Fine. Why don't you head back to the witness room? I need to work with Clifton a bit." Akers stood as if to go, but didn't exit immediately.

"I have the dispatch tapes you wanted. All they say is that there was a shooting at Carver High," Clifton reported.

"There's no indication that the primary suspect is Kevin Ford?"

"None," Clifton said. "When I saw Rodney at the school, he couldn't have known his son was the primary suspect."

I nodded and glanced over Clifton's shoulder—Akers was still lingering in my office. "Was there something else, Officer?" I asked.

"Did you want the gun?" Akers asked.

"No. Let's not disrupt the chain of custody. Just give it to the F.B.I. gun expert who is in the witness room. He'll identify it first, and then I'll move it into evidence through you."

"Okay." Akers finally turned and left.

Clifton handed me a bag of cassettes and continued. "Man, there were a lot of tapes. That crime scene was an event. People were on the rover for hours. But I'm telling you Clay, when I saw Rodney Ford early on, right when the action broke, he said, 'I heard on the rover that it was my son,' and I said, 'Well in that case, you have to leave.' But I was thinking, at that time, no way. There was no way that boy's name could have been mentioned. The police had no idea who the shooter was at that time. Impossible. I'm not saying Rodney Ford killed Bradford. I know Kevin Ford confessed, but something's up. My gut says Rodney was in the school at the time of the shooting."

"Are you kidding me?" I paused to catch myself. "Keep a lid on this and don't yack it up in the witness room. Let's see how it plays out—quietly," I told Clifton. "Who all knows?"

He counted. "You, me, and now Akers."

"Do you know Akers well?" I asked.

"No, he just transferred into our unit," Clifton said.

I was concerned. Three can only keep a secret when two are dead. Akers was a wild card, especially given Rodney's corrupt reach. But there was nothing I could do now; trial was in full tilt. The whole mess made me think about Rodney and his posse. In terms of silencing the truth, Rodney Ford owned his son. But he didn't own Keisha. And with Akers, and any other police officer that I called to the stand, I would just have to call an audible.

"Listen Clay, there's something else you should know." Clifton looked serious.

"What is it?" I asked.

"You know that kid who overheard Kevin Ford brag about the gun, Terrance Overton? Rodney Ford got to his dad. You can't call him as a witness. He won't 'remember' anything," Clifton said gravely.

It did not surprise me and I knew that things could have been worse. I stood up, stretched my legs, took a breath, and began to pack up my briefcase. I looked back at Clifton to wrap up the conversation. "Yeah, I figured that one out months ago. Little Terrance wouldn't tell us anything of value." I snapped the two buckles on my black Kenneth Cole briefcase in unison when I closed it. Love that sound. I continued, "With Rodney, it isn't just 'witness tampering,' it's 'the art of witness tampering.' Just subtle enough so he won't get charged. Rodney does get around, but trust me, Johnny and I have been getting around too. Let's walk to court. Stone always wants the attorneys to be early." I patted Clifton on the shoulder to nudge him through the doorway first.

Annette rushed after us. "Hey, Monster. C'mon over here and talk to me," she said.

I looked at Clifton. He shrugged. "Go ahead."

Annette pulled me aside and whispered hurriedly, "Clay, this Galina bitch ain't playing ball. I got her on the phone. She says she's not coming into court to testify. When I ask her why, she says, you'll know what she's talking about. What do you want to do?"

"Call Johnny. Tell him to go arrest her. I am guessing she's either at her apartment in Virginia or the Kirov Ballet near Catholic University. The addresses are in my Rolodex," I whispered back. "Tell Johnny that I'm sorry but that is the best I can do. Tell him to hit the ballet first. Oh, and tell him she doesn't have a car in case he wants to run a license plate. One more thing: tell Johnny to get those Lucky jeans in a plastic evidence bag, stick an evidence tag on it, and have it signed by Allison Melville of the F.B.I. Also, tell him I'll be calling Pooh as a witness today."

Annette hurried off. Fortunately, the D.A.'s office was on the top floor and the courtrooms were below. Clifton and I jumped on the elevator. I asked him to escort me to the courtroom to shield me from hallway conversations. As I entered the courtroom, the energy level was high, but it was not as tense as the first day. I said hello to Mundy, sat at my table, and unpacked my briefcase.

*

"All rise," Karl Tulkinghorn belted out as Judge Stone entered.

"Gentlemen, good morning," Judge Stone said as he sat down, his black robe puffing momentarily before gracefully settling upon his body. The jurors had not yet entered the courtroom.

Stone fixed his eyes on me. "Mr. Prosecutor, this trial is not complicated—either the gun went off accidentally or it did not. I will not have the members of the jury give up six months of their life to decide a simple question. You have two days to make your case. Now, who will you be calling?"

It wasn't even 8:30 A.M. and already I had to dodge Stone's pimp hand. He'd probably been up since 4:30 A.M., refining this speech while he finished his morning calisthenics.

"Your Honor, I will call the firearms identification expert; the first officers on the scene; David Triplett, the kid the defendant gave the gun to; Isaiah Travers, the kid that heard the defendant say, 'You hangin' with a murderer;' and a couple of quick chain of custody cops. I should be done tomorrow," I synopsized, leaving out Triplett's street-name, Shoeboot, and Travers' street-name, Pooh.

"Very good," Judge Stone said. "Mr. Tulkinghorn, go get the jury. I want to start precisely at 8:30 A.M."

"Your Honor, I was wondering if the prosecution intends to call the detective who took my client's statement?" Mundy asked.

"I may or may not call that detective, depending on how the evidence rolls out," I said evasively.

"Judge, I think I have a right to…" Mundy began, but Judge Stone cut him off.

"Mr. Mundy, I read your client's confession. Your client says the gun went off accidentally. Why should the prosecution put on your defense for you? You have the right to call the detective or whatever other witnesses you deem necessary. The prosecution likewise reserves the right to call to the stand whomever they please. I will not interfere with their case or yours," Judge Stone's volume increased with every breath.

"Thank you, Your Honor." Mundy was unfazed by Stone's morning flame. The jury entered.

"Good morning jurors." His Honor was all smiles. "I trust you all had a pleasant evening and are rested and ready to go." The jurors nodded politely. Then, the smile dissolved, and Judge Stone got back to business. "The prosecution will call its first witness."

"Yes, Your Honor. The prosecution calls F.B.I firearms identifications expert Agent Sakar, who will match the bullet from Mr. Slater's body to the murder weapon," I announced. Judge Stone shot me a nasty look. Of course, Agent Sakar hadn't been qualified and received as an expert yet—one more speech like that and Stone would lock me up. I knew there was a risk, but I wanted to remind Mundy that if he was going to make little speeches, I would too.

"Good morning Agent Sakar. Please introduce yourself and spell your last name for the court reporter, thank you." I was going to push hard this morning, get a breakaway going.

Sakar put the palms of his hands on the arms of the witness chair, pushed up, and adjusted his body as he settled in. He had a medium to slight build, thick, jet-black hair, brown eyes, a wide nose, full lips, and an easy-going and confident demeanor. Behind closed doors, Scott and Alexandra called him Mr. Science from Mumbai. Speak of the devil—I caught a glimpse of Scott in the first row holding a file. We made eye contact for half a second and I proceeded with my direct.

"My name is Agent Sakar—S-a-k-a-r—and I work at the F.B.I. ballistics laboratory. I did my undergraduate degree in engineering at Johns Hopkins University and my F.B.I. training in Quantico, Virginia."

"Where have you worked since graduating from the F.B.I. academy?"

"I have worked in D.C. in the firearms examination unit in downtown Washington, D.C. where I routinely examine weapons."

"Have you ever been qualified in the area of firearms identification?" I asked.

"Yes."

"What is firearms identification?"

"It is the study of guns and bullets. It is different from ballistics, which often focuses on the angle and trajectory of bullets. Firearms identification mainly deals with tracing bullets to specific guns and guns to specific owners. It also deals with specific characteristics of guns such as the size of the bullets, distance they can travel based on the type of gun they are in, gun residue, and point of impact."

"Your Honor, at this time the prosecution would offer Agent Sakar as an expert in the field of firearms identification."

"He will so be received," His Honor said, not even asking Mundy if he objected.

"I am handing you prosecution exhibit number seven. Do you recognize it?" I asked.

"Yes. This is the bullet I examined. I can tell it's the same one, because I see my name on the yellow evidence tag. I matched this bullet to a standard police-issue nine millimeter gun."

"How? How did you match the bullet to the gun?"

"Every gun, believe it or not, has unique characteristics—similar to a fingerprint. As the bullet moves through the chamber, lands and grooves are created on the outside of the bullet. Those marks are compared against the gun that was used," Sakar explained, and the jury took notes.

"I am handing you what has been marked as prosecution exhibit eight. Can you tell us what that is?" I handed him the gun the police obtained from Shoeboot.

"This is the gun I used in the comparison," Sakar said.

"Can you explain that further?" I led him.

"I took this standard D.C. police-issue gun, placed a bullet in it, fired it into water, recovered the sample bullet, and compared it with this bullet, marked exhibit seven," he said, holding it up for the jury. "Both bullets had identical lands and grooves, demonstrating that the bullet recovered from Bradford Slater's body was fired by this gun, marked exhibit eight. I hold this opinion to a reasonable degree of scientific certainty."

"Could you tell us who exhibit eight, the gun in this case, belongs to?" I asked.

Mundy jumped up. "Your Honor, the defense stipulates that the gun belonged to Kevin Ford's father, Rodney Ford." Mundy wisely wished to avoid further testimony on the subject.

"The prosecution accepts the stipulation that exhibit number eight is the police-issue handgun belonging to Rodney Ford and moves for its admission into evidence," I fired back before Stone could even speak.

"It will so be received." Stone swiveled his chair toward the jury box and proceeded to lecture. "Members of the jury, as we have discussed earlier, stipulation means the parties agree regarding a specific matter. In this case, they have agreed that the gun in discussion is the property of one Rodney Ford, a D.C. police officer, and that the bullet that killed Bradford Slater was fired from this gun. I am not saying who did it or whether it was accidental or not; that is another matter that will have to be proven beyond a reasonable doubt. The parties simply agree on these matters so you jurors don't have to sit there endlessly when certain matters of proof are obvious, known by everyone, and not in true contention. The prosecution may proceed."

Rodney Ford would undoubtedly be displeased to hear his name linked to the gun in this way, but it was impossible to gauge his reaction. He was not allowed in the courtroom because both sides had subpoenaed him in case his testimony was needed.

"Mr. Sakar, did there come a time when you examined the clothes of Bradford Slater to ascertain whether or not there was gunshot residue?" I asked.

"Yes, there was a distinct pattern of gunshot residue. Based on that pattern, I determined that the shooter was three to five feet away, almost point-blank range, when the shot was fired."

Sakar and I continued to dance for another twenty questions. I wanted to call Akers quickly to establish how the gun came to the police. I returned to my seat to watch Mundy's performance.

"Mr. Mundy, cross-examination," Judge Stone boomed.

"Briefly, your honor," Mundy practically mumbled. "Mr. Sakar, you are an expert in guns?"

"Yes," Sakar responded.

"But you are not here to tell us if this gun was shot intentionally or unintentionally?"

"Correct. At this time, I cannot testify to that because I was not tasked to examine that issue or look at any information regarding that matter."

"You cannot tell us whether this gun went off accidentally, can you?" Before Sakar could answer, Mundy continued, "Mr. Sakar, I'm holding up the evidence bag, I am looking at the chain-of-custody tag, and it says 'David Triplett,' correct?"

"Yes."

"It doesn't even say my client's name, Kevin Ford, does it?"

"No sir," Sakar said.

"Thank you sir, thank you for coming in," Mundy said and sat down.

Mundy was just doing what he was paid to do, dancing his dance in a loud, confident voice.

"Mr. Prosecutor, any re-direct based on Mr. Mundy's cross-examination?" Stone asked loudly.

"None," I said.

"Call your next witness," Stone ordered without so much as a "please."

"The prosecution calls Officer Akers," I announced. Akers timidly approached the stand. "State your name for the record and spell your last name for the court reporter?"

"Officer Michael Akers, A-k-e-r-s."

"Did there come a time when you recovered this gun from a friend of the defendant?" I handed him exhibit eight, Rodney Ford's gun.

"Yes, I received this from David Triplett when he called the police to turn it in," Akers said.

"Who did David Triplett get the gun from?"

"Kevin Ford."

"Can you identify Kevin Ford for the record?" I asked.

"No, I can't. I have never seen him, so I honestly can't tell you whether that is him or not," Akers said. Akers knew damn well how to identify Kevin Ford. I had intended to ask him some more connect-the-dots-type questions to help flesh out the story for the jurors but at that moment I knew. Rodney Ford had gotten to him. So I sat down with a quick "nothing further," in the hopes that the jury would appreciate Aker's "honesty."

"Mr. Mundy, cross-examination," Stone ordered.

"Yes. Exhibit number eight is a standard police handgun. Do you have one like it?" Mundy asked.

"Unfortunately, yes," Akers said.

"Why did you say 'unfortunately'—have you ever had any problems with the gun?" Mundy asked.

"Well, they are notorious for jamming and accidentally firing. I have had a lot of problems with my gun firing accidentally," Akers said, matter-of-factly ruining my case.

"Nothing further," Mundy said, gladly using the evidence that Rodney Ford had put together.

As I gathered my questions, I handed a note to Annette, who was seated right behind me. She took it and left.

Stone glowered at the officer. The corruption was obvious to him, but the jurors did not have the benefit of his long experience on the bench.

"Anything on re-direct from the prosecution?" Stone asked, practically begging me to clear things up.

"Officer Akers, you have never been found responsible for accidentally shooting a person, either in a lawsuit or by internal affairs, correct?"

"That is correct," he said, not really expecting me to quietly jump on his shit.

"And pulling the trigger, that requires about ten pounds of pressure, like picking up a heavy bag of potatoes at the grocery store?"

"Yes," he said quietly.

"Nothing further," I said. I had come close to asking him if he personally knew Rodney Ford from working with him on the D.C. police force, but it was too risky. Akers the Defector would have said "no" or "yes, but I wouldn't lie for him."

"Members of the jury, this would be an ideal time for our morning break," Stone announced.

As Tulkinghorn took the jury away, Akers approached me and said, "Sorry, man, I don't how that happened. It just sort of came out and I was under oath and all," he said.

"No worries, just give your cell phone number to Annette in case we need to call you again," I said and shook his hand. So much for my morning breakaway. I wasn't going to give Akers the pleasure of freaking out. Besides, I had been here before. I had once walked into the men's bathroom during a trial break and watched the defense attorney pay off a witness. He was literally handing the witness twenty-dollar bill after twenty-dollar bill, counting aloud. But this was not the work of Mundy; this was all Rodney Ford. I just had to gut it out and figure out a counter-punch.

"Like I said, I'm sorry," Akers whined, fearing I might call his commanding officer.

"About what?" I pretended. "It won't make any difference. The jury will understand the situation perfectly after I call Rodney Ford to the stand."

"What?" Akers looked a bit shocked.

"Yeah, each police officer's gun comes with a card. Problems or complaints about the gun are recorded on the card, you know, in case the gun has to be replaced or sent back to the manufacturer. I passed a note to Annette to have the F.B.I. pull the gun card. That'll clear things up."

Akers quickly exited the courtroom (probably to run and give Rodney a this-just-in news update). I packed up my black leather briefcase and headed upstairs to make some calls.

\*

When I arrived at my office, I found just what I needed: Johnny LeGray.

"Galina the ballerina is in the witness room. I heard about Akers," Johnny said calmly.

"Fuck Rodney Ford," I said in a very low tone of voice, looking Johnny square in the eyes. "I'm calling him to the witness stand to tell the jury that his gun was in perfect condition."

"That's my boy. What can I do to help?" Johnny asked.

I was enjoying his support while it lasted. As soon as the trial was over, he would resume riding my ass into the mud. "Go prep Pooh again in the witness room and send in Galina."

"Blondie is all dressed up but doesn't want to dance," Johnny said. "I tried to talk to her but she kept saying she needs to speak to you before she testifies." Johnny shrugged his shoulders. "I couldn't make her laugh. I guess she really likes you." He winked at me.

"Get your game-face on, bring her in, and stay in the room. I want a witness. But don't you say a fucking word. I'm doing the driving today." Johnny left. I called for Annette.

"Hey sweetness, you hanging in there?" Annette asked me.

I nodded yes.

"Agent Sakar checked Rodney's gun card. No reports of malfunctioning," she said.

I thanked Annette for getting the gun card info so fast. "Have Sakar come back to the courthouse. I'll have to call him back to the stand if I need to move the gun card into evidence."

The door had yet to fully close behind Annette when it opened again.

"Hi, Galina, have a seat," I said, pretending to be too absorbed in the papers on my desk to look up. She sat in a chair and crossed her perfect Bolshoi Ballet legs, as though a summery black dress with spectacular décolletage would convince me to grant her a green card.

"You've met Johnny." I nodded toward him as he closed the door.

"He thinks he's funny," Galina said.

I pulled out one of Scott's empty Diet Coke cans from my trash can, put it on the edge of the desk, and asked her if she wanted to smoke.

"I thought you couldn't smoke in here," she said as she immediately grabbed her Marlboro lights and some matches.

"Today's a special day. Your day. I'll break the rules. Here let me get that for you," I said and took the matches from her, lighting the cigarette.

"I didn't bring you here to threaten you. The truth is, you're just doing what a hundred witnesses have done before—spinning me." I shook the match out as a miniature trail of smoke waned.

"What do you mean?" she asked, and then deftly put the ash of her cigarette in the small mouth of the soda can.

"You know exactly what I mean."

"I don't know what I'm going to do on the witness stand," Galina said very quietly, holding to her threat with the predawn discipline that got her to the Kirov.

"I don't know you very well, but this is what I do know. The day I went to watch you at the Kirov Ballet, I experienced something I never thought I'd experience. You have a gift. Bradford Slater, he helped kids like you discover their gifts. You know what that means, to discover your gift, to commit your life to it?"

"I thought it would make me rich, like Mikhail Baryshnikov." Her lie sounded weak, even to her. She knew exactly what I meant.

"Bradford helped hundreds and hundreds of students. He taught them to create, not destroy. He helped them cope with their not-so-creative reality."

Galina pushed her cigarette into the can. The heat of the cigarette met the caramel-colored swill inside, causing it to quietly sizzle. "What happened to our video tape?" she asked, her voice barely audible.

"I threw it away and forgot about it."

"You haven't called," she changed the subject. Johnny, standing three feet away, didn't bat an eyelash. He put two and two together and it added up to zero. He could care less, and he knew I trusted him.

I needed to get this conversation back on track. "Let me tell you something," I said, then paused. "Galina, your testimony is important —not just to me, but to Bradford Slater's students. I am calling you to the stand."

"What are you going to ask?"

"You were the first person to see Kevin Ford with the gun. I need you to identify him, the same way you identified him from the pictures you were shown."

"That is all?"

"That's it," I assured her. "Johnny, take her to the witness room and don't let anyone talk to her."

"You got it boss." As soon as the trial was over "boss" would become "bitch."

"I guess we'll see what happens in the courtroom." Galina smirked.

I pretended to ignore her defiance. "I"ll see you in the courtroom."

Johnny escorted her out.

"Stone's courtroom clerk just called. Morning recess is over. You need to head down there, Monster," Annette said. I bolted toward the elevator. As I entered the courtroom, I saw that the jury was already in the box.

*

"Call your next witness quickly, Mr. Franklin, these jurors want to get through as many witnesses as possible before lunch," Stone grumbled at me. So many people wanted to make me look bad today I felt like telling Stone to get in line.

"The prosecution calls Galina Vishnevskaya as its next witness, Your Honor." I stumbled a little on Galina's last name. The hands of the jurors paused during their writing, struggling with her name as well. Despite her sex appeal, Galina was going to be a tough sell. She oozed the double agent vibe, replete with Euro-accent.

Galina gave her name and spelled it for the court reporter. She paused for a moment and pulled a stray strand of blond hair from her eyelash. Then she continued: "I am from Russia. I am a professional dancer."

"Where were you trained in dance?"

"You mean ballet? Where was I trained in ballet?

"Yes, thank you." Dance, ballet, clogging, stripping—I don't care, just identify Kevin Ford.

"I was trained at the Bolshoi Ballet in Moscow."

"Where do you currently work?"

"Kirov Ballet, here in Washington, D.C."

I hurried through the preliminary questions, not wanting to give her further opportunity to consider whether it was in her best interest to answer. "Did there come a time when you performed at Carver High School?"

Galina didn't answer right away. "Yes, I was there the day Bradford Slater was shot." Her jaw clenched and I could hear the heel of her boot manically tapping the floor of the witness stand.

"Sorry, I am nervous, I have never been in courtroom like this," she explained.

"Take your time, ma'am," His Honor jumped in, "that is perfectly natural." If Galina was planning to tell the jury that she'd had sex with the prosecutor, she was doing a damn good job of building her credibility. My stomach was churning. My little do-the-right-thing speech was horseshit. I knew it and so did she. The case and my career hung in the balance.

"Can you tell the jury what your connection was to Bradford Slater and what ballet you were performing at Carver High School?"

"Mr. Slater wanted us to perform small pieces of famous ballets so his students could see soloist pieces," Galina told the jury, speaking into the microphone.

"Where is the Kirov Ballet, and did Carver High students ever come there?"

"Our company is near the Catholic University Metro stop. Mr. Slater once brought a small group of students, mainly modern or hip-hop dancers that were interested in classical dance. They were very nice kids," Galina said.

"So how many times had you met Bradford Slater?"

"Two times. Once at Kirov." She paused. "And the day of the killing to say hello. Very nice man."

"Did anything unusual happen the second time you met him?"

"Yes, after the performance I heard a loud noise. I thought it was a bomb and then I came out of the bathroom when a young man almost knocked me over. This young man, over there," Galina said, pointing to Kevin Ford.

I pressed forward. "Let the record reflect, the witness has identified the defendant." I turned back to Galina. "Did you notice anything else unusual?"

"Yes, the young man, he had a gun—a big black gun."

"The record will so reflect," Stone said. "You may continue with your next question."

"What happened next?"

"People screaming and yelling that Mr. Slater was shot and lots of running in different directions. There were sounds of a fire engine or police car and the school filled up with police."

"Objection," Mundy said. "What she heard about the shooting is hearsay."

"Your Honor, she said people were 'screaming and yelling.' The statement clearly falls under the excited utterance hearsay exception," I rebuffed Mundy, and he damn well knew I was right.

"Overruled. You may continue," Stone said, without looking up from his note taking.

"What did you do when you heard all the commotion?"

"I ran to get my ballet bag and get out of the school," Galina said.

"Did there come a time when you were shown six photographs and asked to pick out Kevin Ford?"

"Yes," Galina answered.

I handed her a six-person photographic array. "Are these the six photos you looked at?"

"Yes."

"Are those your initials next to the picture of Kevin Ford?"

"Yes, absolutely," she said. Thank you, Absolut Vodka girl.

"Nothing further from this witness," I said and returned to my seat.

The direct had gone well, but I wasn't out of the woods yet. Mundy had the opportunity to cross-examine Galina. Did there come a time when you had sex with the prosecutor in preparation for this trial? Can you identify the prosecutor you had sex with? Let the record reflect, the prosecutor has been identified.

"Ma'am, I am holding up an evidence bag with a gun in it. Can you see it?"

"Yes," Galina said.

"You can't tell the jury if this was the exact gun you saw on that day, can you?" Mundy asked.

"No I can't. I just know it was a black gun that looked like that," she said, credibly.

"Judge, I have no further questions of this witness. I just ask this Honorable Court for a limiting instruction. Kevin Ford has been identified as the student who held the gun, not as the person that pulled the trigger, intentionally or otherwise."

"Mr. Mundy, the prosecution is putting on a piece of circumstantial evidence. The defendant was never identified in the manner you described. The jurors have heard the evidence and will consider it as they see fit. Motion for limiting instruction is denied. Call your next witness Mr. Franklin," Stone ordered.

"Thank you, Ms. Vishnevskaya, you may be excused," Stone ordered, pronouncing her name confidently.

"Mr. Tulkinghorn, would you escort her out and bring in the next witness."

I was so elated, I almost offered to drive Galina directly to the nearest immigration office, although I knew she would easily find another sucker. I had a feeling the next guy would have more money than me anyway.

"The prosecution calls David Triplett," I announced.

Tulkinghorn came back in with Shoeboot (wearing fresh Diesels, of course) and walked him up to the stand.

"Please state your name for the record and spell your name for the court reporter," I said.

"My name is David Triplett and my nickname be Shoeboot," he said. "My last name is T-r-i-p-l-e-t-t."

"Do you see anyone you recognize today?" I asked.

"Yeah, Kevin Ford, right over there," Shoeboot said, pointing.

"How do you know him?"

"I seen him around the hood, up at school," he said.

"Did he give you anything the day of the shooting at Carver High School?"

"A gun," Shoeboot said.

"I am handing you exhibit eight. Do you recognize this?"

"Yeah, that's the gun he gave me," Shoeboot said.

"Tell us about the circumstances."

"He was running from the school. Sirens going off everywhere. I told him I'd take the gun off him and pay him something later. He said, 'Okay.'"

Shoeboot shifted in his chair and began to cough. I grabbed a brown plastic water pitcher, poured him a small cup of water, walked over to the witness stand, and handed it to him.

"Down the hatch," he blurted out quietly and drank the water. A few jurors smiled. Stone gave him a dirty look.

"Is that better?" I asked.

"Yeah, thanks."

"Why did you turn the gun into the police?" I asked him.

Shoeboot shrugged his shoulders. "I changed my mind. I just didn't want it."

"You were in jail when you first met with a detective and me, weren't you?" I asked preemptively to take the wind out of Mundy's sails. I knew Mundy was going to ask Shoeboot about his jail time because I had sent Mundy a memo explaining how I reduced the felony shoplifting to a misdemeanor.

"Yeah, they locked me up for stealing a pair of jeans. But the case got dismissed."

"The person you see in the courtroom today, is that the person that gave you the gun?"

"Yes."

"Nothing further."

"Mr. Mundy, cross-examination," Stone ordered.

"Locked up for theft, Mr. Triplett?" Mundy stood up quickly and the legs of his wood chair screeched against the tile floor. "You like to shoplift?"

Shoeboot didn't answer.

"Mr. Triplett, respectfully sir, please answer my question. Do you like to shoplift, is that your M.O.?" Mundy's voice dramatically escalated as he buttoned his houndstooth sportcoat.

"Not really," Shoeboot said quietly.

"So you like to shoplift, but you just don't like to get caught?"

"Whatever." Leave the 'whatevers' for teenagers. Shoeboot had forgotten my advice on cross-examination.

"You like to steal guns, too?" Mundy said.

"No."

"Well, didn't you grab the gun when you saw it in Kevin's waistband and say you wanted to use it for robberies in the future?" Mundy asked.

"No," he said. I remembered Shoeboot telling me that in jail last December, and I knew the jury would ultimately hear it. Facts are facts, and there was nothing I could do to change them.

"The only reason you called the police to turn that gun in is you realized that Kevin would explain that the gun went off accidentally and tell the police who took it from him—you, Mr. Triplett," Mundy said.

"Whatever," Shoeboot said.

Mundy shot Stone a look that asked for intervention, and he was rewarded.

"Sir, that will not cut it in this courtroom. You are to answer the question properly," Stone jumped in. Shoeboot quickly realized that Stone knew exactly what to do with "whatever." Stone had made a career out of correcting attitudes worse than Shoeboot's. In the past, before gangbangers could answer their first question, Stone would ask, "Sir, are those shorts? Since it is late in the day, I am going to suspend the proceedings. You are hereby ordered to appear tomorrow wearing long pants. Shorts are not allowed in my courtroom. If you don't come back tomorrow, I will send the marshals out to find you and you will sit in jail until you are able to procure a pair of pants." Can't procure pants—no problem—you'll be testifying in an orange jumpsuit.

"Mr. Triplett, unless you are asserting your right against self-incrimination you will answer the questions or I will hold you in contempt of court. Now straighten up and fly right young man."

"Yeah, I figure he'd give it up," said the new-and-improved Shoeboot.

Mundy tossed Shoeboot around for another ten minutes before laying the seed. "And you don't remember Kevin Ford telling you he accidentally shot Bradford Slater?" Mundy put a coat of wax on his defense.

"No," Shoeboot answered.

"And you don't remember Kevin Ford telling you he liked Bradford Slater, that he helped my client develop his painting skills?"

"No," Shoeboot said.

"But you are a guy that likes to steal and plan robberies?" Mundy said.

Mundy tore Shoeboot apart, but I wasn't concerned. Part of what Mundy was doing was show. Rodney Ford paid Mundy a substantial fee (whether he got it from stolen drug money or refinancing his house was anyone's guess), and now Mundy had to earn that money. While Mundy didn't mess with Galina, he needed to show the jurors (and his client) that he was a world-class cross-examiner.

"And you certainly didn't hear him brag about this tragedy?"

"No."

"Nothing further," Mundy said.

Stone ordered me to call my next witness. I called Pooh. Pooh gave his real name, Isaiah Travers, and I quickly got to the money question.

"Did Kevin Ford say anything to you when you were running from the school with him?"

"'You hangin' with a murderer.' That's what he said." The jury took notes and stared at Pooh.

"Nothing further your Honor, I pass the witness," I said.

"Cross, Mr. Mundy," Stone ordered.

"You did not want to speak to my investigator when she went to your house did you?" Mundy asked, trying to intimate something, anything. Mundy did a good job with what he had, but this witness gave him so little to work with.

"I didn't have nothing to say to her," Pooh answered.

"But you weren't in the basement of the auditorium at Carver High School?"

"No."

"You have no way of knowing what happened in that basement?"

"No."

"You don't know if it was an accident or not?"

"No."

As I listened to Mundy's questions I began to wonder about why Kevin Ford had made this crazy, knuckleheaded remark to Pooh. If, as Johnny and I had discussed, Rodney was the killer, why would Kevin brag about it? Rodney was clearly a suspect. He lied about being at the school. He was having an affair with Keisha, and Bradford knew about the affair. As a teacher, Bradford had a legal duty to report a sexual affair involving a minor, so Rodney was fucked.

The truth was finally coming into focus. It occurred to me that as hard as it was to believe, Kevin Ford was protecting his dad by bragging to Pooh. Now I knew I had the wrong person on trial, but all I could do at this point was to trust that Mundy would force Rodney's hand. Stone's voice snapped me out of my trance.

"Mr. Franklin, do you have any re-direct?" he asked.

"No, Your Honor."

"Well then, I think we can do one more witness before lunch," Stone said.

"Your Honor, respectfully, I do not want to interrupt your scheduling, but my next witness is Rodney Ford. I expect his testimony will take a long time, and it is twenty minutes to noon."

"Very well," Stone said graciously. "Members of the jury, we are going to take our lunch break. We will reconvene at 1:30 P.M. Until then, enjoy your lunch."

*

Johnny entered my office. "I hear we're doing good," Johnny said.

"One of my cops testifies against me? Yeah, we're doing just great," I said sarcastically, my tone laced with months of frustration.

"I guess that is why Mundy wants to cut a deal." Johnny smiled.

"What?"

I was surprised that Mundy had placed the call—not that Mundy called Johnny first. Years ago, Johnny famously gave Mundy an interview tape exonerating his client before he presented a copy to the D.A.'s Office. Ever since, the two men had maintained a respectful, if sometimes adverse, relationship. Also, Johnny and Mundy had been around a long time and knew each other long before I came to the office. Johnny knew Mundy would, on occasion, sue the police for police brutality and Johnny wanted to stay on Mundy's good side.

"Mundy wants to discuss a proposal over lunch," Johnny said. "He's over at Subway waiting for my call."

"A proposal for who?" I said.

＊

"Nice cross on Mr. Triplett," I congratulated Mundy as I sat down.

"You mean Shoeboot?" Mundy smiled. "I prefer to use witnesses' Christian names in front of a jury."

"Thanks for the subs," I said, helping unpack our little picnic. "And chips too. You must really be desperate to deal."

"Not desperate—curious," Mundy said. "Why do you want to call Rodney Ford to the stand?"

"Well, since you called Johnny instead of me, I'll let Johnny explain," I said, then added, "Of course, everything we say at this table is covered under Rule 408, so you can't use it in court." I took a big bite out of my turkey sub.

"You got it Counselor," Mundy said.

Johnny jumped in, verbally incontinent as always. "Clay's going to prove that Rodney Ford was at the school when Bradford Slater was killed. We know he lied about hearing that his son was a suspect on the police radio. Rodney was having an affair with a classmate of Kevin's, an underage girl named Keisha. Bradford found out about it, and Rodney shot him."

"That's cold, Clay," Mundy said, his body communicating the resignation he felt.

"No colder than Rodney Ford sticking the murder on his own son," Johnny shot back.

"That's a preposterous theory, but let's play with it a moment. If your office indicted and tried the wrong person, and if Mr. Ford was involved in this terrible event, it raises the same defense of accidental or intentional shooting, and possibly self-defense. That is a real headache for your office and a huge embarrassment—going to trial on the wrong human being." Mundy refused to admit it outright, but his speech affirmed what Johnny and I already suspected.

"Johnny, you don't mind if I talk, do you?" I said. Mundy smiled. "If Rodney pleas to second-degree murder, I'm willing to trash-can the sex offense. The girl's family doesn't care why Rodney Ford goes to jail so long as he's in jail," I said.

"How many years?" Mundy asked.

"Thirty."

"Thirty is too much. I'm not authorized to accept," Mundy said.

"Fine, we'll go back into court, I'll convict his son for a crime he didn't commit and indict the father for a sex offense when the case closes. You want cold? That motherfucker had his henchmen kicked the shit out of me, he carried out illegal searches and seizures, he forced Akers to commit perjury, and God knows what else. Hell, the money he paid you was probably stolen. Nothing against you, Mundy. You're the best I have ever been up against, and you deserve to be paid—but it's thirty years, take it or leave it."

"Okay, thirty years. Judge Stone wouldn't take a deal under that, and he'll probably be eligible for parole in eighteen years anyway." Mundy pursed his lips and shook his head from side to side. Losing gracefully could be as much of an art as winning, and Mundy was keeping it together admirably.

"One last thing: Rodney has a little going away gift for me," I told Mundy, "and I think you know what it is."

Mundy reached into his briefcase and placed a small notebook next to my sandwich. "It's yours. Rodney's notes from an interview with Ray the bartender, including a signed statement by Ray. You can burn it. Now I'd like to get that pair of Lucky jeans in an evidence bag."

"The evidence stays in my personal safe outside the office in case anything happens to me or my family. Rodney might be feeling a little raw, and I don't feel particularly inclined to trust him," I said.

"You don't get if you don't ask," Mundy smiled, reciting an old criminal defense mantra.

"It's not you, Mr. Mundy. It's Rodney Ford, and he's not getting shit from me," I said. "C'mon up to my office and we can work out the details of the agreement."

The three of us walked back to the office and were sweating profusely from the hundred-plus heat. We sat down in my office and took our jackets off.

"Does Rodney want to come in?" I looked at Mundy and wiped the sweat from my brow.

"That's not necessary," Mundy said. "He'll take my advice, you can count on that."

"Here's the actual plea form. Rodney will have to initial all the information on the left-hand side of the page," I said as I slid it across the desk. We continued to hammer out the details over the next half hour, including the fact that Rodney would go into custody the minute the plea was entered.

"Can you come in here for a sec?" I called Annette.

She came into my office. It was apparent that she'd taken extra pains to dress nicely.

"What do you need?" Annette said, sounding unusually professional.

"My, my—you dressed for church?" Johnny teased her.

"My attorney is in trial and I'm proud of him. I want to represent," Annette said.

"Would you please call Judge Stone's secretary and request a meeting in his chambers?" I asked.

"Okay, Sweetness," Annette said and darted out.

*

There was a knock on the office door. It was Alexandra. "Why aren't you in trial? Are you waiting for a verdict? Is the jury out?" she asked impatiently.

"It pled out, but you're not going to believe what happened. Rodney Ford pled to second-degree murder, thirty years," I said. "Dad killed Bradford, then gave Kevin the gun and told him to run. Since Kevin was a minor, Dad decided to use his son and told him if he was caught, he'd just be in a juvenile jail until he was eighteen years old. The best laid schemes of mice and men..." I shook my head and added, "Happy Birthday son, here's a gun."

"Thirty years? It should be life, you wimp," Alexandra jabbed. "You can tell me more about it later. Right now, I have some shocking news of my own."

I smiled. This is what I needed all along—someone to share my unusual victory with. "What's your news? Must be bad; you look a little pissed," I observed.

"Rich Salsbury dismissed several of the priest molestation cases. He set a horrible precedent for the rest of these holy rapists. He ruined our cases," Alexandra said furiously as she held up several of our office files.

No victory lasted longer than a few seconds in this place. I pursed my lips with disgust as I looked at Alexandra. "This fucking office—sometimes it just makes me want to quit." I paused and then asked, "How? Why? What's Salsbury's motive?"

"Why else? Has to be money. I know he's dealing with some of his old cronies at those big firms representing the Church. If he cuts enough deals, maybe he gets a partnership." Alexandra rolled her eyes and took a deep breath. "As far as the 'how' goes, I gave him one case that was easy to win, a lock. He said he was prepping it for trial and asked for another case, and I gave it to him. Then he put them together, dismissed both cases, and sent me a memo that they are going to be settled civilly and the victims are going to be financially compensated. I haven't been able to get in to see Tommy yet. This is bad, really bad."

"Unbelievable. Let me know when Tommy is available. I promise I'm not settling any of my church cases. In fact, the number of years in jail just went up," I said. "Seriously, let me know what I can do. Maybe we can file a motion to withdraw plea offers based on prosecutorial insanity, and have Rich demoted down to juvenile. He'll quit, then his big, international law firm will take him back as an international paralegal instead of a partner."

Annette poked her head in and mimed that people were ready in Stone's chambers.

"We will deal with this later, but we will deal with this," I told my pissed-off colleague and headed down to cut the Ford deal.

I took the back way to Stone's chambers and used my security badge to enter the judges' corridor. I guessed that Mundy was already inside chambers because Rodney Ford was leaning against the wall talking on his mobile. The flip phone closed with a snap as I got closer.

"Calling your friends to say goodbye?" I calmly walked up to him, probably closer than I should have been.

"Got to do the right thing for my son—you know that," Ford said. Swagger to the end and beyond.

"You wouldn't know what the right thing was if you saw it walking down the street," I quietly said. "You're going to the right place, that's all I know, and if anything happens to me or my family —if I am even stopped for speeding by one of your cops on the take —I'll issue a writ to bring you out of jail to bring your orange-jump-suited ass out of prison and into court to indict you for having sex with a teenager. That would be the right thing."

I waited for his response but he gave me nothing. I moved past him into chambers and greeted Stone's secretary. Stella was a prim and proper spinster with her hair up in a bun, high and tight, just like the way Stone ran his courtroom.

"Hello Mr. Franklin, you can go right in; his Honor and Mr. Mundy are waiting," she said, humorlessly as always.

Judge Stones' chambers, unlike Judge Watson's, did not have any horse country décor. It was a no-nonsense place where life-altering decisions were made with certitude.

"Good afternoon gentlemen," Judge Stone said. "Sit down, make yourselves comfortable. I understand you have a deal you want to present to me." Stone had a Bakelite radio tuned to an all-news AM station. He turned it off. "Mr. Franklin, as soon as you called my chambers, I told Mr. Tulkinghorn to tell the jurors to cool their heels —a tall order in this heat."

"Judge, I know you frown on plea bargains once the trial has started, but this is an unusual case. We've learned that Kevin Ford's father, Rodney Ford, shot Bradford Slater. Mr. Ford handed his son the gun thinking he'd get softer treatment as a juvenile offender," I said.

"I read the boy's juvenile waiver report," Stone said. "He seems capable of serious misbehavior, but to direct it against Mr. Slater? I had wondered about his motive all along, but it is not my business to interfere with the strategies of counsel. At any rate, I'm relieved the outcome was just."

"Rodney Ford would plea to second-degree murder with a cap of thirty years," I said.

"I know—I have reviewed the plea paperwork. We'll get to that in a moment, Mr. Franklin." His Honor waived me off with a flick of his wrist. "Mr. Mundy, I understand you are representing Rodney Ford. I believe Stella has the conflict of interest waiver form."

"Correct, Your Honor. However, I would like to delay sentencing. Mr. Ford will plea today and will begin serving his sentence immediately, but I would like more time to adequately prepare for the sentencing hearing."

"Does the prosecution object?" Stone asked me.

"No, I want the smoke to clear on this one. This is not one of the brighter days for our office," I said.

"No, it is not, Mr. Franklin. That police officer saying the gun went off accidentally—that was pathetic. Between you and me, that police officer ought to be indicted." Stone rubbed his temples and continued. "Very well, I am going to declare a mistrial and send the jurors home. I am too old to care about what the jurors or the press thinks."

"That's fine," Mundy said.

"Not for your client," Stone shot back.

"What do you mean?" Mundy asked.

"Bradford Slater was a saint and everyone knew it. If Mr. Franklin is willing to agree to a maximum of thirty years, I'll accept it. But Mr. Mundy if you ask for less than that, you will lose. Mr. Slater was unarmed. He was murdered in a school building. I will see to it that Mr. Ford serves every minute of his sentence," Stone had put his cards on the table. Stone respected Mundy, but the business of justice was going to be taken care of Stone's way.

"I warned Rodney Ford that you were going to put the wood to him. He still wants to proceed," Mundy said.

"Your Honor, the plea paperwork is signed and ready to go, including the criminal complaint for second-degree murder." I wasn't anxious to tell a pack of reporters that I'd put the wrong guy on trial. Still, the formalities were tiresome, and I wanted to wrap them up as quickly as possible.

"We'll complete the plea agreement in a basement courtroom. Then, after Mr. Ford is taken into custody, we'll go back to the ceremonial courtroom. I'll declare a mistrial and dismiss the jurors. I am not going to declare a mistrial until Rodney Ford enters his plea and is in the custody of the U.S. Marshals. Agreed?"

Mundy nodded his head.

"Good," Stone said. "Mr. Franklin, you can announce to the press that it is very likely that the senior Mr. Ford will receive thirty years. I have no problem with that. I will see both of you in the basement courtroom momentarily. Stone shook his head and said, "Okay, you are both hereby excused."

\*

We wrapped up the plea in the basement and then dismissed the jurors. As soon as I hit the hallway, reporters swarmed me. "Mr. Monroe and I will be giving a press conference explaining the complete details of the case. For now, suffice it to say that justice has been served. The person responsible for Bradford Slater's death is in jail and is facing thirty years. It is our sincere hope that the community can eventually move on from this tragedy."

I pushed through the crowd and saw Scott. "Come with me," I told him.

I entered my office and shut the door. "Did you hear what Salsbury did with the priest cases? What a day."

"Yeah, Alexandra told me. I told her never to give that guy an important case. Doesn't surprise me one bit," Scott said, lifting his eyebrows.

"Makes me want to quit. First I almost put the wrong person in jail and now this," I carped.

"You can't quit. What about me? What about Alexandra? If you quit I have no one to make fun of. Our other so-called colleagues might not find my brand of humor amusing, and someone else might take it seriously and file one of those Department of Justice internal complaints against me." Scott offered a half-smile.

"You deserve an internal complaint and court-ordered psychiatric testing," I said as I dialed Alexandra's cell phone. I left her a message to come to my office so we could have a threesome with Tommy.

"Tommy is trying to find you to talk about the Ford case anyway," Scott said. "Not that I am eavesdropping on your phone calls."

Eerily, Tommy Monroe walked in.

"Alexandra and I were just looking for you. When are you going to fire Salsbury, today or tomorrow?"

"C'mon Clay, you're just reacting to a tough day and bittersweet victory," Tommy said.

"Bittersweet? I could have sent Kevin Ford to jail for a crime he didn't commit. And now two priests walk away from crimes they did commit?"

"If my Aunt Mabel had balls, she'd be my Uncle Henry. Stop worrying so much Clay. Take a week off. Let things settle down." Tommy sat down in a chair and crossed his legs. "You just won a big one. Thirty years for the killer of Bradford Slater. I can hit the campaign trail and tell everyone it's like a life sentence because he'll be dead by the time he comes up for parole. A cop in jail, he's screwed. You brought home the bacon son, and I'm proud." He adjusted his tie and loosened his collar.

"Stop blowing smoke." I wanted to deck him out of frustration. "Salsbury dumped two of the priest cases. That could not have happened without your approval."

"I didn't give my approval. The first time I heard about it was Alexandra's voicemail, a few hours ago." Tommy put his hands on his hips and took a step to the right. "You think you know everything Clay? I was surprised, and it is not like you haven't experienced some surprises lately."

"It's so unfair. We put these little teenagers in jail for selling one rock of crack, with ten years mandatory for a second time, and they are barely nineteen years old. We take away the best years of their life for selling something the size of a piece of popcorn so they can take a ten-minute break from poverty, maybe buy a pair of Air Jordans. And now a real criminal abuses the trust of children and their parents, and grooms the kids in church until the time is right to slake their own perverted thirst, and we dismiss their cases? It just makes me want to walk away."

"Now don't go mister-fucking-perfect on me, Clay," Tommy said. "We all make mistakes, sure. Let's get Johnny to tear through the files and you can indict them with a different set of victims. I'll take care of the heat that will come with that."

"And Salsbury?" I asked.

"I'll take care of it. I'm not going to fire him, but I'll make sure he doesn't get his hands on any serious cases. It's not your office Clay, it's mine, and you have to respect that. Don't worry about him. He had one foot out the door anyway."

Tommy walked over and put his hand on my shoulder. "Long day Clay. We'll have lunch next week. Duke Zeibert's on me. You, Scott, and Alexandra, we haven't done that in a long time. I'll take care of this mess, just like I took care of your fight—that's what I do," Tommy said and looked back and forth between Scott and me.

"Okay, I just need a break," I said.

Tommy smiled and walked out. I suddenly heard Alexandra's voice headed our way, and then she bounced in with...Kara. I felt slightly dizzy as an adrenaline rush passed through me.

"Scott, let's go get some coffee," Alexandra said to him, and kissed Kara on the cheek as she said good-bye.

"Nice to see you. Am I going to see you later?" Scott asked Kara.

"Absolutely," Kara said.

I felt scarred and healed, magnificent and scared all at once. My heart was hammering against my chest.

"Good, 'cause he's no fun without you," Scott said, nodding his head toward me, and left.

"Shut the door, thanks," I whispered to Scott.

"Boy, he's all grown up now. Talks like an adult. He used to say, 'Shut the door, whore,' but now he's Mr. Polite," Scott said to Kara, and quietly closed the door. Kara flashed her illuminating smile, and then regained a more somber composure once the door closed.

I walked up to her and embraced her, then took her hand and lead her to a chair. I sat on my desk directly in front of her.

"Where have you been?" I asked, at first frustrated. "Never mind, it doesn't matter." I shook my head and just soaked up her presence. "I'm sorry and I have been sorry every hour over the past six months," I began.

"I know that," she said. "I got the five thousand emails."

"I've been here and there and there and here over this thing, a million times, literally, in my head. I was idiotic, mistaken, and egotistical, but I still want to be with you. I never appreciated the value of a real relationship and the importance of trust. It's all so simple. I can't believe I didn't know it before."

I stopped, took a breath, and stared into her pale brown eyes. "I want to be with you and I want it to be real. I'm tired of being angry at myself and you."

"How can you be angry at me?" Kara appeared bewildered.

"I didn't know if you were dead or alive, in or out. I imagined the worst—" I said.

Kara's eyes softened and gazed downward. I struggled to find something clever to add, something to delay what I knew was coming. Kara's gaze returned to mine as she broke the awkwardness: "Clay, I'm not coming back. I am not going to marry you, I don't want to be cruel but now that I'm actually here, it's even hard to look at you. I've known you for so long and you just discarded that history."

Silence.

Kara continued, "We needed to talk." A slight smile crept on her lips. "You were going to keep hounding my friends until you found me."

"I'm persistent, you've got to give me that." I just wanted to keep the conversation alive as long as possible.

"I might as well confess, I threw your ring in the Potomac." Her tone softened. "I had imagined you threw it into a volcano. I'm okay with a river."

Kara sighed, continuing, "And I really am sorry about the tape. It was just—vindictive. That's not the person I want to be."

Maybe we were reconnecting—maybe she was going to give me another chance.

And then she pursed her lips and looked at me intently, her eyes widening. "But I think you know we're not going to reboot this."

Rimshot.

Emptiness filled my office. More emptiness was waiting for me at the P. Street palace. Kara stood up from the chair.

She offered a small smile and kissed me goodbye—on the cheek. The cheek. She quietly exited, closing the door behind her. For the moment, I felt numbness and a strange sort of relief. I glanced at the guilty plea on my desk and remembered that something good had happened today. But I needed to get out of the office. Couldn't bear the thought of talking to anyone. Even Alexandra or Scott, not yet. Back doors. Stairwells. Rear exit.

As soon as I was outside, the boil of August was upon me and the cicadas screamed in a tree near my parked car. I got in and rolled the window down as the air conditioner initially blew out a hot gust of air. I was hit with a sharp stab of awe, finally hoping that I knew who I was and who I needed to be. For a moment, even without Kara, that was enough.

www.ingramcontent.com/pod-product-compliance
Lightning Source LLC
Chambersburg PA
CBHW070758280326
41934CB00012B/2971